THE SMART ORGANIZATION

THE SMART ORGANIZATION

CREATING VALUE THROUGH STRATEGIC R&D

David Matheson and
Jim Matheson

HARVARD BUSINESS SCHOOL PRESS
Boston, Massachusetts

Library of Congress Cataloging-in-Publication Data

Matheson, David, 1963–
    The smart organization : creating value through strategic R&D /
David Matheson and Jim Matheson.
      p. cm.
    Includes bibliographical references and index.
    ISBN 0-87584-765-X (alk. paper)
    1. Research, Industrial—Management. 2. Strategic planning—
Decision making. 3. Value added. I. Matheson, James E.
II. Title. III. Title: Creating value through strategic R&D. IV. Title:
Creating value through strategic R & D.
T175.5.M334 1998
607.2—DC21   97-10776
                                             CIP

To our clients, who have taught us so much

CONTENTS

PREFACE

I T IS 11:00 A.M. in London, a few days before the manuscript for this book is due at the publisher's office. David has just received a revised version from Jim, sent at 3:00 A.M. California time with this exasperated memo: "I feel like I'm writing a second Ph.D. thesis!" David replies by e-mail: "Not just a second thesis—more like a second, third and fourth!"

Having now finished our labors, we understand what a salmon must feel as it travels upstream, leaping one waterfall after another, driven by a mysterious passion to pursue a vague but familiar scent. We have been equally driven for the past several years—in our cases, by a passion to understand and improve strategic business decisions, and by a belief that the world will be a better place when these are guided by evidence, logic, and good sense. Quality in decision making has compelled our journey and the development of this book.

We have seen many organizations achieve great things during that journey: new, life-enhancing drugs, customer-pleasing designs for new products, and improved process technologies. In these firms we have observed behaviors and practices that energize and inspire people. We have seen the opposite as well: companies that routinely snatch defeat from the jaws of victory; behaviors and practices that suck the creative spirit out of employees; R&D efforts that lead nowhere. What explains these differences? In most cases, the differences are explained by strategic choices and—just as important—*how* those choices are made. Companies that consistently make smart decisions end up ahead. But what does it take for an organization to consistently make smart decisions—particularly in R&D? This question is the scent we have followed and continue to pursue.

Our interest in decision making was first stimulated by academic work done in the 1960s at Stanford, Harvard, and MIT, where many of the concepts of decision analysis were initially developed, and has subsequently been extended by the challenge of applying and perfecting those concepts in the corporate world. There, the outcomes of different decisions can make or break careers, result in institutional vitality or decline, and often determine whether shareholders retire well or poorly.

This book is directed to executives concerned with creating value through corporate renewal and growth. Although it takes new technologies, products, and processes as exemplars, it is relevant to anyone involved with strategic business decisions. For them, it offers both practical tools and fundamental principles. The tools can be put to use immediately. The principles, however, require time—time to ferment in the mind, and time to alter existing behaviors. Though their application is less direct, these principles have the power to change the way executives approach problems and make strategic choices. *The Smart Organization* is based on these principles.

Questions we had hoped to answer for ourselves in writing this book have (in the perverse manner of scientific inquiry) raised new ones. In this sense, the final chapter may be the prologue to another, future volume written by us or someone else. Still, we hope that the ideas brought together here will help readers to improve the ways in which their organizations make decisions, creating a better future for themselves, their shareholders, and their customers.

ACKNOWLEDGMENTS

T HOUGH ANY DEFICIENCY in this book is our responsibility, a number of colleagues, clients, and friends deserve thanks for their valuable contributions to our work.

Don Creswell, who manages the Strategic Decisions Group's R&D Decision Quality Association, supported our efforts to develop new ideas and provided a forum in which our findings could be presented to experienced executives. He was instrumental in launching our book-writing effort and remained an unflagging cheerleader.

Richard Luecke, our writer/editor, worked with us—mostly through cyberspace—during the book's entire development. The desktop publishing department of Strategic Decisions Group (SDG), especially Auralee Dallas and Alex Kos, designed most of the graphics.

Our colleagues at SDG, many who helped create the science and practice of decision quality, made contributions too numerous to detail. They include: Robin Arnold, Terry Braunstein, John Celona, Mark Chang, Patricia Evans, Steve Galatis, Ron Howard, Tom Keelin, Mike Menke, Jennifer Meyer, and Carl Spetzler. We borrowed liberally from material developed by these and other colleagues and hope that they will be pleased to see those ideas and experiences presented, at last, in an accessible volume.

A number of friends and clients in industry also informed our thinking: Tony Alvarez, Vince Barabba, Sheldon Buckler, Ed Finein, Phil Griswold, Erich Helfert, Lynn Lander, Bob Putnam, Derek Ransley, Joel Stern, Leigh Thompson, and Karen Anne Zien.

The editors and staff of Harvard Business School Press, notably Nikki Sabin, Barbara Roth, and Katie Mascaro, handled the manuscript with a professionalism any author would appreciate. The Press's four anonymous reviewers provided useful criticism of the first draft.

Many others have helped in producing this book, of course, and we thank each for his or her contribution. Finally, we thank our spouses and families who have patiently supported us over many months.

David Matheson, London, England
Jim Matheson, Menlo Park, California

CHAPTER 1

BEING SMART

> Because its purpose is to create a customer, the business enterprise has two—and only two—basic functions: marketing and innovation. *Peter Drucker, People and Performance*

S MART COMPANIES do great things. They develop world-beating products and services on a continuing basis, and they deliver them at prices that establish value leadership. Being smart and acting smart may be the best guarantees of business success in this fast-changing and competitive world. We define *being smart* as making good strategic decisions. *Acting smart* is the activity of effectively carrying out those decisions. Peter Drucker proclaimed marketing and innovation as the two basic functions of the organization. Although he identified them as distinct functions, good strategy considers both. Successful innovation addresses strategically important markets and in the process assures the renewal of the entire business.

This book focuses on what it takes to *be smart* in the business activity that, more than any other, determines the future of the organization: research and development (R&D). We use the term *R&D* in the broadest sense to mean any technologically related activity that has the potential to renew or extend present businesses or generate new ones, including core competency development, innovation, invention, product development, and process improvement. The chapters that follow provide an actionable approach to improving R&D decision making, which is based on decades of consulting to R&D-intensive organizations in Europe, Japan, and the United States, as well as extensive work on strategic decisions of all kinds. In the course of that work, we and our colleagues have collectively observed, supervised, or led hundreds of R&D consulting activities. A number of those situations are used here to enrich the text, though they are often disguised for purposes of confidentiality.[1] While it is not a theoretical work, the book is nevertheless based upon years of teaching decision analysis at Stanford University, a leader in decision research, and upon studies conducted for the R&D Decision Quality Association. Although our focus is on "smart R&D" as an exemplar of strategic excellence, the principles generalize to the "smart organization" with implications for all functions and major business areas.

The Transforming Power of Strategic Decisions

A great deal is being written about "transforming" the organization through horizontal management, through self-directed work teams, through visionary leadership, and so forth. To these we add the transforming power of strategic decisions that direct the enterprise to adopt the most appropriate technologies, to develop new products with the greatest likelihood of success, and to rationally manage its R&D portfolio. Imagine how your business would be transformed if its R&D decisions were measurably better than they have been? R&D executives estimate that they can improve the value creation potential of R&D by 20 percent to more than 200 percent with better strategic decision making, and these levels have been achieved in practice. The principles of a smart organization create an environment in which this improved value creation is possible and sustainable.

The good news is that this transformation can be achieved by almost any organization. As individuals, we are only as smart as our genes and our environment allow us to be. But organizations can become "smarter." Their decision-making IQs can be improved, and usually with the current personnel and within a fairly short time. We've seen it happen. All it takes is commitment and the right set of tools and attitudes. In this sense, getting smarter about strategic decision making is no more mysterious than the organizational improvements that companies have made in product and service quality, customer service, and other business processes.

A Little History

Since the mid-1970s, companies have concentrated on *acting* smart, pursuing a long list of nontraditional management systems aimed at improving operating results. Many of these systems came from Japan; others were home-grown. For the most part, improvement-oriented companies have focused on business processes, the activities that turn inputs to outputs. Total quality management, benchmarking, just-in-time, quality functional deployment, cross-functional teaming, reengineering, and other methods have shown organizations how to "do things right," that is, to operate more effectively. While many complain that their attempts to implement these programs have produced mixed results, the larger legacy is one of substantial improvements in product quality, cycle time, inventory management, and customer service. By most measures, operational improvements in both manufacturing and services have raised the level of what customers and shareholders view as acceptable.

The number of prominent U.S. corporations that report benefits from these programs during the past two decades is long and continues to grow. Xerox Corporation was among the first. During the late 1970s, this company found itself in a serious competitive situation with a host of new Asian challengers that were profitably selling high-quality photocopiers in the United States at prices below Xerox's own cost of production. Stunned by this development, Xerox adopted benchmarking as an organization-wide method of improving a number of its then substandard operations. Xerox learned many quality improvements directly from its Japanese partner, Fuji Xerox. These initiatives resulted in major improvements and bottom-line results. At about the same time, Motorola adopted its now-famous "six sigma" approach to eliminating quality problems from its products, which had dramatic bottom-line results. More recently, General Electric has announced a major program of quality improvement, with the goal of eliminating some $7 billion to $10 billion in costs (10 percent to 15 percent of revenues) over a period of a few years. In effect, North American companies, and many in Europe, have passed through a revolution in operational improvement, just as their counterparts in Japan did before them. They have learned how to "do things right."

No amount of design excellence or manufacturing agility or knock-'em-dead customer service, however, can save a company whose decision makers direct it to "do the wrong things," that is, to develop unwanted products or products that it has no capacity to market. For example, NCR was the very best producer of electro-mechanical cash registers during the 1960s and early 1970s, but neither product excellence, nor continuous improvement, nor the state-of-the-art facilities the company built to produce these machines would save it from a near-death experience once computer-based electronic cash registers broke into the market. NCR had decided to dabble with computer technology at the time, but only as a means of breaking into new lines of business. Its strategic thrust was aimed at refining the electromechanical technology on which its core business was based. When DTS, a small newcomer, introduced the first electronic cash register in 1971, the industry changed dramatically. Over the course of the next four years, the market share of electromechanical machines dropped 80 percent, and NCR's revenues and profits plummeted with it.[2]

The travails of NCR are not unique in the annals of industry. On that same note, it is not insignificant that several of the companies featured in the pages of *In Search of Excellence*—the book that prepared many American managers for the quality revolution—were on the slippery slope to crisis even as readers across the country were adopting their practices for operational excellence. Before long, many of the companies praised in the book—Atari, Digital Equipment, Eastman Kodak, Delta Airlines, Texas Instruments, and even Hewlett-Packard—were experiencing serious crises.[3] While these companies performed well on Peters and Waterman's measures of operational excellence, lack of excellence in strategic decision making may have accounted for some of their problems. Edwin Artzt, chairman and chief executive officer (CEO) of Procter & Gamble, said as much when he described his company's program of total quality management:

> The limitation is in the area of strategy: total quality does not
> guarantee that companies will produce winning strategies.
> Winning strategies have to come from the minds of leaders
> and be augmented by input from the troops. Total quality en-
> sures the success of a winning strategy and sustains success,
> but it doesn't automatically solve strategic problems.[4]

More recently, several Deming and Baldrige prizewinners—all masters of operational effectiveness—have experienced similar setbacks, and often for the same reason. For example, Florida Power and Light, winner of the Deming Prize in 1989 (the first non-Japanese company to do so), discovered that its quality efforts had barely translated into improved service to the customer. It had created an 85-member quality department, 1,900 quality teams,[5] and a rigorous system of quality review. Very little of this had an impact on the way customers perceived the company's service. If anything, the details of the quality program shifted attention away from customers.[6]

Florida Power and Light's experience is not an isolated case. An Arthur D. Little survey of 500 U.S. companies found that quality programs were having a significant impact on competitiveness for only one-third of the companies. A similar survey of 100 British firms by A.T. Kearney reached a more dismal conclusion. Only one-fifth of these firms could point to tangible results from their quality programs.[7]

The Next Quality Frontier

To fulfill the quality revolution requires a revolution in the quality of decision making, particularly at the level of strategy. Companies need to examine the processes through which they make strategic decisions and make them as effective as their operational processes. Decision making is, after all, a *process*. Like manufacturing, customer fulfillment, and countless others, this process converts inputs to outputs. And this process can be improved.

Because of the impact of strategic decisions on the fortunes of the business, we consider it a *master process*. Strangely, this critical process has been ignored by the quality revolution. Unlike the ancient Athenians, who recognized the need to develop the body *and* the mind, efforts to develop and improve the modern organization have concentrated on the body while ignoring the mind that directs it. The frequent result is misdirected effort and wasted accomplishment. A classic example of this occurred at Xerox's Palo Alto Research Center (PARC) in the 1970s. Many of the inventions that have changed our world, in fact, came from this lab: the personal computer, the mouse, the user-friendly interface, the computer network, and laser printing. Yet Xerox was unable to take advantage of these technical breakthroughs. As Robert X. Cringley describes it, "the captains of industry at Xerox headquarters in upstate New York were making too much money the old way—by making copiers—to remake Xerox into a computer company. They took a couple of halfhearted stabs . . . but did little to promote PARC technology."[8] By not investing strategically in their commercialization, Xerox failed to capitalize on the excellent work being done in its lab. Instead, Apple, Adobe, 3Com and others saw the potential of these technologies and reaped the benefits.

The Leveraging Power of Strategic Decisions

Quality decision making has tremendous leveraging power, particularly at the strategic level. The bottom-line difference between a good and a bad decision in mergers and acquisitions, R&D, capital budgeting, and market selection is usually many millions of dollars. For example, Ford Motor Company was in a dismal state in the late 1970s. Its car models were uninspiring and of inconsistent quality, giving rise to the acronym FORD, Fix Or Repair Daily. A number of good decisions about design and organization, and the decision to adopt process quality measures, however, turned this situation around over a period of about five years. Following directions set through these strategic decisions, the same people who designed, built, and marketed some of America's most unspectacular automobiles in the 1970s launched the record-breaking Taurus in 1986 and, a few years later, the successful Explorer utility vehicle. Ford went from being Detroit's most troubled auto maker to the most profitable of the Big Three.

When top management hones its strategic decision-making skills even slightly, the leverage at the end of the value chain can be huge. And if a company achieves quality decisions in all functions and at all levels, tremendous improvements in performance can be made. This is particularly true of R&D decisions, since they sit at the beginning of the entire value chain. Participants in our R&D briefings usually estimate that better strategic R&D decisions would easily generate billions of dollars of greater value for the ten to fifteen companies typically represented. What could your company accomplish if the quality of its major decisions improved by only 25 percent?

What We Mean by Smart R&D

Smart R&D is about making quality decisions, which we define as those that produce the best prospects for creating value. Smart organizations make these decisions routinely. Quality decisions proceed from facts and logical analysis, not from "how we do things" or from contests between contending factions or product champions. Consider the result of one company's habit of letting its product champions determine its R&D direction.

In the late 1970s, the R&D lab of a company we know well developed a demonstration microwave clothes dryer. The head of the laboratory liked the technology and pushed it aggressively, justifying it on technical merits and on the ability of microwaves to dry clothes efficiently. "It will save the customer a bundle," he assured dubious colleagues. The company's marketing representatives were not so confident. They had concerns about customers' perceptions about microwaves, but the company had no meaningful process for incorporating these concerns. Aggressive lobbying by the laboratory manager simply closed off discussion of these concerns and ignored the need to develop more complete market information.

The laboratory manager won the battle. The microwave dryer was developed and eventually launched with great fanfare. But the company lost the war in the retail market. Despite substantial investments in marketing and product launch, the microwave dryer was a huge flop. A project postmortem revealed the reason: prospective customers were generally afraid of microwaves. Some thought that microwaves would contaminate their clothes with radiation. Others thought that microwaves should not be used on metal zippers and snaps; to them, the microwave dryer had limited use, even though the microwave dryer in fact did not share this limitation with its cousin, the microwave oven.

Simply stated, the quality of the company's decision was terrible. In its enthusiasm to launch the product, it had not adequately gathered or considered information on customers' perceptions. The company's marketing representatives had articulated concerns about these and "product acceptability," but the company's decision makers had no meaningful process for incorporating these concerns. Confidence in the technical capabilities of the product and aggressive lobbying by the laboratory manager closed off discussion of these concerns and development of more market information. The result was a low-quality decision, which led to a bad outcome.

To prevent a recurrence of this type of mistake, the company wisely adopted an information checklist as part of its decision-making process. This checklist included the items of information on customers' perceptions, competing products, and so forth that would have eliminated the blind spot that was allowed to exist in the microwave dryer situation. Future decisions routinely followed this checklist. This new practice alone, however, resulted in only limited improvement in decision quality. Although the information component of this company's R&D decisions was greatly improved, its powerful managers continued to push through decisions that favored their projects. They simply overpowered objections and biased or disregarded information contrary to their views.

Quality decisions, in contrast, are outcomes of a process, not of a contest. Instead of the too-familiar "winner-take-all" contest that pits opposing viewpoints against each other, decision quality takes the best ideas from many parts and levels of the organization and in so doing creates alternatives that are often superior to those of any single advocate.

The Unique Challenges of R&D Decision Making

While all strategic decisions are important to the future of the enterprise, those involving R&D are difficult because they are usually made in the face of many uncertainties:

▲ the time between the decision point and the point at which the cash register starts ringing is typically long and filled with unknowns;

▲ the R&D process is inherently uncertain (without uncertainty there would be no R&D); no one knows whether and when R&D will succeed, nor the level of that success;

▲ the markets to be served are most uncertain at the time R&D projects are commissioned; and

▲ successful R&D often takes a company into unfamiliar areas requiring partnerships, alliances or acquisitions, and new ways of doing business.

Decisions about research and development are complicated by the fact that they affect just about everything else that matters in the business. Managers cannot prudently make R&D choices without thinking through the implications for marketing, service and support, manufacturing, and finance. R&D decisions might include acquisitions to gain technology or market access. There is hardly a strategic management issue that does not arise in the context of R&D. As a consequence, any process that successfully addresses strategic R&D decision making must address business strategy as well.

This last point is underscored by the experience of DuPont, which has moved to a system that brings R&D and business decisions together. "In the past," according to one company R&D director, "research always drove the innovation process." The result was the familiar hand-off of completed R&D projects to business units, which were not prepared to deal with them. DuPont's new system

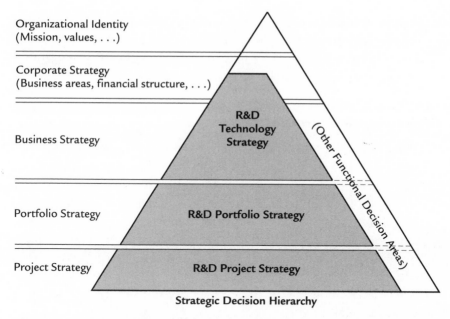

Organizational Identity
(Mission, values, . . .)

Corporate Strategy
(Business areas, financial structure, . . .)

Business Strategy — **R&D Technology Strategy**

Portfolio Strategy — **R&D Portfolio Strategy**

Project Strategy — **R&D Project Strategy**

(Other Functional Decision Areas)

Strategic Decision Hierarchy

Figure 1-1. *R&D and the Strategic Decision Hierarchy*

requires that the corporate business functions get involved from the beginning. "When R&D is finished with its work, the business has already decided to sell it, so we've cut some 40 percent to 60 percent off the time of getting new products to market, because the strategic thinking and commercialization decisions have been made ahead of time. Innovation becomes a business process, not a research process."[9]

Indeed, the unity of R&D and other strategic decisions cannot be overstated. Since everything R&D does should aim to create value for customers, owners, and other stakeholders, its activities must be coordinated with other goals and activities. To help managers appreciate the relationship between R&D and other strategic decisions, we refer them to the strategic decision hierarchy, shown in Figure 1-1.

For the corporation, the top level of strategy is *organizational identity*, its statement of mission and values. Decisions at this level generally focus on the types of businesses the organization will conduct and what it will learn to be good at. Organizational identity is often a given, changing slowly or in response to crises as old paradigms break down.

The next level, *corporate strategy*, involves decisions on what businesses the enterprise will be in, given the enterprise's higher level charter. Corporate strategy is a matter of both desire and capability. The *business strategy* level, in turn, determines how the company will compete in each area. The top of R&D's hierarchy of strategic decisions quite naturally begins within these two levels.

Three Levels of Smart R&D

Three levels of R&D decision making overlap the organizational decisions just described: those that relate to technology strategy, those that determine the content of R&D portfolios, and those that shape individual R&D projects. To be smart, companies must make good decisions at all three levels. R&D technology strategy logically overlaps both the corporate-level and the business-level domains, since technology is a factor in where and how the enterprise competes. R&D portfolio and project decisions are found at lower levels, taking their places alongside the many other decisions that every organization must make.

Technology Strategy

Technology strategy is a vital component of corporate and business strategy that designates the role technology will play in the future. Every business must determine how it will create new value and how it will renew its current products and services. How will it support existing products, generate new ones, and develop entirely new product lines? How will it develop or acquire the necessary manufacturing technologies? Which technology will it develop internally and which will it obtain from outside? What, if any, technological competencies will it rely on to differentiate itself from the competition, and which ones must it excel in just to keep up? Where do technology alliances make sense? How will it shape the R&D organization? Which functions should be centralized or decentralized? How should these functions be spread globally? And what mix of skills is needed in each location?

These questions cannot be answered in the abstract or by the R&D organization alone. They are questions that the CEO and general managers must address as part of business strategy. For example, Xerox PARC, described earlier, was making very good decisions about its portfolio and individual projects. Its teams of researchers and engineers were successfully inventing the computing and communicating processes of the future. But poor decision making with respect to the company's technology strategy—and the connection of R&D activities with its larger corporate plans—undermined Xerox's ability to capitalize on PARC's groundbreaking work.

In contrast, Monsanto, once a traditional chemicals company, realized early on that biotechnology, and especially genetic modification of plants, could become a revolutionary technology. It consciously began to gain competencies in this area and soon became a world leader in plant biotechnology.[10] As early research began to show results, Monsanto began to incorporate those results into products. While the financial benefits of these products were slow in appearing, they are now beginning to roll in. As its highly profitable chemical herbicide, Roundup®, comes off patent, Monsanto is extending its life by genetically modifying seeds to resist the herbicide, which allows farmers to control weeds more easily after the crop has sprouted. The company is also improving the ability of plants to resist diseases.

To capitalize fully on these and related new technical competencies, Monsanto announced plans to spin off its old chemical business lines and transform itself into a life-sciences company focused on human and plant biotechnology, focusing on smarter products through genetic engineering. At Monsanto, technology strategy is completely intertwined with corporate strategy.

Portfolio Strategy

Portfolio strategy deals with interdependencies in the R&D portfolio brought about by the use of common resources such as money and people, participation in common markets, and use of common technology. Portfolio decisions should generate the most value from these resources (rationing) and make the case for increasing or decreasing these resources to create even more value (investing). Portfolio decisions determine how we balance short-term business needs with long-term renewal. Should incremental improvements or broad-based innovation be pursued? Should the focus be placed on the businesses that are producing today's profits, or on areas thought to have the strongest future potential? Does the company have the right set of project ideas to meet its needs, or should it look internally or externally for more? And the ultimate question, Which specific projects should be funded and at what levels?

Many companies fail to answer this last question. For example, a major pharmaceutical organization approved many good projects, but failed to provide sufficient resources for all of them to proceed toward the market in a timely fashion. Nor did it establish a system for prioritizing the use of resources it did provide. The result: all projects were delayed by insufficient laboratory and clinical services. Service managers doled out service to internal customers based on their own narrow priorities such as who had been waiting longest, who was highest ranking, who was owed a favor. There was no system to prioritize according to value creation potential or to determine when to invest in higher capacity. In today's competitive world, either these services need to be fully provided or entire projects should be cut to allow the others to reach the market in the most competitive time frame.

Project Strategy

Project strategy determines how to create and capture the most value from each project or program. It aims to determine the best technical approaches and the best commercialization paths. Project choices may be at the bottom of the decision hierarchy, but they are "where the rubber meets the road." Decision making at the project level considers alternative budget levels, different and possibly parallel technical approaches, alternative paths to commercialization, and optimum timing of introduction to the market.

Each project or program needs a sound strategy at a depth and detail appropriate to its size and stage. While most project work is naturally directed at the R&D content itself, project strategy decisions must balance R&D content and commercial avenues to value creation. This means that about one-half of project strategy work should focus on understanding the paths to commercialization—an unnatural act for many in the R&D community. Once the R&D community understands the path to value creation, it has the knowledge to optimize R&D projects and to determine which risks are likely to be worth the return.

What Is Ahead

The chapters that follow develop the concept of smart R&D and build an actionable model for creating greater value from R&D activities. They are divided into five key parts:

Part I: Decision Quality. Chapter 2 defines decision quality in terms of six dimensions. These dimensions can be used to judge the quality of any decision. Chapter 3 explains each dimension in depth and provides background on key concepts and tools that support decision quality.

Part II: Best Practices. Chapter 4 provides a blueprint of best practices developed from several years of benchmarking R&D leaders. This chapter describes a blueprint of forty-five best practices and how companies measure up to these standards. Chapter 5 begins the exploration of the barriers that not only prevent adoption of the best practice but also prevent these companies from routinely making good strategic decisions.

Part III: Principles. Chapter 6 shows how the underlying principles of smart R&D explain why some companies are able to readily adopt best practices while others struggle with little headway. Chapter 7 explores each principle in depth. Chapter 8 is a self-administered organizational IQ test through which readers can determine the extent to which their own organizations have adopted smart principles.

Part IV: Processes. Achieving decision quality requires the right kinds of interactions among decision makers and doers in the organization. This part shows how dialogue processes can guide organizations to good decisions at each level of R&D strategy. Chapters 9, 10, and 11 develop the processes and illustrate them with real examples at the three levels of technology, portfolio, and project strategy.

Part V: Beyond R&D. The final chapter moves from the R&D setting to that of the larger organization. It shows how principles and processes for smart R&D can guide any organization to routinely achieve high-quality strategic decisions and demonstrates their use with real applications.

PART I

DECISION QUALITY

CHAPTER 2

DECISION QUALITY

> You cannot control the winds,
> but you can control the set of
> your sails. *Anthony Robbins*

S HOULD WE FIRST get approval of our new drug in France, or take longer to get overall European Community (EC) approval?

Should we purchase a new piece of automated test equipment?

Should a larger screen or a longer battery life be the first priority of our next generation of laptop computers?

How many hours each week should we allow researchers to spend pursuing their own projects?

Which is the better option—licensing the new technology from company Z or purchasing Z and retaining its people to form a new competency?

Each of the choices posed above has strategic importance, at least for someone. Some might define the future of the enterprise; others will have less impact. Many of the truly defining choices faced by companies are associated with research and development. In many respects, R&D is the crucible of a company's future and its prospects for satisfying customers and making life difficult for its competitors. It is also the area in which the levels of uncertainty and complexity are greatest and the requirements for decision-making skill are the most demanding. Referring to R&D as the "fuzzy front end" of the enterprise, former Polaroid Vice Chairman Sheldon Buckler has said:

> The fuzzy front end is the source of all business value creation.
> By its nature, it is experimental, chaotic, and unpredictable.
> Making it work requires a high tolerance for ambiguity and
> uncertainty, a willingness to consider the "unreasonable," lots
> of individual activity, and enjoyment of the quest itself.[1]

Understanding the prospects for creating value, given the "fuzzy" nature of R&D work, requires a perspective on every aspect of the business. Consider, for example, a $50 million R&D program to develop a second-generation chemical plant. Smart decisions require that we understand not only the possible technical outcomes, but every step on the road from R&D to profitable commercialization. A next-generation plant might require radical engineering and a long list of important questions:

▲ Should the company look at modular design, fast build time, or a smaller footprint for the plant?

▲ What might the capital and operating costs be?

▲ Are the R&D targets too difficult?

▲ Who will be the customers of the new plant?

▲ How much revenue is possible?

▲ Should we consider joint ventures? If we do, should our R&D focus on identifying and building business relationships with potential partners?

No crystal ball is sufficiently clear to answer these questions with absolute certainty. But these questions need to be addressed because the output of R&D will have a powerful effect on everything that happens in the company.

Measurement, Feedback, and Improvement

To understand R&D decision making, we need to make a distinction between operational and strategic decisions. There are important differences between them; most relate to time. Operating decisions have short feedback loops in which the good or bad results of decisions are known fairly quickly. Feedback is rapid and direct. We try something, observe the results, and make corrections. This is the cycle of plan-do-check-act attributed to Walter Shewhart, and the basis for continuous process improvement.[2]

This approach to decisions assumes that mistakes are not too costly, and that the feedback and adjustment process will move an activity to optimum performance through a succession of incremental improvement steps. The feedback loop in this cycle usually can be measured in months, days, hours, or minutes. The people closest to the activities are viewed as the best source of knowledge and, therefore, the most able to suggest and implement improvements.

This cycle of decision making has its analogy in a mountain-

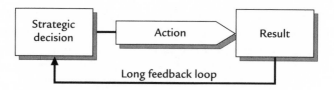

Figure 2-1. *The Long Feedback Loop of Strategic R&D Decisions*

climbing expedition that has to contend with poorly charted trails and variable weather conditions. The climbers themselves have the best local knowledge of the trail and how the weather is developing. If they choose a path that leads down to a valley instead of up toward the peak, they can quickly retrace their steps and try another path. In addition, their new knowledge of the terrain may be useful later.

For such operational decisions, several habits are important:

▲ *Attend to details and follow-through.* The key to improvement is to make sure one is in control of the process and to track very carefully what happens as the process changes.

▲ *Monitor near-term performance.* The near term is what matters, since the feedback loop is short. A succession of good near-term actions will result in a good long-term result.

▲ *Ignore uncertainties.* One will learn the uncertainties fastest by acting and by observing the results. Uncertainty is treated either as statistical variation to be kept within controlled limits or as a set of minor obstacles to be overcome.

▲ *Avoid alternatives.* In high feedback situations, it is better to follow the rule "ready, fire, aim" than the rule "ready, aim, fire." If you miss the first time, try again. Contemplating alternatives could lead to unnecessary delay.

These skills are appropriate for some operational decisions. For strategic decisions, they are not. Strategic decision making is qualitatively different. By definition, it involves large commitments of resources over many years before the results can be known. The feedback loop, as shown in Figure 2-1, is impossibly long. In the military aircraft industry, for example, initial decisions and final results can be separated by twenty years. In pharmaceuticals, a twelve-year gap is common. The decision by Britain's Pilkington Glass in the early 1950s to find a process for continuous casting of plate glass launched a decade of R&D and tremendous capital investments. The result was a breakthrough process that gave the company unassailable competitive superiority for years to come. But the outcome was uncertain until very near the end.[3]

In these cases, mistakes can be costly, and waiting to learn from results is impractical. As Peter Senge has written, "When cause and effect are distant in time or space, and results are ambiguous, then learning is nearly impossible."[4] Furthermore, results are inevitably clouded by intervening events and successive decisions, making it difficult if not impossible to sort out cause and effect and trace results back to the soundness of a particular decision. Often the decision makers themselves will have moved on or retired, with consequent loss of institutional memory. More important, large gains or losses will have already occurred.

Thus, the opportunity for continuous improvement based on results is much more difficult for the strategic decision maker. By the time the results become visible, it is too late to change the strategy that launched them. Decisions to merge or divest, to shift the focus of research from the central nervous system to the cardiovascular area, or to commit to a particular computer architecture are difficult, if not impossible, to reverse. Thus, the quality of strategic R&D decisions, and of the many that follow in any project, must be exceptionally high. And every project and every portfolio contains many of these decisions.

Returning to our mountain-climbing analogy, the strategic decision is like the choice of which mountain will be climbed. The climbers must also select the appropriate route, the best time of year, personnel, equipment, and the like—all in concert with the strategic objective of reaching the top. A poor choice will be costly. Rerouting the expedition from one mountain to another, for instance, would cost dearly in time and resources. In fact, there may be no opportunity to recover from such a false start. The entire expedition may have to be written off as a failure.

Many organizations have already reached a very high plane of operational effectiveness and must stay there simply to be competitive. Thanks to process improvements such as those described earlier, they are already "doing things right" and opportunities for operational improvement are few. For them, the most effective way to create new value is through improved strategic decision making, which calls for a quite different set of thinking skills:

▲ *Focus on the important issues.* Because the strategic landscape is vast, decision makers must stay focused on the major important features.

▲ *Consider long time horizons.* Make sure that the decision will get you where you want to be in the long term. Make sure the near-term actions are consistent with your long-term goals.

▲ *Account for uncertainty.* In the long term, the riskiest path may be formed by a sequence of least risky steps. By understanding uncertainty, decision makers can select the direction with the best risk-return relationship.

▲ *Choose carefully among alternatives.* Take the time to create several alternatives and then pick the best one. If you only have one shot, aim carefully.

Decision Making in Long-Feedback Situations

People often have trouble shifting from operational to strategic decision making. Almost all managers spend their formative years in operational pursuits. There they learn how to make operational decisions. But habits developed in that realm often create difficulties when managers advance to the level of making strategic decisions. For example, one good operational habit is a bias for action: Try something, get going, correct or improve later. In operations, "He who hesitates is lost." At the strategic level, a good habit is a bias for thinking: Achieve clarity of action before proceeding. "Look before you leap."

Each habit works well in its own setting. But executives who are promoted for their operational skills sometimes have trouble reorienting their habits to strategic situations. A good strategic decision process explicitly examines the likelihood of success and failure *before* the green light is given. It weighs risk and potential return, and does so in terms of the organization's ability to contend with financial losses. This deliberative process is unnatural for executives who have developed a deep-seated bias for action.

The fundamental distinction between decisions and outcomes is not always clear to action-oriented people. They are accustomed to judging decisions by their results. If a company makes an investment and fails to make money, they are tempted to say that it was a "bad decision." In a long-feedback world, we say that it was a "good decision" when it was made, but that the result was a "bad outcome." As

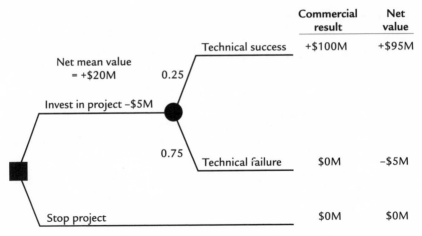

	Commercial result	Net value
Technical success	+$100M	+$95M
Technical failure	$0M	-$5M
	$0M	$0M

Net mean value = +$20M

0.25

Invest in project -$5M

0.75

Technical failure

Stop project

Note: This project has a 25 percent chance of technical success. The net mean value is calculated by multiplying the commercial result by the chance for technical success, then subtracting the initial investment.

Figure 2-2. *A Technical Failure and a Good Investment*

an example, think about teaching a teenager about the importance of not drinking and driving. When the inebriated teenager comes home without getting into an accident, do you reward or punish him? And what about the unfortunate nondrinker who has an accident? This individual certainly suffered a bad outcome after what we would call a good decision not to drink before driving. Who should be punished or rewarded? We can increase the odds of a safe return by teaching teenagers not to drink and drive, but in an uncertain world following these rules cannot guarantee safety.

A simplified example illustrates this point. Suppose that an R&D project for a large company has a twenty-five percent chance of technical success, which leads to results worth $100 million to the company, and costs $5 million to pursue. Is pursuing the project a good decision? Absolutely. It is a great bet. The mean value, one measure of prospects for value creation, is $20 million ($100 million × .25 − $5 million). A large company would like to have this sort of opportunity on a regular basis, even though the most likely result is technical failure. See Figure 2-2.

Business and R&D strategic decision makers need a method to ensure that they are making the very best decisions *at the time they make them*. They need a framework for determining decision quality.

Decision Quality

How do we know a good decision when we see one? One answer is provided by Dr. Arno Penzias, chief scientist at AT&T Bell Laboratories, astrophysicist, research scientist, and Nobel Prize-winner. According to Penzias:

> Scientists ask me, "How do you know you're working on a good project?" I say, "Simple: Imagine that what you're going to do will be 100 percent successful; find out how much money it's going to be worth; multiply by the probability of success, divide by the cost, and look at the figure of merit." When I originally said this, everybody became hysterical. Everybody got mad, saying, "How would we know the probability? How would we know what it's worth? What if we don't know who the customer is?"
>
> But if you don't know who needs something, why are you doing it? If you don't know what the chances are of success, why are you doing it? If you don't know how much it's going to cost—not just in resources but in years of your life—why are you doing it? You ought to know all three things![5]

Here is another way of thinking about the question. A document containing the final recommendations on the company's most important R&D decision lies, unread, on the table in front of you. You have neither the time nor expertise to understand *all* of the issues or their details. Nevertheless, your decision will determine the organization's future. Given this scenario, what questions would you want answered before you felt confident that you could make a good decision?

We and our colleagues have asked this question of hundreds of R&D decision makers and executives over the years. Here are some typical responses:

> Are the assumptions clearly identified?
>
> What are the probabilities of technical and market success?
>
> Does this course of action fit with the company's strength and larger objectives?
>
> Have alternatives been identified and evaluated?
>
> Have different areas of the company been heard from on this issue?
>
> Will the decision result in a clear competitive advantage?

What is the risk/return relationship?

Is there a feasible plan for implementing the decision?

Did staff recommendations consider all the important factors?

Are the alternatives based on reliable information?

What is the expected value of the decision we're about to make?

Is each of the important variables well understood?

What is the cost of failure?

Have we asked the right questions and gotten valid answers?

Is there a recovery plan in case of failure?

Have we obtained a cross-section of good information?

Is there a clear logic to the way we are approaching this decision?

What does our financial model tell us?

Does the decision feel right?

Can the organization get behind the decision?

We have consolidated responses like these, brought in the latest thinking of academics, and tested them with clients in actual situations. In the end, we have found that the quality of a decision can be summarized in six dimensions, as shown in Figure 2-3. Each dimension forms a link in a chain of decision quality.

The *appropriate frame* is the correct background, setting, and context for a decision. It was addressed through several of the previous quotes: "Have we asked the right questions?" "Are the assumptions clearly identified?" "Have different areas of the company been heard from on this issue?" "Does this course of action fit with the company's strength and larger objectives?" The frame is subtle. It is defined by the questions, the assumptions, the business purpose, and the people involved. Since the frame is a "window" we look through, it is the hardest dimension to see. But the right frame helps us avoid solving the wrong problem and often guides us to breakthrough thinking.[6]

Creative, doable alternatives are preconditions for any decision. If there are no alternatives, there is no decision. This dimension is illustrated by the earlier quotes: "Have alternatives been identified and evaluated?" "Is there a recovery plan in case of failure?" "Is there a feasible plan for implementing the decision?" This dimension requires tapping into the greatest source of potential value: the undiscovered alternative.

Meaningful, reliable information requires that the right information

Figure 2-3. *The Decision Quality Chain*

is brought to bear on the decision. This dimension is illustrated by the following quotes: "Have we asked the right questions and gotten valid answers?" "What are the probabilities of technical and market success?" "Have we obtained a cross-section of good information?" and "Have different areas of the company been heard from on this issue?"

Companies are usually good at bringing what they know to bear. The key to quality in this dimension is information about what is *not* known, that is, the limits of our knowledge.

Clear values and trade-offs are found by establishing criteria for measuring the value of alternatives and how the company will make rational trade-offs among them. For most corporations, cash flow is the ultimate measure of value generation over time. Trade-offs among other forms of value are best made by assessing the corporation's willingness to pay for these things out of cash flow. The company must also assess its preference for money now versus more money later. And because greater returns usually are accompanied by greater uncertainty, trade-offs have to be made. Being explicit and quantitative about each of these trade-offs helps ensure thoughtfulness and consistency.

The dimension of values and trade-offs is illustrated by the following quotes: "What is the risk/return relationship?" "What is the expected value of the decision we're about to make?" and "What is the cost of failure?"

Logically correct reasoning requires bringing together the inputs of the previous dimensions to determine which alternatives will create the most value. Since the world is too complex to rely on intuition, a formal model is usually required. "Is there a clear logic to our approach to the decision?" and "What does our financial model tell us?" At the end of the evaluation, the result must be a clear, understandable recommendation—a concise story that's right. The "clear competitive advantage" is apparent and the decision "feels right."

Commitment to action moves decisions to activities. The best decision is useless if the organization will not implement it. This dimension is illustrated by the following quotes: "Have different areas of the company been heard from on this issue?" "Can the organization get behind this decision?" and "Is there a feasible plan for implementing the decision?" The best way to achieve commitment to action is through quality in the other dimensions and meaningful involvement of the right people in the decision process.

The Strength of the Whole

The decision quality chain is only as strong as its weakest link. If a decision is good in all dimensions except the frame, it is still of low quality. For example, in times of change, companies are often blindsided when they fail to frame their decisions properly. The ice companies that were a common fixture of urban life early in this century disappeared as "iceboxes" gave way to electric refrigerators. Perhaps they would have survived had they framed their businesses more broadly—as refrigeration companies instead of ice makers.

Likewise, creating powerful new alternatives will never ensure a company's future if commitment cannot be mustered. Most companies have smart R&D people with good ideas, but good ideas that lack the organization's commitment produce no value.

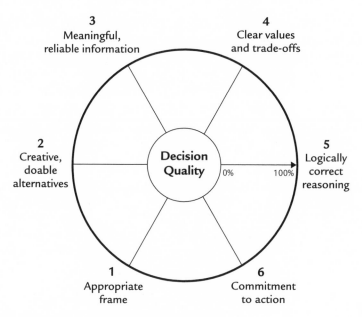

Figure 2-4. *The Decision Quality Spider Diagram*

If You Can Measure It, You Can Manage It

Measuring decision quality makes the process of making strategic R&D decisions manageable. It closes the feedback loop by critiquing decisions as they are made, long before the results are in, and provides data for continuous improvement of the decision process. It *sets standards* for specific decisions so that attention can be focused on the weakest dimension of decision quality.

To use decision quality as a metric, we convert the chain into a *spider diagram*, as shown in Figure 2-4. Here, zero percent quality in any dimension is in the center, and 100 percent quality is on the exterior.

The spider diagram helps us to rate a decision on each dimension, either as a historical audit or as a current assessment, where 100 percent is the point at which additional effort to improve this dimension would not be worth the cost. For instance, it is always possible to improve the frame, by discussing the issue with more people, by getting more perspectives, and so on. The same can be said about information; we can always gather more information, commission more research, and so forth. At some point, however, we experience diminishing returns. Eventually, further improvement is not cost effective.

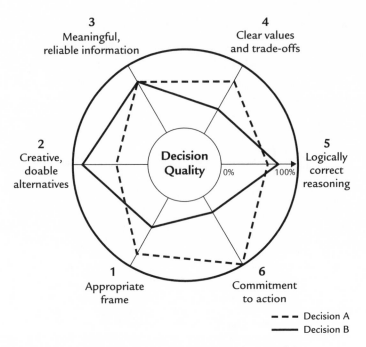

Figure 2-5. *A Spider Diagram Comparing Two Project Decisions*

Generally, we create spider diagrams by interviewing the many individuals involved in a particular decision. This can be done for a specific decision (ongoing or as a postmortem) or to appraise the decision quality of the organization in general. This rating system is not exact, but it helps us to understand and identify strengths and weaknesses.

A sample spider diagram for a company we benchmarked appears in Figure 2-5. This diagram compares two project decisions (called A and B) concerning major R&D efforts intended to develop new business areas. The thoughts and comments of interviewees associated with the ratings are shown in Table 2-1.

In the example, decision B is weak on commitment, which is a symptom of weaknesses in other dimensions. The big tip-off is the low quality of the frame. Because it sets the context, it can throw off the other dimensions. When decisions have weak frames, the focus should shift to that dimension.

In general, because the overall quality of a decision is only as good as its weakest link, the weakest dimensions should receive the greatest attention. For example, project A is low on the alternatives. This would be a good place to focus attention. Doing so would probably force the issue in logically correct reasoning, the other low dimension for project A, because developing several compelling alternatives would create a requirement to evaluate them.

Another purpose of the spider diagram is to understand why particular dimensions have high or low ratings. As we consider each dimension, we have a reason to think about and discuss the contributing factors (see Table 2-1). For example, project B is in an area unfamiliar to the company, which makes the frame, values, and commitment low. A good question is, "Why does our decision process not help us frame decisions in unfamiliar areas?" This kind of question and diagnostics help keep a decision on track and improve an organization's decision-making process over time.

Table 2-1. *Interviewees' Comments on Each Dimension of Decision Quality*

	DECISION A	DECISION B
Frame	Incremental business; felt confident that we have the background and expertise	Fundamentally unfamiliar with this business area
Alternatives	"Satisficed"; picked first alternative that looked "good enough"	Put a lot of effort into investigation and understanding; used exploratory research program to generate many alternatives
Information	Gathered good information, understated uncertainty	Gathered good information, understated uncertainty
Values	Clear how new business could fit it	Unresolved trade-off; fear of risk of doing something new versus excitement about new potential
Reasoning	Emotionally ready to accept without much of a case	Good fact-based case
Commitment	Familiar territory, easy to get authorized	Organization lined up to do it; management agrees that it makes sense; but funding decision getting stalled

In a major European paper company, we used spider diagrams to conduct a number of postproject decision audits and used the analysis to improve the company's decision process. In effect, this was a decision quality health check. For each of several R&D groups, we identified one or two recent strategic decisions and talked group members through the decision quality spider. Comparing the spider diagrams across the groups, we recognized a striking pattern: Decision makers did not understand the value-creation potential of their projects. The company undertook to improve its process so that R&D value measurements are made.

The Case of Company X

The value of periodic diagnosis of decision quality was made clear to us in a case we encountered not long ago. The corporation, Company X, had a dynamic, thriving research organization with a long history of successful products, and a strong tradition in a few important technical areas. Recently, however, it had run into trouble. Two of its major products had gone off patent and it had no major near-term products in the pipeline. Why? The company's R&D department clearly had a large portfolio of projects, but somehow it had not been able to identify and nurture any with commercial viability. The authors conducted a decision quality health check to find out what was going on.

We soon found that the company had no explicit technology strategy. In the absence of this, it simply aimed to "work hard and be opportunistic." Unfortunately, the company's core competence in an important technical area was no longer highly relevant to its industry. This competence had shifted from being a source of competitive advantage to something that could be readily outsourced. Yet the head of R&D had a strong background in this technical area and, as a result, the area was never questioned.

These problems showed up quite clearly in our diagnosis. Using a special decision quality questionnaire, we examined decision quality at three levels: technology strategy, portfolio strategy, and project strategy. Figure 2-6 is the actual spider diagram for Company X's technology strategy process, which was sadly lacking in quality. Company managers understood the importance of R&D to their business, but were never clear about goals. They framed their strategic decisions well, but never really made choices. The quality in all other di-

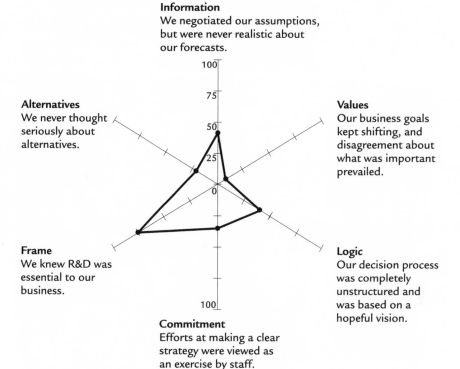

Information
We negotiated our assumptions, but were never realistic about our forecasts.

Alternatives
We never thought seriously about alternatives.

Values
Our business goals kept shifting, and disagreement about what was important prevailed.

Frame
We knew R&D was essential to our business.

Logic
Our decision process was completely unstructured and was based on a hopeful vision.

Commitment
Efforts at making a clear strategy were viewed as an exercise by staff.

Overall technology strategy decision quality is 25 percent.

Figure 2-6. *Company X's Technology Decisions*

mensions was low. We rated the quality of this technology strategy process as about 25 percent by taking an "average" of the six dimensions that weighed the weak links heavily. (Technically we use the harmonic mean.) This was an appalling score, given that the benchmark for best-in-class on technology strategy process is 70 percent. The median companies are at 50 percent and the bottom decile of companies is at 30 percent. Company X was, in fact, among the worst companies we have surveyed for technology strategy!

Without a commitment to a well-defined technology strategy, setting an appropriate frame and establishing clear values at the portfolio level was bound to be impossible for this company. Lack of clarity about a technology strategy resulted in a vacuum of meaningful guidance about portfolio decisions. Figure 2-7 shows the spider dia-

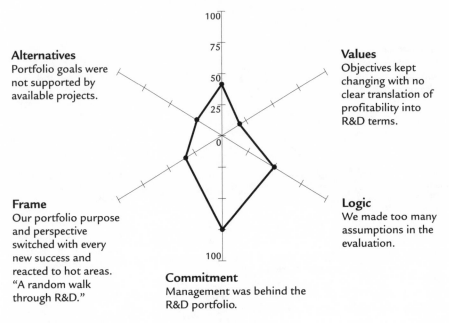

Information
There was too much negotiation of information and not enough scenarios.

Alternatives
Portfolio goals were not supported by available projects.

Values
Objectives kept changing with no clear translation of profitability into R&D terms.

Frame
Our portfolio purpose and perspective switched with every new success and reacted to hot areas. "A random walk through R&D."

Logic
We made too many assumptions in the evaluation.

Commitment
Management was behind the R&D portfolio.

Overall portfolio strategy decision quality is 30 percent.

Figure 2-7. *Company X's Portfolio Decisions*

gram for the same company at the portfolio level. Notice an emerging pattern: Value measures keep shifting, and information is negotiated rather than based on evidence. Company X's score of 30 percent for portfolio strategy placed it among the worst companies in our surveys.

Only at the project level did this R&D organization approach average decision quality (Figure 2-8). The R&D staff had reasonably good projects and were skillful at making decisions that maximized the value of individual projects. However, the failure to obtain and operate with reliable information, a disconnect between R&D and broader business objectives, and weaknesses in alternatives and logic kept this company from making high-quality decisions at the project level. Company X's 48 percent score for project strategy placed it in the middle of the pack for this type of decision.

When we look at all three diagrams together, patterns emerge.

DECISION QUALITY

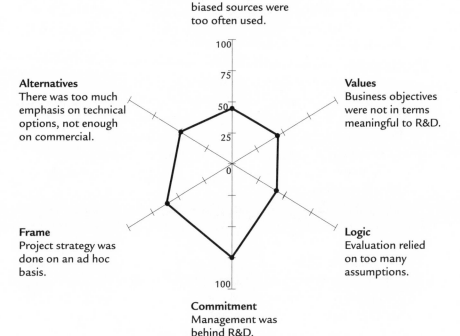

Information
Point estimates from
biased sources were
too often used.

Alternatives
There was too much
emphasis on technical
options, not enough
on commercial.

Values
Business objectives
were not in terms
meaningful to R&D.

Frame
Project strategy was
done on an ad hoc
basis.

Logic
Evaluation relied
on too many
assumptions.

Commitment
Management was
behind R&D.

Overall project strategy decision quality is 48 percent.

Figure 2-8. *Company X's Project Decisions*

Each decision is low in the information dimension, and for similar reasons: Assumptions are negotiated; point estimates mask underlying uncertainty in information; and information sources are biased. This organization had difficulty discussing uncertainty and had little basis for calibrating its forecasts. One participant put it quite directly: "We tend to believe our own b.s."

Company X was in serious trouble.

The prescription for a company like this is never obvious. Like doctors on first seeing a late-stage cancer patient, we kept thinking, "Why didn't this guy come in earlier?" In fact, the company soon entered a period of crisis. Shortly after we conducted our work, the company was acquired and taken apart. Employment dropped from approximately 5,000 to 800. The great irony is that Company X was acquired for the great technical strength of several of its research areas.

A Prescription for Quality Decisions

Regular self-examination is the best prescription for quality decision making. If a bad decision is made, find out why, and prevent the same mistake from recurring. This sort of vigilance prevents an organization from reaching the point of no return, as Company X did.

If you want your organization to be Olympian in its decision making, monitor individual decisions. Do a decision quality test on each decision, track the results, and take steps to improve the process. The challenges are likely to come when the steps required to improve decision making run counter to the current culture of the organization. This will require surfacing and directly engaging aspects of the culture that represent barriers to decision quality. For example, if your company has a planning culture that prevents discussing uncertainty, you will need to address the counterproductive aspects of the culture.

The decision quality chain defines our goal: what we want to achieve on every strategic occasion. It allows us to critique the quality of a decision at the time we make it. The next chapter discusses the six dimensions in depth. Subsequent chapters explain the *process* for systematically reaching high-quality strategic decisions, which is based on the *best practices* of R&D decision making, and *nine principles* that enable the cultural and organizational transformation to make it happen.

CHAPTER 3

THE SIX DIMENSIONS OF DECISION QUALITY

A S THE PREVIOUS CHAPTER ASSERTS, the quality of decision making and its several dimensions can be measured, creating an opportunity for better management. This section considers each dimension of decision quality in detail, explains the standards of quality, and describes the practices that create it.

Appropriate Frame

A "frame" is a window through which we view a particular problem. Unless we make a deliberate effort to do otherwise, we frame problems in terms of our beliefs and prejudices, predisposing ourselves to see these problems in certain ways, reality notwithstanding. Hammer and Champy underscored the danger of this predisposition when they wrote, "The changes that will put a company out of business are those that happen outside the light of its current expectations."[1] Inappropriate framing leads to inappropriate perceptions, interpretations, and decisions.

One Project, Three Frames

It is not unusual for a single R&D project to be seen through different frames. The challenge for the decision maker is to determine which is most appropriate. For example, an R&D project aims at making a 10 percent cost improvement for a crucial process. The project has reached a stage gate in the company's process[2] and is up for evaluation. The project frame will have a major impact on its chances of passing the gate and the ability of the company to capitalize on its results. Here are a few ways in which decision makers might frame the project.

> *Frame 1:* If the project is successful, the company will enjoy increased margins. A ten percent cut from operating costs will

go straight to the bottom line. For a few years, the company will enjoy extra cash flows.

This frame leads to some natural questions: How much is 10 percent worth in actual dollars to the bottom line? How long can that extra margin be sustained? Which plants have the most potential for benefiting, that is, where would it be worth implementing the process?

> *Frame 2:* The improved process represents an opportunity to enhance our competitive position. Low costs can put us in a preferred supplier position. If we pass on some of the savings to customers, the immediate result will be increased market share. If we continue innovations along these lines, we will stay ahead of our competitors on the cost curve and be able to price to retain a dominant market position.

This frame leads to an entirely different set of questions: How many customers would switch suppliers for a 10 percent price reduction? How long can they be retained? Can the company realistically keep ahead of its competitors on the cost curve, or will they soon catch up?

Suppose that a 10 percent savings is not a great deal of money in absolute terms, but that price is the basis for competition. The first frame might well kill the project. On the other hand, the project might get a "go" decision as an important but low-priority, continuous improvement project.

The second frame could lead the organization to large value. In order to assess the volume impacts of a price reduction (and to gain commitment to make it happen), the project would need to involve people from marketing, and could become a high-profile cross-functional priority.

> *Frame 3:* The new technology has the potential to improve the company's global position. The company has avoided entry to an important region of the world because established suppliers here enjoy economic advantages. With the new process, it may be possible to compete effectively with those competitors.

This third frame leads to an entirely new set of questions.

This cost improvement example illustrates how the frame defines the purpose of the decision, as well as the organization's perspective. These are also defined implicitly by the people involved, as the following example, attributed to Russell Ackoff,[3] illustrates.

Slow elevators were Complaint Number One among employees at a particular company, and the executive committee brought in the engineering team to solve the problem. A few weeks later, the engineers made their report.

"We've measured the speed of the elevators in terms of average and longest waiting times, and we've examined the equipment, which is very old. Elevator speeds are much improved in newer systems. Even in old slow systems like this, however, new approaches to elevator dispatching can dramatically reduce waiting times."

"So what can we do?" asked the chief executive.

"Our recommendation is to upgrade the cables and motors and add express elevators. To minimize disruption, we recommend refurbishing one shaft at a time. We were able to get an excellent quote from a contractor, who should be able to complete the job in about eight months for only $6 million."

"That's too much time and money!" cried the chief executive.

"It's the best possible option," replied the engineer.

The chief executive knew that doing nothing was not a viable option—it would have a devastating impact on morale. "Unless anyone has any better ideas," he said with resignation, "we will have to go ahead with this plan."

"Let's try another perspective," suggested the human resources manager. "I know an industrial psychologist who might help us. Let's give him a week and see what he comes up with."

The chief executive could not imagine a psychologist having much to say about what appeared to be a mechanical issue. But, he wasn't thrilled about paying $6 million for faster elevators either. "Okay," he said, "but if he doesn't come up with anything within a week, we'll proceed with the engineers' plan."

The psychologist spent the greater part of one day observing people in the waiting areas, and he spoke with a number of them. He reported back to the executive suite the next morning.

"The problem is not that the elevators are too slow," he told the chief executive, "your people are simply bored. Have you spent much time in the elevator lobbies? They are dull and sterile. I'd suggest a little redecoration—some plants and a few mirrors."

The chief executive, a hard-crusted engineer, regarded the psychologist blankly. "Plants and mirrors?" he thought to himself with repressed amusement. "It sounds crazy, but I'd rather act crazy than spend $6 million." He agreed to try it.

Within a few weeks, the elevator lobbies were upgraded. Employees stopped complaining about the wait, and they were pleased that management had responded rapidly to their Complaint Number One. Morale improved.

As this anecdote suggests, different people with different perspectives implicitly frame decisions in different ways. Some frames are more productive and appropriate than others. One good way to evaluate and improve the quality of the frame is to expose the problem to people with different points of view.

Requirements for a High-Quality Frame

Quality in framing requires several shifts in thinking habits.

Do not simply accept the problem as first presented. Many R&D projects present themselves as technical opportunities. With some work, they can be framed as business opportunities, such as the 10 percent cost reduction cited earlier. Developing the full frame usually requires some cross-functional, assumption-challenging thinking. One R&D manager we know was very excited about automating a particular measurement process. "It will go ten times faster than doing it manually!" he exclaimed.

"What good will that do?" we asked. He looked at us as if we were idiots. The question challenged his assumptions.

"It will be good for the business," he responded vaguely.

We later explained this opportunity to the head of the business unit. "That would be good, I guess," he replied, "but it's not the real issue. We rarely get bottlenecks in that step, and when we do, we can hire temps."

By accepting the initial frame of "automation makes things faster," the R&D manager had been working on the wrong issue for months. It only took us a few minutes to question the frame. In a few days we were able to identify the real issues and help him adopt a better frame.

Advocates often subconsciously select the frame most advantageous to their point of view. Always question them.

Frame strategic and operational problems differently. Avoid an operational frame to a strategic problem. Always ask, Is this decision an operational one, or is it strategic?

Stage gate processes help prevent this mistake, if used properly. The passing of each gate creates a sort of strategic break from business as usual—a time to question projects from a strategic perspective. Used in this way, the stage gate is more than a project management and tracking tool. It creates an opportunity to make real value-creating strategic decisions. Any planning process can be used this way: stage gate process, budget cycle, planning cycle, or commercial and technical reviews.

At the strategic level, approach R&D activities as long-term investments, not as expenses. Many executives, especially those with nontechnical backgrounds, view R&D as an unavoidable "tax" on corporate resources. This frame shapes their decisions on project funding. These executives should view R&D activities as strategic investments, like those in manufacturing, marketing, and the like. When R&D is viewed as a tax, executives are motivated to minimize it. When R&D is seen as an investment, executives may see it as a good place to put money.

A true shift of frame requires that we explicitly measure the value of R&D and in terms comparable to those of other corporate investments. This means thinking beyond a narrow technical perspective and aligning business strategy and R&D strategy—which we call technology strategy. These are best developed jointly, with one frame informing the other. The Xerox PARC example illustrates some of these issues.

Although Xerox's Palo Alto Research Center invented laser printing, Ethernet, the personal workstation, and the graphical user interface, it is not a player in any of these businesses today.[4] In the 1970s, when it made these inventions, Xerox was a copier company and these projects did not really fit its corporate strategy. Consequently, other companies brought these inventions to the world and captured their value, often raiding Xerox's talented staff to do so. The only business into which Xerox really made solid inroads was laser printing, which was fairly close to its core copier business.

It would be wrong to conclude that R&D should be in lock-step with current businesses and strategies. R&D is capable of renewing businesses and changing industries. That is, itself, a strategic opportunity. Xerox could probably have done better with a business strategy suited to the results that were being delivered by its lab rather than with its traditional strategy. Its problem was a strategic disconnect in decision making—a mistake in framing earlier strategic decisions. In a private interview, a senior R&D executive at Xerox PARC at the time said that the company only had the resources to pursue either laser printing or the workstation. It chose laser printing. Perhaps this was a good decision, given the situation. But it was poor strategy to allow an organization with the resources of Xerox (at the time) to reach a situation in which it could only pursue one of many revolutionary new businesses.

Even in the decision to pursue laser printing over workstations, Xerox had a limiting frame. It saw itself as constrained by limited resources. By comparison, the upstart companies that commercialized Xerox PARC inventions had miniscule resources. But they saw themselves as able to raise resources to pursue these new businesses. Different frames produced different results.

Include multiple perspectives in establishing the decision frame. Engineers and scientists typically have narrow technical perspectives. These must be expanded through cross-functional representation in framing strategic R&D decisions. Cross-functional teams are common in R&D operations, and they are equally powerful in the creation of R&D strategy. The elevator example given earlier showed how adherence to one discipline's point of view can lead to decision-making myopia. The example of the 10 percent cost improvement likewise required the insight of another business discipline—marketing—to frame cost reduction as a basis for competition.

Creative, Doable Alternatives

The operational culture typically seeks a single viable choice. "We've done all the research and we've asked everyone involved, and *this* is what we recommend." The single viable choice puts top management in the position of saying either "yes" or "no." Saying "yes" reduces the executive role to one of mere approval. Saying "no" may demotivate the people who brought forth the choice.

For example, an electronics manufacturer was immobilized by a set of narrow choices. The engineering group wanted to upgrade one of the company's plants; it developed an elaborate proposal and took it to senior management. The proposal was presented as a tightly bound package needing only executive approval. Because of its expertise, senior management could have made a valuable contribution to the content of the proposal, but it had no constructive way to contribute. So it questioned the proposal and its justification in great detail. Eventually, a flaw was found in the proposal. Unable to say "yes" to the plant upgrade as presented, senior management had to say "no, go back and rework the proposal along these lines."

The engineers felt that management was nitpicking, but reworked their proposal to the point of being "bullet proof." A few months later, they returned for management approval, only to have management uncover another flaw. This cycle lasted for *two years*, to the great frustration of all concerned.

The fundamental error in this situation was that there were no alternatives, hence no basis for comparison or discussion. There was no real choice.

A contrasting scenario is the case of a pharmaceutical company that used multiple alternatives in the evaluation of its portfolio. For each project, this company developed four alternatives, each with a different directive:

1. a substantial increase in the budget,
2. a substantial decrease in the budget,
3. budget continued as is, and
4. stop the project while preserving salvage value.

Each project team was challenged by these directives to develop a set of significantly different project strategies. This unleashed their creativity, gave more options to upper management, and ultimately generated a 30 percent increase in the value of the portfolio.

Creativity as a Source of Alternatives

Much human progress can be attributed to individuals who have sought and found creative and practical solutions to humankind's thorny problems: Edison in the field of lighting; Henry Ford in manufacturing; Lister, Pasteur, and dozens of others in the field of human health. Creativity is not as mysterious as it seems. In many cases, creativity involves nothing more than looking at a problem with fresh eyes, seeing in it something others have missed, and refusing to accept the apparent solution. Creativity frames problems differently.

Perhaps no better example of triumph through dogged refusal to accept the apparent solution is found than the case of longitude—a problem that had vexed mariners and the scientific community alike for centuries.[5] In 1714, Britain's Parliament established a prize of £20,000 for whomever could devise a practical method for determining longitude at sea. A board of scientific luminaries, including Sir

Isaac Newton and Astronomer Royal Edmund Halley, was established to judge the merits of submissions.

Excepting far-fetched proposals—such as one to anchor cannon-firing signal ships at regular intervals across the Atlantic Ocean—most serious contenders sought an astronomical solution to the problem. Indeed, the board itself was heavily weighted with astronomers who naturally favored this approach. The actual solution, however, came from John Harrison, a self-taught London clockmaker who approached the issue from a different angle. Harrison devised a unique timepiece, the marine chronometer, capable of keeping near-perfect time through rolling seas and dramatic shifts in humidity and temperature. With knowledge of the exact time at their home ports (or Greenwich time), navigators could then use standard astronomical fixes to determine their positions east and west on the globe.

Field tests of Harrison's solution clearly indicated its practical effectiveness. But the fact that it did so through unconventional means impeded the board's awarding of the prize—and the adoption of Harrison's superior method for navigation—for several decades.

Alternatives Must Be Doable

Creativity can take us only so far, however. In the end, alternatives must be doable. There must be some foreseeable path to commercialization. Many suggestions are not doable, but this does not always stop them from advancing far into the planning process.

One client's top R&D project involved the design of a huge, next-generation plant at the heart of which lay a radical new process capable of unheard-of efficiencies. At the client's request, we projected the project to commercialization, only to discover that the scale of the plant required investments beyond the reach of the largest companies on earth. It was not financially "doable." The research program needed alternatives featuring reduced capital costs and plant sizes. The project was ultimately cancelled, but not before the project team lost credibility for dogged advocacy of what was clearly not a feasible proposition.

A Good Set of Alternatives

A good decision-making process creates multiple alternatives for management's consideration. Alternatives should be

▲ broadly constructed, and not simply minor variations of a single concept;

▲ reasonable contenders for selection, not ridiculous extremes meant to make some other alternatives appear obviously superior; and

▲ sufficiently numerous to represent true choice, yet not so numerous as to confound the ability to evaluate and choose.

An example is a computer firm that recognized it needed a technology strategy. It had been dabbling in many different business/R&D areas. Its strategy was *de facto* a collection of activities initiated by various developers and business units—some in hardware; others in software. Some projects were aimed at PC users; others addressed the needs of Macintosh users; still others addressed users of UNIX systems. Among the products being developed, some would be sold through retail channels while others would serve OEM and industrial customers. In fact, this company had no strategy.

Initially, R&D and marketing personnel generated hundreds of strategies, based on logical combinations and permutations of platforms, hardware, software, and target customers: alternative overkill. Managers and researchers then attempted to define and defend a single strategy, with a few minor variations. "Let's return to our core business. We have complicated our situation and lost track of our real capabilities." This was also low quality on the alternatives dimension, with only one alternative being developed, and with too much detail.

Their third response finally achieved high quality. Here they stepped up to the hard work of thinking through alternatives for their business. "Return to core" was one strategy. Several others were also developed: focus on hardware; support emerging PC networks; develop crossplatform protocols; and so on. Each of these represented a comprehensive strategy that implied choice in each of the many decision areas for platform, hardware/software, and target customers. Each strategy was developed in detail.

Requirements for High-Quality Alternatives

Quality in the creative, doable alternatives dimension requires that we do three things:

1. Generate a good set of alternatives—not retreaded old ideas. Separate the creation of alternatives from their evaluation. Evaluating

alternatives as they emerge tends to kill good ideas before they are
fully conceived.

2. Make sure that each alternative represents a comprehensive and feasible strategy. Each alternative should provide direction for each
major functional and business area. Some should make the business
stretch. Each alternative should be specified in sufficient detail to be
clear, but not enough to be cumbersome.

3. Generate alternatives that are significantly different, spanning the
range of possibilities. Typically, there should be three to seven alternatives. Chapter 9, Technology Strategy, demonstrates the use of
strategy tables, an effective tool for creating and describing a set of
strategies.

Meaningful, Reliable Information

What are the facts about the future market for a new drug? What are
the facts about the efficiency improvements achievable through a
new but untried assembly process? What are the facts about the future regulatory environment?

Unfortunately, there are no facts about the future, and so there
can be no facts about any of the above. Strategic decision making requires information about possibilities that are fundamentally uncertain: future markets, level of technical success, competitors' actions,
and regulatory changes, to name a few. In lieu of unobtainable facts,
decision makers must make do with information that provides insight into the future. That information must be meaningful in the
sense that it selects only what is helpful in illuminating current decisions, while avoiding needless complexity. At the same time it must
be objective and reliable, incorporating the best judgment of people
in the best position to know.

Traditional Forecasting Is Not Good Enough

The operational habit of searching for the facts and collecting extensive data has limited value. Taken to its extreme, this habit buries decision makers under historical data and point projections of present
trends, but arms them with neither intelligence nor perspective. One
company we know of kept a record of every customer's use of its
product. It projected customer usage trends into the future and
planned accordingly. When the regulatory environment changed,

this company found its data of no value in finding a new direction. It was overwhelmed by irrelevant data and unable to make good decisions.

The usual approach to forecasting is to take a best guess and assume it will happen. This is typical in project justification, a process familiar to most readers:

▲ Start with the assumption that the technical approach will work.

▲ Assume no insurmountable complications.

▲ Look at historical market size and project a market share figure.

▲ Adjust the assumptions to obtain a positive net present value.

▲ Believe that your numbers are real.

Understand the Drivers of Uncertainty

Information quality involves a shift of emphasis from the tangible world we know to the potential world we seek to understand. Most organizations are excellent at bringing the information they know to bear. They are less than excellent at talking about what they do not know.

The first step in the transition is to be explicit about what information is required for a good decision. This can be done by using an influence diagram, which maps uncertainties. Figure 3-1 shows an influence diagram for a typical pharmaceutical project decision. What the company in this figure ultimately wants to know is the commercial value of a potential new product. This value is a function of uncertain development costs, revenues, cost of goods, and expenses. Revenue in the figure depends on two other critical uncertainties, price and number of patients. The major factors influencing price are the health-care environment and clinical trial (phase III) results, which indirectly influence the number of patients through share. In this way, one identifies the map of key uncertainties. Phase III results, for example, influence commercial value through multiple paths. This type of map can be applied to decisions in any industry.

Be Clear about Definitions

Uncertainties must be clarified. Unless one is clear and unambiguous about terms, information can be misinterpreted. Referring to Figure 3-1, what does "health-care environment" really mean? Or consider

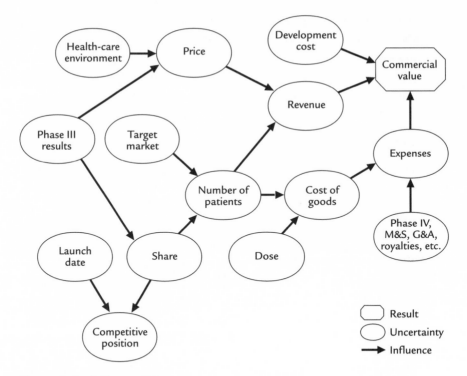

Figure 3-1. *Influence Diagram*

"technical success." To a researcher, the term *technical success* may mean a result suitable for publication. To a marketer, it might mean development of a product that delights customers. One specialty chemicals company we worked with debated for months about its chance of technical success with a particular project. Why so long? Project members were unclear as to the meaning of the term with respect to the project. The production manager questioned the project, saying that the chance of technical success was low. The project leader acknowledged the project's uncertainty, but averred that his team could handle every technical hurdle. Each was right. The project had three technical hurdles, each with a 90 percent or greater chance of success. By this definition, there was a 73 percent chance of technical success. Thus, the project leader was right in that the project had a reasonably high chance of technical success. However, the customer required a product that would meet certain price points and performance criteria. Therefore, if the product could not be manufactured at sufficiently low cost, it was of no value to the company. The probability of overcoming all of these performance hurdles was about 65 percent. Putting these hurdles together with the previous ones resulted in a 47 percent chance of ultimate success. Thus, the production manager was also right—they had less than a 50 percent chance of creating a marketable product. When the uncertainty was stated clearly, there was little disagreement on the assessments.

Quantifying Uncertainty

Each of the many uncertainties associated with a project must be quantified.[6] Quantification forces people to structure the issues; it also surfaces additional issues and sources of uncertainty.

Quantification of uncertainty has a long history. Napoleon assessed his probabilities of victory at Waterloo in 1815. Napoleon's hopes for victory hinged on keeping the English and Prussian armies separate so that they could be attacked and defeated individually. At Ligny, he attacked and defeated the Prussians, but not completely. As day dawned on the field of Waterloo, where he was preparing to fight the English, he believed he had removed the Prussian army as an effective fighting force. At breakfast, he told his officers that he thought his chances of victory were ninety out of one hundred, although he believed, erroneously, that the English outnumbered him. When he later learned that the first elements of the surviving Prussian army were joining the English in the battle, he said, "This morning we had ninety chances in our favor. We still have sixty to forty."[7]

The operational habit is to create a point estimate for each variable. The result is unreliable information. It is better to establish *ranges* for important variables. Instead of saying, "The cost of development is estimated to be $1.25 million," say, "The cost of development should fall into a range between $0.80 million and $1.35 million." The range itself should reflect all judgments about possible sources of uncertainty. Consider the following lighthearted example.

When did Attila the Hun die? Before you go running for the encyclopedia, think about what you know and do not know about Attila. In doing so, you will be assessing *your* level of uncertainty about the year of his demise. Given that level of uncertainty, establish a range within which Attila most likely died. For example, "Attila probably died in some year between x and z." As a low figure, pick a year (x) for which you estimate only a 10 percent chance that the actual year of Attila's death would be lower. Now establish the high end of the range. Pick a year (z) such that you believe there is only a 10 percent chance that the actual year would be higher. Now, the chance that the actual year will occur inside your range is 80 percent. This range is an expression of your uncertainty about the year of Attila's death.

Finally, establish a median figure. Pick a year (y), in which the actual year of the Head Hun's death is equally likely to fall above or below. This range is a rough probability distribution; it reflects your uncertainty about when Attila died.

Few people are trained to express uncertainty as probability. Yet probabilistic information is what decision making about the future requires. Extensive psychological research into how people express and make judgments about uncertainty shows the value of information expressed in this way.[8]

Avoiding Bias

Individual estimates made in the face of uncertainty are subject to biases. Consider the *overconfidence bias*. People systematically put too much credibility in their point estimates and create ranges that are far too narrow. This means that the "actuals" often fall outside their ranges.

A little analysis explains the mechanics of the overconfidence bias. People make an initial assessment of some variable, say the lifetime of a manufacturing plant. They cognitively "anchor" on this initial estimate and create a range around it to adjust for their uncertainty, as shown in Figure 3-2. This range is usually inadequate.

Fortunately, practice makes perfect. More experience with ranges and communicating about uncertainty leads to more reliable assessments. Weather forecasters, for example, make daily predictions of the probability of rain. The actual frequency of rain matches their predictions extremely well. When they predict a 50 percent chance of rain, it rains 50 percent of the time. Besides practice, it is also possible to use special "debiasing" procedures in a structured interview to get more reliable ranges.

Assumptions Hide Uncertainty

People often disagree violently over point estimates. These same people, however, are likely to agree on a carefully assessed range or probability distribution. The reason? A range has fewer assumptions.

Assumptions are integral to the way we think. As a result, people

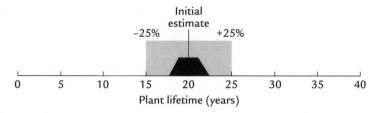

Figure 3-2. *Range Anchoring with an Initial Estimate*

adhere to them and fight in their defense. Unfortunately, assumptions cover implicit beliefs, which must be made explicit to understand the true uncertainty.

Avoid the Precision Trap

Except for the few truly critical issues, decision quality rarely requires great precision: a well-informed approximation is usually adequate.

For example, a client company knew that successful commercialization of one of its R&D projects would require a major capital investment. But how major? Our job was to make an assessment. We began with the engineering department. It had developed cost estimates for the different parts of the plant, using engineering rules of thumb. From these it has distilled a single cost estimate. When we inquired about the underlying numbers, the response was, "If you can get funding for a half-million dollar engineering study, we can get more precise numbers."

The engineering department was precisely wrong. The one thing we could be certain of was that the more precise numbers would not prevail. We did not want them; instead, we wanted to understand the *possibilities*, which a rough range of cost estimates would have indicated. Had the engineers felt comfortable talking about uncertainty, substantial effort would have been saved.

As it turned out, capital costs were far less important than market uncertainties to the actual decision. In this case, efforts spent dealing with capital costs would have been better directed at understanding the market.

Requirements for High-Quality Information

In summary, quality in the dimension of meaningful, reliable information requires the following:

1. Understand the drivers of uncertainty. Talk about what you do not know.

2. Be clear. Do not confuse ambiguity with uncertainty.

3. Express uncertainty as ranges and probability distributions—not as point estimates. In a strategic setting, it is better to be approximately right than precisely wrong.

4. Use the best experts with the least bias. Use assessment procedures to minimize cognitive illusions.

5. Focus on the information material to the decision.

Clear Values and Trade-offs

Two important R&D projects came up for funding at the same time. Since both required the same resources, only one could be funded. Each project's champion submitted a credible analysis.

"My project has a superb strategic fit with our long-term goals," said Alice in her analysis, "and our strategic position will be secured through the many patents we will produce." Bob spoke highly of his project as well, "My project fills a clear unmet customer need in a niche where we should be able to produce high profit margins."

Which project would you fund? Obviously, there is not enough information here to make a good decision. Each project leader is arguing his or her case using two different measures. Alice has chosen patents and strategic fit; Bob has chosen unmet need and profit margin. There is no basis for comparison.

Clear values mean that alternatives are measured against a common metric that represents what the organization aims to achieve. In virtually all business settings, this is shareholder value, appropriately calculated by net present value (NPV) of cash flows.[9] The use of multiple metrics often confuses decision makers. This problem is prevalent in R&D management. In fact, one study found thirty-three metrics being used to measure R&D value.[10] Unfortunately, many of these do not directly measure the overarching organizational objective. Other metrics are simply means to this objective. Had Alice and Bob rendered their reports on a comparable basis, the choice for decision makers would have been much clearer. For example, Alice's presentation could have been, "Because of its fit with our strategic objectives, this project will help us enter new markets and create new value worth $120 million." And Bob's analysis could have been, "Meeting the unmet customer need at the margins we foresee creates $15 million in new value for the company."

Connecting the results of R&D to ultimate business value in this fashion can be a tall order. But it is being done by leaders in R&D-intensive organizations in many industries.[11] The point is to be clear about objectives and to measure projects consistently.

Means versus Ends

The first step in being clear about values is to separate means and ends. The best measures of value focus on final objectives. Consider market share. It is common to measure projects against their ability to generate market share. Unfortunately, you cannot take market share to the bank, and taken to an extreme, the pursuit of market share can lead to excessive spending and few profits. Often, however, a sizable market presence is a first and necessary step to subsequent profitability, possibly with the next product. In the computer industry, for example, companies with high market share are viewed by customers as safer purchases; the perception is that these companies will remain in business and, therefore, be available for customer support and product upgrades. Getting a high market share in the short term, then, creates additional revenues later.

Within a limited arena, it is possible to construct an intermediate (or means) measure, like market share, as a surrogate for a more fundamental ends value measure. For example, Eli Lilly measures many of its development results in terms of "days until approval" of the new drug. On average, pharmaceutical companies spend more than $200,000 per day taking each new chemical entity through to approval.[12] In certain stages of development, each day is worth millions in terms of potential profit.[13] This measure works fine. It also avoids the burden of tracing every decision through to its final implications.

So-called intangibles may also serve as surrogates for value. They almost always reflect some poorly articulated relationship to ultimate value. For example, in making an investment decision for an electric utility, the project leader said that automated control equipment was justified by improvements in operator effectiveness. What did he mean by "operator effectiveness?" After some discussion, we determined that this equipment would allow the utility to reduce head count, which would lower costs. It also allowed better control at low output levels; better control, in turn, would increase revenues in some situations. Based on a quick calculation of the economic value of these effects, relative to cost, the project was approved.

In most cases, however, it is possible to trace the effects of R&D through to their impact on cash flows, which are a better measure of value.

Trade-offs

Even when objectives have been quantified in comparable terms, such as cash flow streams, trade-offs still must be made between short term and long term (time preference), risk and return (risk preference). These distinct trade-offs are often combined inappropriately.

While most people imagine that uncertainty is directly related to time and its extension, this is often not the case. In R&D, the early stages are the most uncertain, and uncertainty diminishes as hurdles are overcome. For example, a 10 percent probability of success would be very high for early-stage drug development and a 90 percent probability would be on the low side when the same drug reaches regulatory approval. Confusing time and risk can kill a company's ability to gain long-term strategic advantage from its innovation process.

The typical approach to discounted cash flow analysis incorrectly undervalues R&D by confusing risk preference with time preference. The source of this error is the tendency of analysts to combine *both* time preference and risk preference in the discount rate. To make our example clear, consider a corporate cost of capital of 5 percent (before inflation) and (incorrectly) crank it up to 20 percent to account for project risk. This erroneous discount rate combines the time preference, the cost of capital, and a crude attempt at risk adjustment.

Now consider what happens to an R&D project. Suppose that a project calls for a $1 million R&D investment and lasts two years. If successful, the project will create a process improvement for a major plant in a stable, long-lasting business. Implementing the process will require a $20 million capital investment, but will produce $5 million per year in cost savings for twenty years starting the year following the investment. Owing to the stability of this business, there is little business risk.

Does this sound like a good investment? It would be but for one thing: There is only a 50 percent chance of technical success. If the project fails, the original $1 million R&D investment is lost. This structure is shown in Figure 3-3.

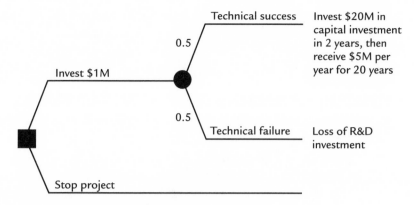

Figure 3-3. *The Expected Value of an R&D Project*

Since this is a risky R&D project, if we (incorrectly) use the 20 per-cent "risk adjusted" discount rate and apply it to the cash flows re-sulting from success, we obtain a net present value of –$0.8M. Since the project has negative value, it should be stopped, right? Wrong. This way of measuring value grossly misrepresents the trade-offs be-tween risk and return, and between cash flows received earlier and later. The problem lies in adjusting the R&D risk using the discount rate. The best way to value this project is to separate time discounting and risk adjustment. Combining them in a discount rate, in this "naive NPV approach," overpenalizes the future and, by extension, the upside potential of R&D.[14] Here is the correct approach.

First, consider time preference. Using the same corporate cost of capital of 5 percent (before inflation), the NPV of the technical suc-cess branch is $34.7 million. It looks like a real winner if it works! Next, adjust for uncertainty. For most R&D investments, the best way to represent the impact of uncertainty is to apply the expected value.[15] This is the probability-weighted average of the various scenar-ios (branches). For this example, the expected value is $16.8 million, (0.5 × $34.7 million + 0.5 × (–$1 million)). This large positive value contrasts sharply with the negative value given before, which erro-neously understates the value of the project.

Using the correct calculation in the example shows an expected re-turn of about $17 million on a $1 million investment. Most compa-nies should pursue as many of these opportunities as possible. The R&D project has a large chance of failure, to be sure, but failure would result in only a small loss. The upside potential of a successful outcome, in contrast, is huge. Confusing time and risk results in lost opportunities for value creation.

Requirements for High-Quality Values

Quality in clear values and trade-offs requires the following:

1. All alternatives should be valued in terms of the same measure (or metric).
2. The measure of value should represent the desired end objective of the enterprise. Metrics for means objectives should either be avoided or be clearly defined as a surrogate for an end objective. Intangibles should be valued explicitly, for example, by willingness to give up cash flow to achieve them.
3. The effects of strategic decisions should be traced through business activities to cash flows. Cash flow is usually the most important end sought by corporations.
4. Cost of capital, not adjustments for risk, should be used as the discount rate in calculating the time value of money.
5. The expected value should be taken across many scenarios to value uncertain prospects. In cases where the uncertainties in payoffs are large compared to the corporate wealth, this value must be adjusted to reflect corporate risk aversion.

Logically Correct Reasoning

"Most major business decisions," warned John Maynard Keynes, "are taken as a result of animal spirits—of a spontaneous urge to action rather than inaction, and not as the outcome of a weighted average of quantitative benefits multiplied by quantitative probabilities."

A logically correct reasoning process considers alternatives, information, risks, and values in the context of the decision frame, and reaches a conclusion based on the evidence. Its objective is to organize and analyze inputs, sort through complexity, and scientifically understand which choice is likely to create the greater value. In practice, this rational process must often proceed through an obstacle course of project advocates (champions) and organizational politics.

Advocates and Politics

The head of engineering labored mightily to make a case for his project: development of a new chemical process technology. He placed all of his "facts" on the table and argued passionately in favor of the project and the better future it would create for the company. When the analysis was complete, however, it was clear to all that the new technology and the manufacturing plant it was designed to serve would be extremely expensive, and would only pay off under the most optimistic scenario. Management was inclined to shelve that project in favor of something else.

Undaunted, the engineer went back to his numbers. Within a few days he produced and delivered—with a straight face—new reports suggesting that the capital costs would be about one-fifth those of his earlier projections! These new figures, he explained, would show that the business was now attractive, and that funding for the R&D project should proceed. Was this individual lying with these figures, or had he simply talked himself into believing the unbelievable?

A decision-making approach like the one just described follows the western tradition of legal advocacy, where justice (the right choice) is seen as emerging from sparring among advocates of different positions. In this system of winners and losers, the advocate's goal is to win the case through argument and persuasion. For this approach to work effectively, each advocate must be counterbalanced by an effective adversary. Thus, others in the organization, usually top management or its staff, must act as quality inspectors—looking for holes in the advocate's evidence, assumptions, and conclusions. Besides causing frustration and stress for all concerned, this decision-making approach often slows time to market.

Organizational politics has its own decision-making logic. Every organization we have benchmarked has one or more low-value projects lying around that should have been stopped long ago. Many began as "the boss's idea," and were never questioned. Because no one wants to cross the boss, these become the projects that "will not die."

Scientific Logic

Decision analysis provides guidance for logical reasoning. Over the last quarter-century, decision analysis has emerged as the only quantitative methodology capable of dealing with the uncertainty and complexity of major corporate and government decisions. While it is beyond the scope of this book to describe decision analysis and its applications in detail, examples of its use and methods are given in chapters 9, 10 and 11.[16]

Managing the Focus of Attention

Left to their own inclinations, people focus on what they find interesting, without thinking about what is important to the decision. Decision analysis helps keep people focused on the right issues. Consider the example of a large oil company.

In the 1960s—long before it became a legal requirement to do so—a major oil company was faced with deciding whether to offer unleaded gasoline. They had studied the proposition on and off for some time, but without resolution. Finally, the CEO authorized a project team to spend up to $1 million on research to resolve the matter. Following the natural inclinations of its members, the team spent $950,000 on plant simulations and engineering tests. It optimized the refinery and determined the lowest possible cost of production. The remaining $50,000 was spent examining the market.

The project team in this case spent its resources on tasks with which it was comfortable. But because offering unleaded gas in anticipation of regulation was at its core a marketing play, with technical implications, the team's effort was misdirected and failed to inform the decision.

The antidote to situations like the one just described is to manage the focus of attention. Determine which factors are the most important. Focus on these, develop insights, and iterate. Develop more detail and information on the important factors. (Chapter 9 illustrates this process in the context of a project strategy.)

Requirements for High-Quality Reasoning

Quality in the dimension of logically correct reasoning requires the following:

1. Shift from political and advocacy logic to a scientific and systematic search for value based on evidence. Use the tools of decision analysis to clarify and illuminate key issues, not to defend points of view.

2. Require an open process. Subject the inputs and analysis to critique and review.

3. Use a rigorous quantitative process.

4. Use initial insights to focus later efforts. Start with simple models. Use these results, and various forms of sensitivity analysis, to inspire better alternatives, focus attention on critical information, and clarify value measures. Conduct analysis at the level of detail required for clarity of action, not at the level required for operations.

Commitment to Action

Commitment to action gives purpose to decision making. An autocratic leader can command that a decision be followed. But autocracy does not work well, particularly in today's more collaborative working environment. When researchers are uncomfortable with a decision, they can usually find a way to work around it. (How many killed projects still lurk in your organization?)

Superficial Agreement

Commitment is not simply a matter of having the right approvals. It is about having genuine intentions to carry out a course of action. All too often, we encounter situations in which the intentions of participants are not genuine, but are "superficial agreement."

For example, a manufacturer decided to install automatic control systems in several related plants. Initially, the equipment would be installed in one plant, where it would be tested and evaluated prior to systemwide installation. The installation at the first plant had been approved two years before we began working with this company. The engineers and researchers involved in the project were excited about the work and eager to carry it out. They had budget authority and other necessary resources. Yet nothing happened. The decision, for some reason, had not been implemented.

The project was justified anew during the second year. During the budget process, the project leader strengthened his arguments and offered even more detailed financial analysis in support of the previous year's decision. To no one's surprise, the project was again approved. The project team remained enthusiastic. Yet, again, nothing happened. Why?

We found that the barrier to implementation was an unofficial veto by the manager of the plant slated for the first installation. This manager always found some reason to delay the equipment installation: tight production schedules in the plant, problems with suppliers of the equipment, and so on. The project had executive approval, but lacked the full commitment of the individual who could prevent implementation. Closer scrutiny explained his lack of commitment: The decision process that approved the equipment installation failed to recognize the plant manager's concern that the installation would throw a monkey wrench into plant operations. But the project leader's zeal to justify this project blinded him to this concern. For example, everyone knew that a competitor had installed similar equipment with the result of substantial plant downtime and financial losses. That competitor had abandoned the program. Our client's project leader had thinly papered over this issue, asserting that "It won't happen to us. We will manage things better."

The decision process had failed to address a key concern: What was the risk of installation failure? How large was the potential for financial loss? With these questions unanswered, the plant manager would not support the decision. This is not surprising, given that he was responsible for his plant's performance.

Real Commitment

Once an organization has achieved real commitment, things move smoothly. The commitment of senior management and the implementors to a sensible course of action provides the basis for trust and empowerment. When the inevitable project glitches come up, people know the intention of the project and adjust accordingly.

So, how does one get commitment? The people who make or can veto the decision need to be involved in the process. Key implementors also need to be involved; it is the only way they can really understand the intent of the decision. In most cases, these implementors can make a tremendous contribution to the decision process. They have practical information that should not be overlooked, and they are good judges of the feasibility of the alternative.

Commitment means that decision makers will provide agreed-on resources and foster broad understanding of the decision's strategic intent. And they will refrain from readdressing the decision at each incremental approval stage. Only significant new roadblocks or opportunities should signal a reassessment of the basic strategy.

Commitment also means that those charged with implementing the strategic intent will be given the resources and authority to get the job done without micromanagement from above.

High quality in other dimensions of decision quality is essential to getting commitment. Often, as in the automated control example above, people drag their feet to prevent the organization from doing something they perceive as stupid. Perhaps they have information that has not been considered. Or they may know of a better alternative. Others may be critical of the whole situation.

Finally, if the logic is not right, people will not commit. They know the project advocacy game and view it with suspicion. If there is not a sense of due process, open review, and fair weighing of the evidence, people will withhold commitment. In the worst case, they become cynical and demotivated.

Requirements for High-Quality Commitment

A high-quality commitment requires the following:

1. Both decision makers and implementors should be included in the decision-making process.
2. Decision quality, trust, and confidence must be built during the process; it cannot be injected in at the end. "Official blessings" are not a substitute for the personal commitment of decision makers and implementors.
3. Quality in the other dimensions is required for wide-based commitment.

The Smart Decision

If you can recognize a good decision when you see one, you have made the first step in understanding each of the six dimensions of decision quality. Since the weakest link of the decision quality chain is the most important, you will know where you should be focusing your attention.

But what should you do? Chapters 9, 10, and 11 use case examples to describe approaches for getting decision quality right the first time. If you have a tough decision, you might jump to those chapters. But it is one thing to use these processes to make a single good decision, and quite another to use them to build decision quality into the fabric of the organization, making it routine.

We presented the decision quality framework just described at the first meeting of the R&D Decision Quality Association, in 1989. "This all sounds great," members responded, "but if you can measure it, you should be able to benchmark it and find the best practices for making decision quality a routine event."

We took up that challenge, and the outcome—benchmarking research and best practices for R&D decision making—are described in the next chapters.

PART II

BEST PRACTICES

CHAPTER 4

BEST PRACTICES FOR
R&D DECISIONS

HEWLETT-PACKARD. GILLETTE. Merck. 3M. Shell. General Electric. AT&T. DuPont. Procter & Gamble. Motorola. Dow. IBM. Xerox. Intel.

These companies have extraordinary R&D "hit rates." They know how to place their bets and how to turn those bets into winners. Hewlett-Packard, for example, garners almost 60 percent of its revenues from products that were introduced in the last five years. Gillette and 3M normally look to their new products for 25 percent to 35 percent of their annual revenues.[1]

What is it about companies like these that make their R&D initiatives more successful than others? Why is it that they routinely produce high-quality decisions? We and the R&D Decision Quality Association conducted a multiyear, multiphase benchmarking study to find the answers to these questions.[2] Benchmarking has been applied over the years to just about every business practice from manufacturing to customer service with the goal of identifying practices that are superior and transferable to other situations. To our knowledge, this is the first application of benchmarking to R&D decision making. What we found, in a nutshell, is a strong association between R&D decision quality and a number of "best practices." This association held across companies and across industries. Each of the successful organizations we benchmarked had a decision process that used these best practices in ways that supported its success.

In all, we found forty-five best practices that many companies are using routinely to create decision quality, improve performance, and generate competitive advantage. These can be consolidated within nine logical components. As we will soon see, these form a blueprint for making and executing high-quality R&D decisions. The nine component areas in which best practices are found are:

1. the decision basis
2. technology strategy

"Say...look what they're doing."

Figure 4-1. *Why Benchmark?*

3. portfolio management
4. project strategy
5. organization and process
6. relationship with internal customers
7. relationship with external customers
8. R&D culture and values
9. improving decision quality

Before we discuss the individual practices that fall within these nine components, let us consider how we found them.

Methodology

Figure 4.1 illustrates the purpose of benchmarking research, which is to find great ideas that can be implemented in our own organization to improve results.

BEST PRACTICES

Our study was conducted in five phases, identified in Table 4-1 with their main results.

Table 4-1. *Phases and Results of the Study*

PHASE	MAIN RESULT
Brief survey	Nominations for interviews
In-depth interviews	Blueprint for doing the right R&D Forty-five best practices
Best practice questionnaire	Statistical benchmarks on practices Diagnostic tools
Validation	Confirmation and validation of results
Extension	Principles of Smart R&D

Over the course of these phases we surveyed and interviewed hundreds of decision makers in hundreds of R&D organizations, some of which are listed in appendix A. Figure 4-2 indicates the broad range of industries included in the research.

Figure 4-2. *Industries Covered in the Benchmarking Study*

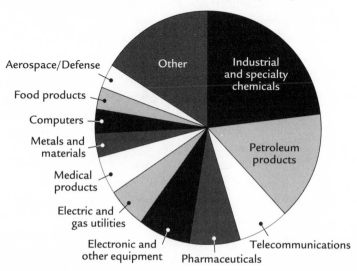

Which Are the Best R&D Companies?

The brief survey phase focused on R&D decision making, measurements, and improvement areas. Our main challenge here was to identify organizations worth talking to in greater detail. To accomplish this we used a nomination system, asking participants (about 250 senior people in mostly North American companies) to identify R&D organizations—both inside and outside their industries—that in their experience exemplified high-quality R&D decision making. This nomination procedure produced a rank-order list of twenty-two target companies shown in Figure 4-3. 3M topped the list, being nominated by over 50 percent of the respondents. Each of the companies in the upper part of the list—3M, Merck, Hewlett-Packard, General Electric, AT&T, DuPont, and Procter & Gamble—is one that was nominated by a broad base of participants. Others, such as Pacific Gas & Electric (PG&E), were nominated exclusively by others within their industries and represent insider knowledge about good companies.[3]

Learning from the Best

The goal of the in-depth interview was to learn from the leaders identified earlier. To do this, Strategic Decision Group (SDG) sent teams to interview decision makers and decision process managers at five of the top eight companies and at eight of the remaining group. To ensure breadth, a few companies outside of the top twenty-two were also interviewed. Each interview was conducted with three or four representatives from the organization over a period of about four hours. Responses were recorded in the participants' own words. The results of these many interviews were analyzed during a retreat of several weeks. From the interview records we identified approximately 200 raw practices, many of which appeared in several companies in slightly different forms; that is, the basic intention and function of the practice were the same, but they were implemented in a different way. These raw practices were consolidated into forty-five master practices.

Once we had identified the practices, we realized that all of the top companies were using various practices to achieve certain broad functions. We organized the practices around these broad functions and developed the nine components for doing the right R&D. All of

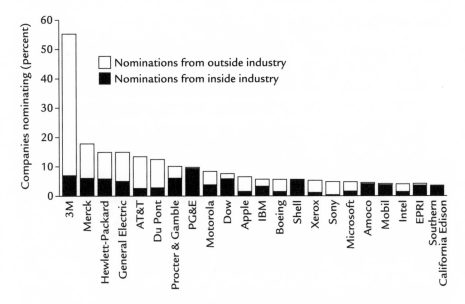

Figure 4-3. *Companies Nominated for Excellence in Strategic Decision Making*

the top companies used various of the best practices in harmony to create an integrated decision process that cut across all of the nine components.

Benchmarks on Best Practices

In the next phase of the study we sent out hundreds of questionnaires designed to collect data on company performance and the application of the best practices. Once received and tabulated, these data made it possible to create statistical benchmarks for each practice. These benchmarks, and the questionnaire itself, are then the basis for diagnosing the performance of any organization.

Researchers are always concerned with the validity of their results. To allay our own concerns on this score, we added a validation phase in which we repeated the study with different groups, most notably with companies represented by the Quality Director's Network of the Industrial Research Institute and companies located in Western Europe. These additional studies confirmed our original results and conclusions.

Blueprint for the Right R&D

Earlier, we listed the nine components within which best practices can be logically organized. Figure 4-4 shows how these components form a blueprint that companies can follow in diagnosing and managing R&D decision making. Some of these components direct us in making good decisions. Others indicate how we can organize for decision quality. Still others address the issue of improving decision quality.

Making Quality Decisions

The category "Making quality decisions" is about making specific decisions well. Each of the companies interviewed in our study had harmonious processes that enabled it to make specific decisions well. One component concerns the basis of a decision. It covers best practices for each of the elements of decision quality, from framing to commitment. For example, all but one of the companies interviewed framed their decisions strategically, in terms of technology strategy, portfolio management, and project strategy. The practices in the decision basis component address issues that cut across all three kinds of decisions. Since the different kinds of decisions have special characteristics, there is also a component of the blueprint dedicated to each. These components have associated best practices. For example, one of the main challenges in portfolio decisions is balancing short- and long-term R&D, and there is a practice that addresses this. Thus, the blueprint has components to ensure a quality decision basis, develop good technology strategy, manage the portfolio well, and develop good project strategies.

Organizing

The category "Organizing for decision quality" concerns the supporting structure, organization, and culture required to have a healthy R&D organization. This provides the ability to tee up decisions routinely and bring to bear the right kinds of information, processes, capabilities, and intentions. The best of the best have the organization and processes that make good decision making part of the company DNA, have a strong relationship with both internal and external customers, and define their R&D culture and values in a particular way. There is a component for each of these aspects of organizing for decision quality.

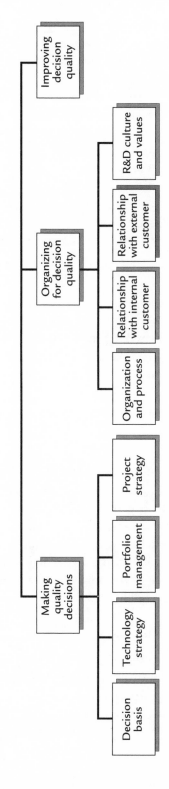

Figure 4-4. *A Blueprint for Doing the Right R&D*

Many best practices relate to both doing R&D right and doing the right R&D. Take, for example, the use of cross-functional teams. Many R&D organizations routinely use cross-functional teams in their R&D projects. One company we benchmarked was superb in this practice from an operations perspective, but failed to apply it to strategic decisions; that is, it used cross-functional teams to implement decisions, but not to make them. Once this company recognized the oversight, it was a small step to extend the practice to the strategic realm. In other words, doing R&D right set up a foundation for doing the right R&D.

As we will see later, most companies are doing better at practices in the "Organizing for decision quality" than in "Making quality decisions." This reflects years of attention to the operational excellence of R&D.

Improving

The category "Improving decision quality" is about learning and improving the decision-making process over time. The practices in this component ensure that people in the organization sustain and improve decision quality and adapt to the changing business environment.

Best Practices

Figure 4-5 lists all forty-five of the best practices identified in our study, each organized under the blueprint component it primarily supports. Not one of the organizations interviewed used all of these practices well, but each used a number of them as building blocks for a process that routinely achieves decision quality.

Although discussion of each best practice is not possible within the scope of this chapter, let us consider a few and how companies use them to achieve high-quality R&D decisions.

Quantitative Project Analysis

Practice PS-2, "Evaluate projects quantitatively," is one that many organizations already have on their short lists of things to improve. Quantitative evaluation of projects is essential for clear communications and optimal prioritization of projects. The best companies combine economic and technical evaluations, which include market

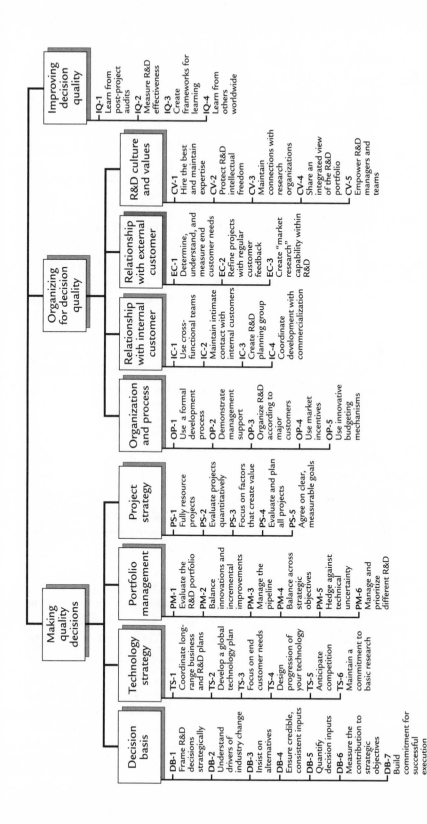

Figure 4-5. *The Forty-Five Best Practices*

71

potential and technical hurdles. Uncertainties are addressed in the language of probability. Most projects are compared on the basis of expected net present value and a productivity indicator, such as net present value divided by expected R&D cost.

Our interview records describe how specific companies implement this practice:

▲ *Use a comprehensive, quantitative evaluation process for all candidate projects.* This process requires a clear definition of the R&D project and of the objectives it must meet to be successful. The process also requires decision-making criteria based on explicit performance goals, the most important being expected profitability.

▲ *Develop an economic evaluation model for R&D programs.* An economic evaluation model helps managers focus on costs versus benefits and can be indispensable for setting priorities, assessing potential value, and allocating resources.

▲ *Select and prioritize projects using expected net present value.* Choose and prioritize R&D projects based on incremental expected profitability, selecting those with the highest expected shareholder value. Expected shareholder value is a function of the probability of success, development time and cost, and value given success. Among many possible indicators of success for an R&D project, expected net present value (ENPV) is the strongest. When properly derived, using an appropriate model, ENPV reflects many contributory factors that have been quantified.

▲ *Take the time to determine the implications of success and failure.* When both management and project champions are enthusiastic and ready to charge ahead, take the time to perform a thorough and dispassionate evaluation of the upside and downside implications of the project.

▲ *Incorporate risk when prioritizing projects.* Make sure that the analysis used to establish priorities incorporates risk in its information base. In addition to deterministic information, include the results of probabilistic reasoning about uncertainty. This makes it possible to compare and select projects according to informed and reasonable assessments of their expected values.

▲ *Define, formulate, and evaluate risk explicitly.* Explicit definition, formulation, and evaluation of risk is essential for R&D decisions—so much so that this task may need to be performed at regular intervals. Since risk assessment involves expert judgment, draw on the best expertise available.

▲ *Perform standardized financial analyses of projects and new product lines.* A fully developed business case should be developed and analyzed for every project and new product line. These should be multiyear analyses that project various scenarios (including best and worst cases) and incorporate the rate of return on sales, the economic value added of each scenario, and other relevant measures.

Portfolio Evaluation

Another practice on many a company's "to do" list is PM-1, "Evaluate the R&D portfolio." Portfolio evaluation is a key practice that categorizes, compares, and analyzes the portfolio as a whole. This practice requires that we compare alternative portfolios on probability distributions of net present value, in terms of expected product launches over time, patterns of resource requirements over time, and the ability of the portfolios to meet corporate objectives. This approach provides a clear sense of the value of the entire R&D portfolio and leads to significantly better portfolio investment decisions.

Other Measures of Effectiveness

A common theme in the practices just mentioned is the measurement and quantification of R&D results. Two other practices that relate directly to this theme, underscoring the connections among a number of best practices, are IQ-2: "Measure R&D effectiveness" and DB-5: "Quantify decision inputs."

For practice IQ-2, "Measure R&D effectiveness," the best organizations devote substantial attention to measuring the effectiveness and productivity of their R&D. Knowing where they stand in terms of effectiveness helps them to focus future improvement efforts. These measurements are both retrospective and prospective. The best retrospective measures relate to commercial success; for example, the percentage of revenues and profits generated by new products. The best prospective measures relate to the position of R&D in future company operations; for example, expected net present value and contribution to strategic goals.

Practice DB-5, "Quantify decision inputs," is a challenge, but a worthwhile one. Although expressive, language has ambiguities that can lead to confusion, misunderstanding, and poor decisions. Whenever possible, decision inputs should be quantified to ensure clear and precise communication. When information is uncertain or subjective, ranges of inputs and probabilities can be used.

Best Practices Work in Harmony

The particular set of best practices described above indicates how they can be used in harmony to cover multiple components of the blueprint. For example, one company selected expected net present value of cash flows as a prospective measure (IQ-2). Its analysts and R&D personnel evaluate each project by quantifying the market and technical inputs (PS-2). They develop ranges to describe the size of potential markets; major technical hurdles are identified and success in overcoming them is expressed in terms of probabilities (DB-5). Using an economic model, they develop a probability distribution for each project's net present value (PS-2). Based on this analysis, the company reorders individual project priorities and focuses on R&D targets having the greatest potential for value creation.

Having moved to a consistent set of measures, this company now finds it relatively easy to compare projects on a portfolio basis (PM-1) and to measure R&D effectiveness (IQ-2).

In following such a program, this company has been able to adopt several other best practices with little additional effort:

▲ Quantification of both technical and market inputs has led to the use of a crossfunctional evaluation team (IC-1).

▲ Direct comparison of projects ensures consistency of inputs (DB-4), which has already been largely achieved by the quantification procedure.

▲ The evaluation process was readily adapted to a formal development and decision process (OP-1).

▲ General agreement on portfolio priorities has resulted in many projects being killed while others are fully resourced (PS-1).

By implementing several practices in conjunction with a decision process, this company has moved closer to becoming an organization that routinely achieves high-quality decisions.

Benchmarking for Best Practices

To benchmark the best practices, we conducted hundreds of detailed surveys with R&D executives in many organizations in many industries and in many countries. These surveys provided the statistics on two dimensions: actualization, and potential contribution to decision quality. In our definition, *actualization* is a measure of how well a particular practice is utilized by a particular company. To have a highly actualized practice, a company must use it frequently and execute it well. Our surveys gathered self-assessments on the *frequency of use* and *quality of execution* (on a scale of 0% to 100%), and multiplied these two factors together to get the actualization measure.

Potential contribution to decision quality is a measure of a practice's value. We obtained data on this directly from the surveys.

Best Practices Cut Across Industry Lines

One of the important findings of our survey is that the best practices are the same across industries. The correlation between actualization or potential contribution across industry segments is weak. This finding supports what many understand intuitively: R&D decision makers face the same types of issues in many industries; thus, the best practices for addressing them are similar. For example, R&D decision making is fundamentally about managing uncertainty. As a result, practices are needed for understanding the probability of technical success, potential market size, and so on. The context of the R&D decision-making process changes from industry to industry, but the content of the process does not.

The fact that the best practices are the same across industries means that a company can adopt a practice being successfully applied in a completely different industry. If its competitors are not already using it, that practice might be a source of competitive advantage.

Best Practices Are Achievable

Another finding of our study is that each best practice is achievable. We reached that conclusion as follows. First, we identified a set of best practice companies—companies that were in the top 10 percent of actualization for each practice. These companies believed they were doing a particular practice well and often. Each practice has a group of companies that are best at it.[4] For example, companies A, B, and C might be the best practitioners of IQ-1, while companies C, D, and E might be the most adept at practice PM-2.

Next, by plotting what individual companies perceived as the potential contribution of best practices against their actualization,

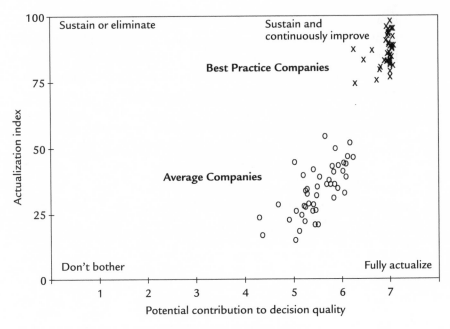

Figure 4-6. *All of the Best Practices Are Achievable.*

we found that companies successfully actualize practices they perceive as beneficial. The cluster of Xs in the upper right of Figure 4-6 shows the mean results for these best practice companies. Many of the forty-five practices fell on top of each other at a potential contribution of 7, and can be found as a vertical band in the figure's upper right corner.

The standards set by the best practice companies are quite high, with actualization of 75 percent or above! This sets a benchmark for what is achievable. The best practice companies also value the practices highly. The contribution for every practice, in the opinion of these companies, is 6 or above! This is important information about how highly other companies should rate each practice. If a company believes that a particular practice, say PM-1, does not have much potential, it should think again. The companies that have fully actualized it—those that have experience with it—claim lots of value.

The cluster of Os in the lower right-hand corner of Figure 4-6 shows the mean (or average) of all companies. The lowest O, Practice IQ-1, is at the 15 mark and is one of the most poorly actualized. It is perceived as contributing to decision quality at a level of 5—still a contribution, but less valuable than perceived by the best practice companies, which rate it at 7. The highest O, Practice OP-3, is the most highly actualized on average, with a score of about 60 percent.

The gap between the two clusters represents the benchmarking gap, indicating how far average companies must go to match the level of the best practice companies.

Much Room for Improvement

According to our data, most companies excel at only a few of the best practices. No company achieved the 75 percent benchmark for all practices, indicating that every company has room for improvement—even the best.

The surveys also showed a relationship between performance and actualization of the practices: Increased actualization correlates with increased performance.

The easiest way to see this relationship is to divide companies into two broad categories, high performers and low performers, as shown in Figure 4-7. Companies that score above the median performance

Figure 4-7. *Distribution of Self-Assessed Performance (Combination of self-ratings on number of new products, return on R&D, and percentage of sales from new products)*

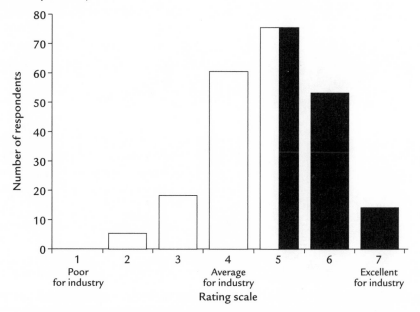

Note: White bars indicate low performers; black bars indicate high performers.

score are classified as high performers; the others are classified as low performers. (We used a seven-point scale where 1 equals poor for industry, 4 equals average for industry, and 7 equals excellent for industry.) The performance score is the average of responses to three questions in our questionnaires:

1. Relative to your industry, where is your organization on number of new products released each year?

2. Using the same scale, relative to your industry, where is your organization on return on R&D?

3. Relative to your industry, where is your organization on percentage of sales from new products?

After dividing the companies into two categories, we took the mean actualization score for each practice for each group. Figure 4-8 shows that virtually every practice has a larger actualization for high performers than for lower performers. The practices on the left side

Figure 4-8. *Actualization: High Performers versus Low Performers*

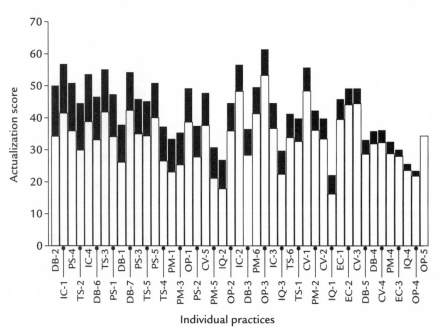

Note: White bars indicate low performers; black bars indicate high performers.

BEST PRACTICES

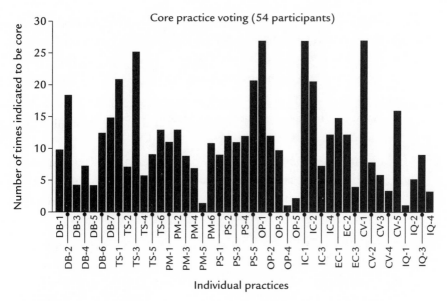

Figure 4-9. *Core Practices*

of the graph have the largest gaps; those on the right have the small-est gaps. Only one practice, OP-5, shows no difference. The over-whelming message here is that higher actualization of the practices correlates with better industry performance.

Some Practices Are Core to Any Decision Process

Although all practices are correlated with performance, they have dif-ferent importance in different organizations. SDG did further re-search on the best practices, surveying a set of seventy-two outstand-ing R&D organizations. We asked each of these companies to indicate which practices were core to their decision processes, and tal-lied the results for each practice. The results are that some practices are core to many companies while all are core to some companies, as shown in Figure 4-9. None of the practices are used by all organiza-tions. This means that it is possible to be an admired company and build a decision process that emphasizes a subset of the practices.

The practices that are core to many companies may be require-ments for competition. In that case, if your competitors are using these and you are not, watch out—you may be behind! The following are among these core practices:

▲ Coordinate R&D and business plans (TS-1).

▲ Focus on end customers' needs (TS-3).

▲ Agree on clear, measurable goals (PS-5).

▲ Use a formal development process (OP-1).

▲ Use cross-functional teams (IC-1).

▲ Maintain intimate contact with internal customers (IC-2).

▲ Hire the best and maintain their expertise (CV-1).

Other practices may be a source of competitive differentiation. These are the practices core to relatively few companies. Some organizations have made this a core part of their decision process, so we know the practice works. These practices include:

▲ Insist on alternatives (DB-3).

▲ Quantify decision inputs (DB-5).

▲ Hedge against technical uncertainty (PM-5).

▲ Use market incentives (OP-4).

▲ Use innovative budgeting mechanisms (OP-5).

▲ Create a market research capability within R&D (EC-3).

▲ Share an integrated view of the R&D portfolio (CV-4).

▲ Learn from post-project audits (IQ-1).

▲ Learn from others worldwide (IQ-4).

So, what should you do? Benchmarking is all about finding good ideas to implement. In an ideal world, all forty-five best practices would be implemented and actualized 100 percent. But this is clearly impractical. Since it is possible to use a subset of the practices, one need not do everything at once. The question is, Which practices will provide the most gain for your organization?

One approach is to diagnose your organization in terms of the forty-five best practices, finding where it stands on each. This diagnosis will determine the "benchmarking gap" between the best performing companies and your own. A large paper company recently conducted such a diagnosis across its many divisions, asking each to identify the best practices on which it was strongest *and* weakest. Clear patterns for the entire organization quickly emerged: The divisions were universally strong at cross-functional teaming and universally weak at measurement and portfolio evaluation. This diagnosis told the paper company where to begin to improve its R&D performance.[5]

Strategic Decisions Group has bundled the best practices into coherent processes that can be applied to various kinds of decisions: technology strategy, portfolio strategy, and project strategy. If your decision process needs an overhaul, you may want to adopt one of these. Chapters 9, 10, and 11 illustrate these integrated processes with case studies of several real companies.

Get On with It

At the end of the day, what really matters is implementation. Speaking at one of our executive forums that first revealed the conclusions of our study, Ed Finein, retired vice president and chief engineer of Xerox Corporation—and one of the founders of benchmarking—offered this advice:

> The key now is to take [this] information and begin applying [it] to your corporation. . . . Excellent companies will do that. One of the reasons they are excellent is that they do that on a continuous basis. The companies that are not very good probably will not do it. They will go out and find fault with the study and try to find new information and continue studying forever without making change.

CHAPTER 5

IMPLEMENTING BEST PRACTICES

> We have met the enemy, and
> he is us. *Pogo*

READERS WHO GREW UP in agricultural regions of the United States during the 1960s and 1970s may recall the frequent and highly publicized visits made by Soviet farming experts. By the hundreds, managers of Soviet collective farms visited family farms in Minnesota, Iowa, Kansas, and other highly productive areas, where they observed the practices that made U.S. farming the envy of a hungry world. Photographs of smiling commissars at the controls of huge John Deere tractors or sitting at the dinner tables of midwestern farm families appeared regularly in American newspapers and magazines.

At the conclusion of these fact-finding visits, hands would be shaken and toasts given to the friendship of Soviet and American farmers. Then the experts would go back to Russia or the Ukraine or someplace else, where backward and inefficient agricultural practices would remain virtually unchanged. Soviet farmers had plenty of wonderful soil, and they had seen the best farming practices at work, but they never put the two together. Their system operated under principles of organization, decision making, and doctrine that made adoption of American practices next to impossible.

The inability of organizations to embrace superior practices is a common feature in industry, science, and other fields, and examples can be found through human history. Richard Luecke has provided an illustration of this perennial problem through an episode drawn from late medieval times. He describes the tactical development of mass archery by Edward III and his successors, the havoc this practice wrought on their French opponents, and the stubborn refusal of the French to adopt the same practices.[1]

The English discovered the military potential of the longbow in decades of border warfare with the rebellious Welshmen, who were experts in its use. The Welsh longbow had twice the range of its continental counterpart, higher projectile velocity, and much greater penetrating power. English commanders learned through painful experience how effective this weapon could be in defeating their own most potent asset—the armored horseman.

The English wisely recognized the longbow's value and made it a key component of their own tactics. Archery was made a compulsory hobby for male commoners, and was encouraged through competitions throughout the kingdom. So, when King Edward took a small army into France in 1346, an estimated 60 percent of his men were well-trained yeomen archers, the rest being mounted knights and heavily equipped men-at-arms. This lightly armed force met and defeated a far larger host of French knights at Crecy in one of the most lopsided victories in European military history to that date. Edward's bowmen literally decimated the charging ranks of the armored French aristocracy.

Crecy was but the first of a series of lopsided English victories, including the battles of Poitiers and Agincourt, that occurred over a period of eighty years. In virtually every case, archers provided the winning edge. But through it all, the French refused to alter their tactics. Something prevented them from adopting massed archery, which would not have been a difficult technical feat. According to Luecke, adoption of English practices by the French was blocked by the fact that doing so would have upset the rigid social order of medieval France, which put the armored knight at the apex of a tightly knit social, economic, and political order. "To do so would give ground to the idea that a peasant in a leather helmet with a bunch of slender arrows in his belt was in some way a match for his social superior. The cult of chivalry and the unbending pride of the nobleman would not open the door an inch to that idea."[2]

Paul Lawrence observed a similar phenomenon in the resistance of people to technological change in the workplace, noting that resistance has less to do with technology than with the altered social arrangements it produces.[3] Thus, managers who must lead the implementation of observed best practices may resist practices that shift decision-making authority or greater autonomy into the hands of teams or lower level employees (the yeomen of the modern corporation). "If we adopt this practice," they may tell themselves, "then I will become less important." Machiavelli may have said it best when he wrote that "The reformer has enemies in all those who profit from the old order," that is, current practices.

Like the touring Soviet bureaucrats and the medieval French military system, business and R&D organizations may actively resist adoption of best practices when those practices threaten to upset established relationships involving power, prestige, or control. But our research indicates that the barriers to effective implementation are more various and complex. And there is wide variation in the success of implementation.

Some companies observe a set of best practices, pick the handful that make the most sense to them, and begin implementation—learning as they go. Others make no headway. Champions of these best practices become discouraged when their recommendations fall on deaf ears. Worse, the practices are implemented half-heartedly to little effect.

Why are some organizations successful at implementing practices that make sense to them while others are not? Our research has found that companies that successfully implement observably superior practices have different organizational and cultural foundations than those that cannot. We call these foundations the principles of smart R&D. For companies that operate with these principles—the ones with the right attitude, behaviors, and support systems—implementation is straightforward. Counterproductive attitudes and behaviors, on the other hand, overwhelm any attempt to create meaningful change. This insight holds true for organizations of all kinds.

Uncovering Barriers to Implementation

Strategic Decisions Group has conducted several studies on implementation of best practices, the most recent being a 1996 survey of the most highly regarded companies and their implementations of core practices. In this study we asked respondents to comment on the difficulty of implementing practices they considered core to their current decision processes. The responses were revealing. Here are a few:

> "Because they have been integral to our organization from the beginning, it has not been very difficult to spread them."

> "Implementation of each key practice required three to four years."

> "These practices have been coming up from our long experiences and company culture."

"It has been difficult to get wide acceptance because the corporate culture required substantial change to implement these ideas."

"Spread of the practices met moderate resistance initially, but as the results associated with their implementation yielded measurable improvements, acceptance has noticeably increased."

The contrast in these statements is remarkable. The first says that implementation is easy. The company offering the second quote says that implementation is so difficult that it takes three or four years. Several statements point to company culture as a key factor. That is, if the practices are well suited to the company culture, implementation is easier; if they are not, then implementing them requires cultural change.

Change Is Not Easy

Data gathered since 1991 indicates that resistance to implementing best practices are deeply imbedded. Even the highly regarded companies identified for study in the previous chapter do not fully actualize practices they *know* to be highly beneficial, as shown in Figure 5-1. This figure appeared in chapter 4, but is repeated here to show another important insight. The vertical axis shows how well each practice is actualized, on a scale of zero to 100. A score of 100 means that a practice is used frequently and executed well each time. The horizontal axis shows the potential of each practice to contribute to decision quality, where a 7 means that if the practice were fully actualized it would make a "great contribution" to decision quality. The cluster of forty-five Os in the lower right-hand corner shows the average results from our database of several hundred organizations.

Consider IQ-1, "Learn from post-project audits," for example, located at the bottom of the cluster. Companies do not actualize this practice well, even though they believe it would contribute to decision quality. This practice has an average actualization of only about 15 percent and a potential contribution of about 5, meaning that its potential to contribute to decision quality is between "moderate" (a score of 4) and "great" (a score of 7). There is tremendous room for improvement.

People sometimes tell us that the best practices amount to nothing more than common sense. If so, following common sense is really difficult. The lesson in Figure 5-1 is that companies are unable to meet their aspirations for best practices.

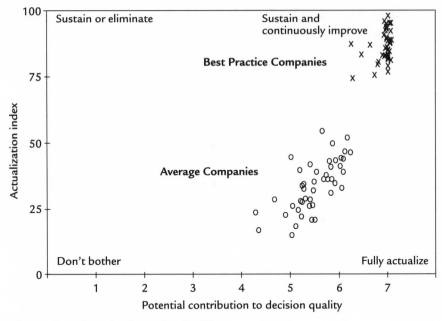

Figure 5-1. *Practice Screening Profile*

A Common Set of Barriers

At various R&D executive meetings, we and our colleagues have gathered data on the barriers to implementing best practices. The same barriers turned up over and over again in discussions with R&D executives. We have listed a selection of them here.

Short-Term Focus

Several executives described their difficulties in implementing best practices as follows:

"We confuse the urgent with the important."

"Process improvement is perceived as higher cost in the short term."

"Our short-term reward systems keep us from focusing on the long term."

Take a practice like IQ-1, "Learn from post-project audits." In a culture of excessive short-term focus, there is no time to learn. The audit is always skipped because something more pressing drives it out.

Or consider practice DB-3, "Insist on alternatives." In a culture of short-term focus, it is easy to go with the first alternative considered. Time devoted to examining alternatives looks like foot-dragging.

Perceived Difficulties in Measurement

Executives tell us that:

> "It's difficult to quantify R&D value."
>
> "It's hard to agree on measures and success criteria."
>
> "People are afraid of making the wrong prediction, so they don't make any."
>
> "It's hard to normalize results from different contributors."
>
> "We have problems discussing uncertainty."

Organizations that view "doing the numbers" as extra effort or wasted effort find that practices related to quantification never take off. It becomes a self-fulfilling prophesy: If it is too hard to quantify, people avoid quantification, which means that they never learn to quantify. Continuing the current easier approach is more appealing than adopting something that requires more work. So efforts to implement these types of practices are met with cynicism and given half-hearted efforts.

Organizational Boundaries

Much has been made of the dysfunctional behaviors that occur in organizations with strong functional "silos." These behaviors include roadblocks to implementing best practices. Executives say:

> "The psychological walls between R&D and marketing are too great to permit collaboration."
>
> "Our functions have conflicting performance targets."
>
> "R&D won't take direction from marketing, and marketing won't listen to R&D."
>
> "Business plans are not integrated with R&D."

A practice like TS-1, "Coordinate long-range business and R&D plans," cannot take root in an organization with these functional barriers. To be sure, a long-range plan can be created, but it will not influence people in the different functions if they are unable or unwilling to cooperate.

A practice like PS-3, "Focus on factors that create value," is also difficult to implement in these circumstances. Lacking an effective link to marketing, for example, R&D must guide itself by its own sense of what is valuable, which usually has a strong technical bias. The customer's perspective can easily be overlooked.

Table 5-1. *Common Barriers to Best Practice Implementation*

Short-term focus	Executives tend to "confuse the urgent with the important." Reward systems focus attention on short-term results.
Perceived difficulties in measurement	Companies think it is difficult to quantify R&D value and, therefore, shy away from attempts to measure results explicitly. Political forces inhibit efforts to deal with objective methods.
Organizational boundaries	Functional "silos" create dysfunctional behaviors, such as conflicts between R&D and marketing, and isolated performance targets that are not fully integrated with business unit strategies.
Internal focus	Organizations either fail to find or reject ideas and information from the outside: "Not Invented Here" syndrome.
Lack of credibility	Information sources, recommendations, and reports are perceived as political or biased and not taken seriously. Decisions are viewed by those in the organization as political and biased.
Secrecy	A needs-to-know culture prevents people from developing a general perspective on important decisions and denies access to information required for specific situations.
Lack of proper skills	The people involved in the best practice implementation are assigned with little regard to training or skill. There is little training or support from experienced people.
Lack of resources	Attempts to implement best practices are made without providing adequate resources. People are asked to do things "in their spare time."

These three and other important barriers to implementation are listed in Table 5-1.

Lessons from Best Practice Companies

The barriers just described are not easily overcome. Yet some companies manage to do so. Do they face fewer barriers? Are their barriers easier to overcome? What are the characteristics of companies that successfully implement best practices? To find the answers, we

Lack of discipline	Management will not kill projects; the process to choose among projects is inconsistently applied; there are many "special cases." In this last instance, many decisions are made outside the normal decision process.
Lack of strategy	Corporate strategies are vague vision statements or overspecified long-term plans. Neither provides much guidance. The result: conflicting priorities, and general confusion.
Metrics are misused	Predictions are turned into commitments. Uncertainties are represented by misleadingly precise forecasts. Historical measures are used for punishment rather than learning.
Tendency to oversimplify	We face increasingly complex situations and systems and less time for really understanding them and developing perspective. Faced with too much data and not enough information, people tend to oversimplify to deal with overload.
People are reluctant to change	The new practices upset the status quo; people move to protect their positions and interests. Making a change leads those who built the current system to feel that they did a poor job.
Power and politics	Loud advocates, fear of accountability, resistance to relinquishing control, fear of being seen as disloyal, and lack of trust all conspire against best practice implementation.

worked with the Quality Director's Network of the Industrial Research Institute in a benchmarking study of companies that were good at specific best practices.[4] In this study we examined implementation of four practices:

▲ measurement of R&D's contribution to strategic objectives (DB-6),

▲ evaluating the R&D portfolio (PM-1),

▲ coordinating long-range R&D and business plans (TS-1), and

▲ agreement on clearly measurable goals (PS-5).

Earlier studies with the Quality Director's Network helped us to identify companies that excelled at these practices. These included AT&T, Avery Dennison, Chevron, DuPont, Elf Atochem, Exxon, Grumman, and Henkel.[5] These became subjects for detailed interviews. We found that three common characteristics enabled these companies to implement the best practices:

1. all had explicit decision processes for aligning R&D with corporate strategy and for creating economic value;
2. all used metrics that quantified this alignment and value creation; and
3. each company had an organizational setting that supported decision quality and the implementation of improvement efforts.

Decision Process

The decision process serves several functions. First, it translates business objectives into terms meaningful to R&D. Second, it operationalizes these values by implementing decisions on specific projects and for the overall portfolio; few if any decisions are made outside of the process. Third, the process monitors and tracks the results over time. This provides, among other things, feedback for learning and improvement. The decision process is disciplined, effective, and follows up.

With a process like this in place, it is easier to adopt best practices. One company, for example, had a process flowchart on the wall; proposed improvements were constantly suggested and incorporated. When a new practice came along, say to evaluate the portfolio, it fit into an established process framework and a tradition of improvement. Barriers to implementation, such as "power and politics" rarely came up.

If a company lacks decision-making discipline or has no tradition of process improvement, attempts to install a process challenges the tradition of the company ("how we do things"). This makes implementation very difficult.

Metrics

The metrics used by high performers were found to vary from organization to organization and situation to situation; they are tailored to specific company requirements. Yet they have a few important characteristics in common. The metrics help to align R&D objectives with corporate strategy and value creation. The measures express the view of customers on the speed, quality, value, and cost of R&D efforts. They take full advantage of the experience of managers and staff in both R&D and business areas, providing useful feedback on what is important at any given moment.

What is important about these metrics is what they represent about the organization. The metrics show what creates value, and people strive to improve it. The organization has a tradition of pursuing value systematically. Employees use the metrics to understand what creates value and go after it. They use the metrics to track value and therefore learn: What improves value? What delivers value?

Metrics like net present value and economic value added (EVA) bring employees face to face with the sources of value to the firm and its customers, and continually remind them that creating value is the purpose of their work. Once these measures become part of the culture and everyday "shop talk," R&D personnel have an internal compass that directs them to new sources of value. And they are more inclined to seek out other practices that will help them in their work.

For example, one R&D organization in our study used a measure based on revenues from new products developed for its business units.[6] It received regular scorecards indicating the revenue those products had generated over a moving five-year period. With this tradition of value creation and measurement, implementing a best practice such as "Evaluating the R&D portfolio" was relatively straightforward. For the example company, it was a small step to start evaluating its R&D portfolio on the basis of forecasted revenues.

For companies that lack a tradition of value measurement, barriers are likely to spring up. Skeptics will resist, fearing that the proposed metrics will be misused. If their resistance is somehow overcome, the measures and the numbers produced by the metrics are likely to be treated cynically, undermining their effectiveness.

Setting

All of the organizations we studied had organizational settings that supported decision quality. One of the most important of these was a process and quality language. For example, one company had recently redesigned its decision process to include the best practices mentioned above. Implementors said the critical success factor was their disappointing experience with a popular quality management course. Everyone in the research organization had gone through this course, but few liked it. The result was a high level of cynicism and frustration with quality programs.

Within a few years, the course was all but forgotten. So when the implementors suggested improving the decision process, they carefully avoided any mention of "quality." However, people understood what they were trying to do. The course had given them a language for process improvement. The implementors received constructive feedback about how to design the process and obtained the consensus required to make it work. Without the quality course, people would not have understood what they were talking about and the entire effort would have been a nonstarter.

Our study with the Quality Director's Network provides some important clues as to why implementing best practices is difficult, under what circumstances the barriers arise, and how best practice companies successfully implement. These clues lead us to this conclusion: Cultural and organizational elements are at the root of implementation success or failure. In other words, the issue is not so much that the practices are intrinsically either difficult or easy to implement; the issue is the context that companies set for or against implementation.

PART III

PRINCIPLES

CHAPTER 6

ORGANIZATIONAL PRINCIPLES

> The aspects of things that are
> the most important for us are
> hidden because of simplicity and
> familiarity. *Ludwig Wittgenstein*

A S WE CONCLUDED in the last chapter, the key to implementing best practices is the organizational context. This context is determined by the principles that operate in a decision situation. These principles are subtle and work at many levels, influencing the way people think and act. They determine whether people are excited or cynical about adopting a new best practice. In effect, they are enablers of best practice implementation and, thus, the foundation of good decision making.

To appreciate how these principles operate, consider an analogy. One of the authors, David, played soccer as a child. He knew the various plays and tactics—the best practices of soccer. His coach did what good coaches do: He explained how to dribble, pass, and shoot. He drilled David until he could execute the moves.

Nevertheless, David was a terrible soccer player. He was as fast as the other children. He had the same stamina and skills. What he lacked was a sort of "team decisiveness." In soccer it is important to act decisively in either taking the ball or leaving it to a teammate. David did not have the instinct for those decisions. When the ball was in his vicinity, he moved ambiguously. His teammates could not tell whether they should support him or whether he was supporting them.

David simply did not get it. No matter how many plays and skills he learned, his overall success was limited by his lack of the principle. Fortunately, David was very good at other things and did not pursue an athletic career.

Just as there are principles of good athletics, there are principles of smart R&D. These principles provide the organizational readiness that every company must have if it wants to be a top performer in R&D decision making or in anything else.

Educators use the term *reading readiness* to describe the cognitive skills required by youngsters as a condition for progress in reading. Until children develop these skills, time spent teaching them to read is largely wasted. But once they have developed these skills, they learn to read fairly quickly. In business, certain organizational and cultural skills are also necessary preconditions for adopting the practices that support decision quality. When the principles are lacking, the organization cannot address important strategic initiatives in a disciplined way. When the principles are in place, the organization is capable of making and implementing quality decisions.

These principles are difficult to see in an organization because principles are intangible and operate beneath the surface. They are bound up in the philosophy, people, culture, and support systems of the organization. Nevertheless, they exert a powerful and undeniable influence on peoples' behavior.

Overview of the Principles of Smart R&D

Our research on best practices and decision quality has led to a specific set of principles for strategic R&D decision making. They apply to any organization that has its future tied up in the success of innovation, research, technology, or corporate renewal. To make high-quality decisions routinely, an organization must have this set of principles in place. Otherwise, attempts to institutionalize the practices for good decision making will encounter significant barriers and the quality of strategic R&D decisions will be left to chance. The greater an organization conforms to this set of principles, the more systematically it will be able to make good strategic R&D decisions.

Value Creation Culture

A "smart" organization has a purpose. Everyone in the organization understands that purpose and uses that understanding as a final test of whether their strategies and actions are creating value for the organization and its customers. Value creation is a compelling argument for change, overriding barriers thrown up by tradition, functional boundaries, personal ambitions, and even budget limitations.

Creating Alternatives

A soundly reasoned decision can only be made as a choice among a good set of competing alternatives. Without alternatives, there can be no true choice. Smart R&D demands the creation of alternatives and will not take strategic action before multiple alternatives are created and evaluated.

Continual Learning

Change is one of life's few certainties. *Being smart* means continually learning how to create more value in the face of change. Employees respond to potentially threatening information in nondefensive ways. The organization identifies opportunities and paradigm shifts, and finds new and better ways to create value.

Embracing Uncertainty

There are no facts about the future, only uncertainties. People in a smart organization understand how to work with uncertainty. They measure what they do not know and manage the associated risks. They do not deny uncertainty, but recognize it when making decisions. Uncertainty is understood, communicated, and managed.

Outside-In Strategic Perspective

People typically start their thought processes by assessing where the organization is and then think about where it is going. In facing important strategic decisions, however, we should begin by understanding the broad territory in which the organization operates. The smart organization begins with the big picture—where the world is going, how its customers and industry are changing—then works inwards toward the implications for itself.

Systems Thinking

Albert Einstein said that we should make things as simple as possible, but no simpler. Unfortunately, most important strategic situations are complex. The development of a new technology, product, or process creates changes in the world of customers and competition, stimulating a chain of competitive reactions, next-generation products, and so forth. The smart organization uses systems thinking to understand the long-term (and often counterintuitive) implications of its decisions. Systems thinking encourages us to follow Einstein's maxim and to simplify to the point of maximum insight for decision making.

Open Information Flow

It is often impossible to tell in advance which information is important, or how some apparently disconnected piece of information will trigger a new and creative insight. The smart organization creates open and virtually unrestricted information flow to all of its parts. The habit of hoarding information as a source of power is driven out. In a value-creating culture, everyone needs open access to information to do his or her job.

Alignment and Empowerment

Traditional hierarchical, command-and-control structures are too slow with fast-moving global competition. They repel talented people who seek participation and purpose in their work. And they require excessive micromanagement. The standard antidote of these traditional structures, of course, is "employee empowerment." However, empowerment without alignment around common goals and understanding results in chaos and haphazard results. The smart organization uses participation in the decision-making process to achieve the alignment that makes empowerment effective. A common understanding of the strategies for value creation coordinates the organization.

Disciplined Decision Making

The opportunity or need for a strategic decision is often difficult to discern. A smart organization builds in processes to recognize the need for strategic decisions before it is overtaken by events. It then applies systematic, disciplined processes that delineate the steps to reach sound conclusions; these processes involve the right people, and their involvement secures their commitment to the final decision.

Systematic Evidence for Principles

Anyone familiar with contemporary business literature will recognize many of the nine principles as subjects of a number of popular books, articles, and even successful consulting practices. For example, Chris Argyris and Peter Senge have addressed the principle of continual learning in eloquent detail.[1] Likewise, Russell Ackoff has laid the foundations of systems thinking for modern corporations in a number of publications.[2] The importance of value creation and its measurement have been articulated by Collins and Porras by the consulting firm of Stern Stewart & Company—the latter having popularized the financial concept of economic value added.[3] Joseph Juran and the late W. Edwards Deming built a major movement around the idea of quality processes. Methods for embracing uncertainty in a rational way were developed in the 1800s by Pierre-Simon Laplace and Daniel Bernoulli, and have been described since the 1960s in dozens of publications on decision analysis and cognitive psychology.[4]

In pulling together the principles of smart R&D, we are going beyond what these authors have said and are making the claim that for an organization to routinely make high-quality decisions, it must have this *set* of principles in place. Otherwise, attempts to institutionalize the practices for good decision making will encounter significant barriers and leave the quality of strategic R&D decisions up to chance. The greater an organization conforms to this set of principles, the more systematically it will be able to make good strategic R&D decisions. This is a strong claim, so it is worth explaining briefly how we arrived at this set of principles and discussing the evidence we have used to test them.

Various studies on the implementation of best practices suggested that there were some root causes for good decision making in an organization. We reviewed our databases, interview records, and case studies. In these we observed patterns of behavior, which we developed and coalesced into the principles of smart R&D. This effort was fundamentally synthetic and inductive, extracting patterns from data. We initially identified a large set of principles. Realizing that some were closely related, we restated them and kept iterating.

The final result: a set of nine principles that support the best practices. The fact that we have nine principles instead of some other number is fairly arbitrary. In developing these principles we tested many different possibilities and made choices about which set of principles concisely covered the important behaviors. Whether there could be eight or ten or some other number is less important than the fact that there is no single panacea, but a coherent set of principles, and that following this set of principles can make any organization more powerful and effective.

We tested our hypotheses (the nine principles) in several ways. First, we tested the link between the principles and the barriers to best practice implementation by reviewing an existing database on barriers to implementation. This review indicated that if the principles were operative, the barriers would not be relevant. We applied the same test to organizations not represented in the database. In workshops with R&D executives, we had them generate lists of implementation barriers experienced by their organizations. We then asked how things would be different if they had the principles in place. In every group, the executives told us that the presence of the principles would have overcome their barriers to best practices.

The second kind of evidence is based on the measurement of "organizational IQ." We developed a survey instrument based on observable behaviors that measure the degree to which each principle is in operation in an organization. As explained in chapter 8, this IQ test discriminates among companies and demonstrates that conformance to the principles is measurable Some organizations are better; some are worse.

The third kind of evidence is based on case studies of specific decision-making situations. As described in the previous chapter and elsewhere, we have found ample examples of situations where good decision making was impossible because of behaviors that did not conform to the principles. If a decision process has gone awry, our experience indicates that some specific counterproductive patterns of behaviors are in place (The long-range planning case below is an example.). Removing or addressing the pattern rectifies the decision process. In other words, changing behavior to conform to the principles of smart R&D removes barriers and improves decision making.

The fourth kind of evidence tests the set of principles *together*. Negating any one of them creates barriers to good decision making. For example, consider the opposite of creating alternatives: dismissing alternatives, which directly undermines decision quality because a quality decision requires a set of viable alternatives. In an R&D setting, dismissing alternatives is often the operating principle of the project champion, who does whatever it takes to get a project approved. Almost by definition, the champion vigorously defends his or her position against alternative uses of resources.

We pulled together all of these threads of evidence into a coherent picture of how principles really work in organizations.

Figure 6-1. *Best Practices Implementation Matrix*

Counterproductive Principles Lead to Poor Results

Many executives who attend our workshops start with the view that they can somehow manage their way through barriers to best practices without changing their organizations and their collective attitudes. In some cases it works; but it can take a lot of effort and the success rate is low. The barriers are not the issue, in any case. They are merely symptoms of counterproductive organizational principles. The prescription is not to overcome the symptoms—the barriers—but to deal with their underlying causes. This requires a deeper understanding of how counterproductive principles lead to poor decisions.

When a company attempts to implement a best practice it is requesting individuals to change their behavior. In some cases, however, the best practice may be smart for the organization but not smart for the individuals. If it does not serve their interests, they will either withhold their support or actively resist implementation, perhaps covertly. Individuals act in ways that are smart for them, and will not sacrifice for the organization—at least not for long. Initiatives that put the interests of the organization and its individual members in conflict are doomed to failure.

The upper left quadrant of Figure 6-1 indicates the way many organizations approach implementation, by implicitly asking individuals to sacrifice for the organization. It is the classic win-lose situation. An organization that tries to implement the best practice without the right principle in place will find itself in this situation. The lower right-hand corner describes the usual result, with individual interests not working for the common purpose. If a practice is discovered that falls in the upper right corner, not smart for either the individual or the organization, it is quickly recognized as a mistake and is easily corrected.

Smart principles shift the context. When the right principles are in place, a request to implement a best practice is seen as smart for both the organization and its individual members. In the figure, this occurs in the lower left corner. The best practice is supported by the organization and readily embraced by individual employees. This is the win-win situation that leads to organizational effectiveness.

Instead of the typical response to barriers—"manage" them or overcome them through hard work—managers should recognize barriers as opportunities for diagnosis and correction at the level of principle. Instead of pushing against the barrier directly, they should work on the underlying principle. Shift the principle, and the barrier simply goes away. This moves the organization out of the failure mode in the lower right corner to the effective organization in the lower left corner.

The Long-Range Planning Case

A client engagement in 1990 illustrates how behavior that undermines corporate goals is created when organizations put employees in the win-lose situation described above. It also illustrates how looking beyond a barrier to the level of principle can lead to a breakthrough.

The long-range planning (LRP) process of a large R&D-intensive corporation had for years produced a single option for its technology strategies in each of several business divisions. The CEO, however, had come to suspect that developing alternatives would improve the process and lead to better decisions; he asked us to assist in developing and evaluating these alternatives.

The company portfolio spanned several business areas. We worked with the heads and key staff members of each business to identify and forecast the shareholder value associated with different alternatives. We then consolidated the results, which are shown in Figure 6-2.

Each strategy was evaluated in terms of its risk and return, which

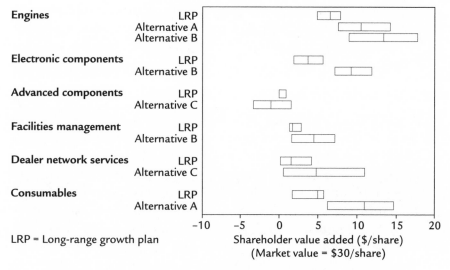

Engines — LRP / Alternative A / Alternative B
Electronic components — LRP / Alternative B
Advanced components — LRP / Alternative C
Facilities management — LRP / Alternative B
Dealer network services — LRP / Alternative C
Consumables — LRP / Alternative A

LRP = Long-range growth plan

Shareholder value added ($/share)
(Market value = $30/share)

Note: Vertical lines that divide the bars indicate median returns.

Figure 6-2. *Long-Range Plan (LRP) Alternatives*

are represented as bars in the figure. For example, for the engines division, the long-range plan had a median return (vertical line in the bar) of about $6 per share, with a range of uncertainty from about $5 per share to $7 per share. Alternative A for the engine division had a median return of about $11 per share, with a range from about $8 per share to $15 per share.

For five of the six business divisions, the alternatives had a higher median return than the initial LRP! In many cases, such as for the consumables division, the best-case result for the LRP was worse than the worst-case result for the alternatives. All of the alternatives had greater uncertainty, but the "risk" was largely on the upside.

The CEO was initially elated by these alternatives. With a few months of work, his organization had discovered new value that would have a major impact on the share price. He would be a big hero, and his organization would move to new levels of financial performance. But in the afterglow of this elation the CEO's mood darkened. "These opportunities have probably been here all along," he reasoned, "and our executives haven't said anything about them."

During the next meeting of key managers, the CEO's distress erupted. "You guys have been holding out on me! Why didn't you come forward with these ideas earlier?" he demanded. There was fear and silence in the room. "I should fire the whole lot of you!" he bellowed at the silent and blank-faced suits.

Finally, someone spoke up. "You did it to us."

This stopped the CEO in his tracks. "What?" he asked incredulously.

The manager continued, "You did it to us. Every year we go through this LRP process, and in making our recommendations, we have a choice. We can either go for conservative growth and keep our jobs or take a shot at something big and possibly get canned."

The manager went on to explain in detail just what he meant. The single LRP for his unit would provide returns of about $8 million in the current year and produce about $100 million in shareholder value by the mid-1990s. Adopting a more aggressive plan would give his unit an opportunity to gain market leadership. However, this would *cost* $10 million in the current year. But if the aggressive plan worked, the shareholders would be $150 million to $300 million richer by the mid-1990s.

"Our competitors are tough," he continued, "and the chance of our making that aggressive plan is about 60 percent. Even if it didn't work, we would create between $100 million and $150 million in shareholder value—far better than the conservative growth strategy." (See Figure 6-3.)

The CEO had been listening closely. "So why didn't you recommend the more aggressive plan?" he asked. "We'd be better off whether you succeeded or failed."

"Because it's *too dangerous*," the manager shot back. "As soon as I let you know about this alternative, you would latch onto the scenario in which we fully succeeded, and turn my forecast into a commitment. The next thing I'd hear would be that my new goal had become $200 million in added shareholder value. And I'd only have a 60 percent chance of making that goal." Then came the zinger: "And we all know what happens to people around here who don't make their goals." The other managers murmured their support. They all knew colleagues who had moved on to "pursue other interests" or to early retirement.

"I'm not going to risk my career on a 60 percent chance when I can offer a respectable conservative growth strategy."

The CEO was stunned and confused. "You should have explained it to me!"

"We've tried," was the response. "It doesn't work. Every year we do

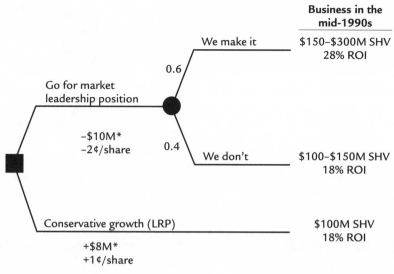

Figure 6-3. *The Manager's Choice*

a long-range plan and six months later we do a budget. At every budget cycle you tell us to cut. The $10 million I'd need to make the market leadership strategy work would be cut to perhaps $6 million or $7 million. Then I'd have *no* chance of making my goals because I wouldn't have the resources. So rather than risk our careers, we give you the conservative growth strategy," the manager concluded.

The counterproductive principles at work in this organization violate two of the principles of smart R&D. They violate Create Alternatives because the situation makes it dangerous even to offer good alternatives. They violate Embrace Uncertainty because the CEO converts forecasts into commitments.

There was hope in this case. The CEO and the managers had an opportunity to change how they behaved and change the principles under which their organization operated.

Principles Come First

This episode illustrates the main implication of the principles: The more an organization is imbued with the principles of smart R&D, the fewer barriers stand between it and best practice implementation.

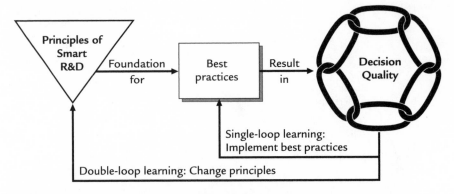

Figure 6-4. *Single- and Double-Loop Learning*

Using smart principles is a precondition to real progress, as shown in Figure 6-4. When organizations guided by the right principles see a best practice, they can adopt it directly—a process called *single-loop learning*. Organizations that do not have their principles in order must practice *double-loop learning*: They must first learn and adopt the principles. Only then will they be in a position to adopt and implement the best practices for decision quality.

The second learning loop is by far the hardest. It requires changing entrenched attitudes and behaviors. The previous chapter posed this question: Why do some organizations implement best practices relatively easily, while others struggle ineffectively? The answer: Organizations that implement with the least difficulty have good organizational principles for decision making; the others do not.

Simply recognizing the underlying principles is a great step forward in a double-loop learning situation; awareness opens the door to change. The participants in the managerial discussion above only recognized through a dramatic confrontation how counterproductive principles had trapped them in a system of counterproductive behavior. That recognition was their opportunity for positive change.

When a barrier occurs, one needs to shift the context, making the practice smart for the organization *and* for the individual. The following case suggests how this can be done.

A company that hired David as a consultant was committed to measuring the risk and return of its projects—a commendable goal. David quickly discovered that while this would be smart for the organization—and central to decision quality—it might threaten a powerful individual. The only way to overcome this barrier was to shift the context.

David interviewed the technical leader of one of the company's R&D projects, and after discussing its many technical factors, the technical leader assessed the chance of technical failure at 30 percent. As they finished their meeting she said, "Don't show this to Frank!"

"Why not?" David inquired.

"He wouldn't like to see that we might fail. In fact, he would think I was being disloyal or unenthusiastic about his project."

Subsequent conversation revealed that Frank was a strong project champion and a powerful person in the organization. Crossing Frank would not be smart from a career perspective, and saying that his beloved project might fail would only make him angry. Other members of the project team followed the same line. "We cannot use this information," they said.

Everyone, in fact, was acting in accordance with an operative principle of this organization, which was to support its project champions. David's suggestion that the technical leader behave differently—by talking openly about risk—would put her in a position of personally sacrificing for the organization, something she was not prepared to do. She was, however, prepared to withhold her information about risk, preventing the organization from benefiting from her insight.

The way out of this dysfunctional situation was to engage all parties at the level of principle. At a meeting of the project team, David pointed out the contradiction between their behavior and their commitment to dealing more objectively with risk, and everyone reluctantly agreed to work toward change.

When David and the team met with Frank and showed him their risk assessment, he reacted strongly, making everyone nervous. As with the others, David engaged him at the level of principle.

"You're the project champion, right?" David asked.

"Yes. And I believe strongly in this project! It's crucial for the company's success that we keep up the momentum."

"That's an important role," David agreed, "but I'm asking you to play a different one right now, one of an outsider looking in. Like a shareholder, perhaps."

This was a new thought for Frank, and he agreed to follow David's suggestion. In Frank's company, the entire team then discussed the implications of not being able to have a conversation about the risks in a project. In the end, and to the relief of his colleagues, Frank decided that it was more important to be able to discuss risks than to maintain a positive outlook at all times.

Frank's eventual willingness to deal openly with risk was a win for him and for his colleagues. Once it became possible to discuss possible project failures, it became possible to question some of the basic product performance goals. That discussion led to a consensus that high performance was not nearly as important as achieving a basic viable product. Frank and the technical leader were able to move forward with what they agreed was useful guidance for the project. The principle of embracing uncertainty proved itself.

Engaging at Many Levels at Once

The preceding example illustrates the need to engage at the level of principle as well as at the level of practice and process. Our perspective on implementation is to work at several levels, as shown in Figure 6-5:

▲ *Skills.* Specific practices may require specific skills, such as decision analysis, and these may need to be acquired through hiring or training.

▲ *Methodology.* In building a high-quality decision process some methodological issues may need to be resolved. For example, how will value be measured, by net present value or by some other method?

▲ *Process and practices.* The decision process itself is composed of many practices that must work in harmony. Implementing best practices requires changing the current process, for example, to include quantitative evaluation of projects.

▲ *Principles.* As our consulting anecdotes make clear, implementation may run afoul of current organizational principles. These need to be altered in favor of principles more conducive to making good decisions—the principles of smart R&D. If the implementation effort does not operate at this level, dealing with barriers will be extremely difficult. Be prepared to recognize and act upon opportunities for double-loop learning.

If effective implementation of the practices requires the principles of smart R&D, what are they exactly? How would you know if you

Figure 6-5. *The Several Levels of Effective Implementation*

Skills	Management
	▲ Recognize and require decision quality
	Doers
	▲ Ability to deliver decision quality
	Specialists
	▲ In-depth knowledge of processes and methodology
	Contributors
	▲ Understanding of their contribution to the process; internalization of the principles
Methodology	Management
	Common tools and techniques
	▲ Net present value
	▲ Decision analysis
Process and Practices	Meetings, reviews, participation
	Formats for contribution and presentation
	Criteria for identifying a strategic decision
Principles	Value maximization culture
	Continual learning
	Creating alternatives
	Disciplined decision making
	Alignment and initiative
	Embrace uncertainty
	Systems thinking
	Strategic perspective

had them in your organization? And why do they lead to better decision making?

These are the topics of the next two chapters. Chapter 7 goes through each principle in depth and shows what a productive pattern of behavior looks like and what kind of capability these patterns enable. Chapter 8 defines these patterns operationally in an organizational IQ test that will help you recognize the patterns in operation in your organization.

CHAPTER 7

THE NINE PRINCIPLES OF SMART R&D

> Beliefs create perceptions;
> perceptions create behavior.
> *Tom Guarriello*

T HE NINE PRINCIPLES of smart R&D comprise the worldview required for routinely achieving high-quality strategic decisions. Each principle represents a coherent theory that organizes a particular set of beliefs and, therefore, behaviors. This view permeates an organization, defining elements of its culture and setting a context for decision making on many levels. When smart principles are in place, behaviors tend to support decision quality. Other principles are often in operation in an organization, but they tend to create barriers to achieving decision quality. This chapter examines each principle in depth, addressing the questions:

▲ What is this principle?

▲ What productive pattern of behavior does it create?

▲ Why does it lead to better decision making?

Because nine principles are a lot to digest at once, we have divided them into three groups, organized loosely around three generic functions any organization must accomplish: achieve purpose, understand the environment, and mobilize resources (Figure 7-1).

Principles Relating to Achieving Purpose

Organizations face vague and conflicting purposes. CEOs give speeches. Stockholders want returns. Customers demand better products and services. Achieving purpose is about clarifying what is valuable and striving always to increase it.

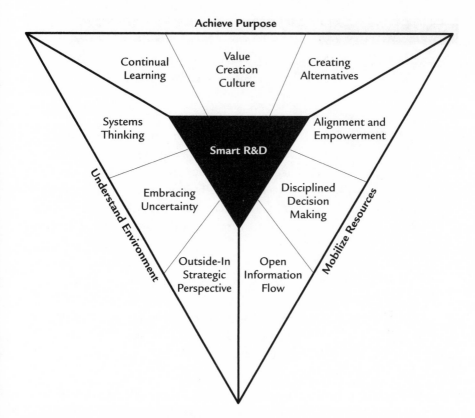

Figure 7-1. *Nine Principles of Smart R&D*

Three principles are related to achieving purpose: Value Creation Culture, Creating Alternatives, and Continual Learning. Valuing creation culture is having an orientation toward the ultimate value created by the organization and using value creation as a compelling argument for change. Creating alternatives requires taking the time to create a valuable set of options, from which the best will be selected. Continual learning means seeing the world as constantly changing, and responding by learning new ways to create more value.

Aim Always for Value Creation

PHILOSOPHY — The purpose of the organization is seen by everyone as maximizing the value created for customers and captured by the enterprise. The focus of decisions is on creating value. Tradition and politics take a back seat. R&D is seen as a key source of value creation and business renewal.

PERSONAL PERSPECTIVE — Every person sees his or her ultimate job as creating the greatest value. Requests for changes and exceptions to the rules are made when the rules stand in the way of creating value.

ORGANIZATION AND CULTURE — The culture rewards those who work to create more value, even if this means changing or breaking the rules. Different functions collaborate to create value. Disagreements are resolved in favor of the greatest value.

SUPPORT SYSTEMS — A very few practical metrics of value creation are regularly used in decision making. Specialized staff provide information and technical assistance in calculating value.

A colleague of ours recently visited a friend employed at Disneyland, who offered to give him a behind-the-scenes tour of the Magic Kingdom as soon as he came off duty. Halfway through the tour, they noticed a visitor who appeared anxious and unhappy. "I need to take care of this," said the friend, excusing himself. The visitor could not find her group because she was at the wrong film stand. The Disneyland employee cleared up her confusion and helped her find her friends.

Why did this off-duty employee go to the trouble of helping the visitor? "Disneyland is the happiest place on earth," he said. "That's our motto. If someone is unhappy, I can't stand by without helping."

Like Disneyland, every organization needs a clearly articulated purpose, one that employees from top to bottom understand and believe in. Creating value must be an integral part of that purpose. Collins and Porras show that organizations dedicated to a vision of how to serve customers created more shareholder value than other excellent organizations that make shareholder value creation their primary purpose.[1] These visionary organizations have justifiable faith that serving the customer well will serve shareholders best. Henry Ford recognized this long ago when he said, "A business that makes nothing but money is a poor kind of business."[2]

When value creation defines business purpose, employees in all functions have a common compass against which to check the direction of disparate activities and strategies. Value creation is also a common purpose around which agreement can be made: Disagreements can be settled in terms of which alternative creates the greater value, not in terms of who has the greater power. While the forces of tradition, internal politics, and other constraints will inevitably exist, they can be subordinated to the value creating impulse.

The Metrics of Value

Determining the value generated through a long value chain is difficult and often complex—especially for R&D, which makes investments over time in many projects. Profits from these efforts are only recognized after many years and after further investment for commercialization. Financial theory has proposed many approaches to measuring economic gain, but these seem to be converging on net present value of cash flow as the best primary economic measure. NPV accounts for the cash flows of the entire development and commercialization process as well as the "interest" on net investment or profit balances. In an R&D setting, it is crucial to apply NPV carefully and correctly: Naive applications are misleading.[3]

A closely related measure, Economic Value Added (EVA), calculates a business or business unit's after-tax operating income less the cost of capital actually used in its operations.[4] EVA, or similar systems, have been adopted by Polaroid, Coca-Cola, Honeywell, AT&T, Quaker Oats, Monsanto, and dozens of others to measure management performance and/or determine compensation. This discipline has helped more than a few firms discover that some of their businesses are actually value destroyers. In extreme cases, companies have sold these businesses and redeployed capital to more productive activities.

Useful though it may be, even the proponents of the EVA approach find that the long time horizons of R&D make development of meaningful and motivating incentive programs difficult. However, they agree that for decision making (about the future), the net present value of ultimate cash flow will produce identical results to the EVA approach.

It is not surprising to find that many companies use different value-oriented metrics to accomplish the same end. At 3M, for example, value creation is one of three key metrics considered in its system for prioritizing projects (the 3M Pacing Program); the others are project completion time frame and technical differentiation. The need for these metrics was clear. According to a company executive, "We found we were spending as much on a program that might be worth $1 million as one that was worth $20 million or more." To estimate the value of potential projects, 3M has adopted a metric called Shareholder Value that applies net present value and outcome probabilities to individual projects.[5]

An excellent example of the power of focused metrics in value creation is provided by Eastman Chemical, which won the Malcolm Baldrige Quality Award in 1993. For years the R&D of this company routinely produced good results. When the quality movement came along, it introduced many quality metrics in the hope of increasing R&D productivity. However, Eastman continued to produce R&D results at about the same pace. The multiple measures did not send a clear message. Finally, Eastman decided, as part of a highly integrated quality effort led by management, to focus on a single metric of value creation: carefully applied NPV. In only a few years, the productivity and output of R&D more than doubled. Figure 7-2 records Eastman's dramatic increase in value creation through R&D.[6]

This example illustrates that it is crucial to have only a few metrics for value. Having too many is almost as bad as having none. Given a list of possible metrics, project champions will select measures that make their projects look good, biasing the decision. In addition, multiple metrics make it impossible to compare and prioritize projects; they confuse the organization about what is important. They do have their uses: Metrics in addition to value creation can be useful surro-

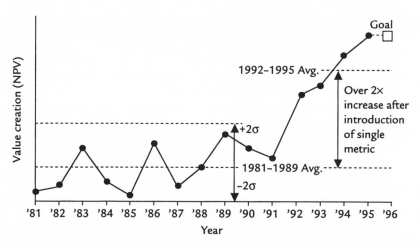

Figure 7-2. *Estimated Value of New Product and Process 1981 through 1995*
Source: *Eastman Chemical Company. With permission.*

gates where real value is hard to measure. The critical issue is to know which direction is true north and not be confused by the waypoints.

The principle of Value Creation Culture overcomes many of the barriers to best practice implementation. If the culture is truly focused on value creation, disagreements and differences of perspective are subordinated to the common goal. Conflict is resolved by appealing to value creation, not through politics or power.

For example, one organization we worked with initiated a critical R&D project aimed at developing enhancements for its chemical separation plant. The commercial and R&D sides of the company disagreed about the focus of this project. The commercial side wanted to increase greatly the range of material the plant could process; the R&D side wanted to reduce costs. Rather than settle the issue through the usual political approaches, the company decided to focus on value creation. It formed a team of people from both sides to examine objectively each perspective in terms of its potential for creating value. Many of the team members had never worked together before.

When the project was completed, both sides realized that the most value was created by doing something neither side had initially considered—to use the plant to provide a fundamentally new kind of service. The project proceeded on that basis. The focus on value creation overcame the boundaries and settled the conflicts. The usual politics never materialized.

Create Valuable Options

PHILOSOPHY — Choice means creating several good alternatives and selecting the best one.

PERSONAL PERSPECTIVE — Everyone routinely generates several good alternatives for every important decision. People stretch themselves to be creative and then understand which ideas produce the greatest value.

ORGANIZATION AND CULTURE — Creativity and new ideas are welcomed. The decision process requires generating multiple alternatives before evaluating them. No one will accept a recommendation without knowing what was considered and rejected. Organizational norms prevent people from second-guessing those who developed alternatives.

SUPPORT SYSTEMS — Facilitators are capable of applying alternative-generating technology and methods. Analytical support is available to evaluate alternatives.

Continuing with the example of the chemical separation plant, note that the approach that created the most value, using the plant to provide a new service, was on neither side's agenda when the project started. But the search for value required exploring other alternatives. The evaluation team developed several alternatives to those initially held by the opposing camps. These corresponded to different ways the plant could be used and how it could best serve them. This discussion led to a "revolutionary" alternative that reframed their thinking by modifying the original purpose of the plant and offering new services.

Both sides found this revolutionary alternative disturbing, and many individual team members proposed dropping it. Only abundant evidence supporting the premise and the team's commitment to creating alternatives prevented this option from ending up in the trash bin of ideas. To the surprise of many, this revolutionary alternative proved, in the end, to be the most valuable. Its prospects for value creation stood at more than $1 billion in lifetime NPV—better than any other alternative. The R&D and commercial sides of the project reorganized their thinking around this alternative to mine its potential.

The principle of Creating Alternatives is about making the quest for high-value alternatives desirable, safe, and rewarding. It also requires a commitment to evaluate alternatives honestly and without prejudice. Many organizations discourage employees from suggesting alternatives: Individuals who suggest them are viewed as weak, indecisive, uncommitted, or incapable of producing a single winning plan. The person who tells the boss she can think of four credible ways of going with her project is likely to be told, "Come back when you've done your job and figured out which one is best." These organizations make it risky for people to offer multiple alternatives, especially when hindsight makes a rejected alternative appear superior.

For example, Frances, the leader of an important project for an electric utility, created two attractive alternatives for her project. One involved an incremental improvement and the other a more radical plan with greater technical risk but higher potential payoff. The choice was difficult, and opposing camps developed around each. Frances realized that she could not satisfy both camps, and so chose the route that appeared best: the high-risk/high-return alternative. Six months later, her team reported that it had tried all known approaches for overcoming that alternative's biggest technical hurdle, but none of them had worked. The leader of the rejected incremental improvement camp used this failure against Frances, making the case that he, and not Frances, should get the next major assignment since "she had shown poor judgment." The irony is that by introducing alternatives, Frances opened herself up for criticism. A smart organization does not tolerate this sort of second-guessing.

More Good Ideas Than Resources

Smart organizations have many great but unpursued ideas lying around. In creating many options, they reject some good ones in favor of even better ones. Indeed, the value of the unpursued options is a measure of their success! On a project level, this phenomenon is easy to see. General Motors has applied a decision process that requires participants to generate a wealth of options in the product development process. In any given case, the best of these would create significant additional value for GM. In many instances, however, participants have created "hybrid" alternatives that combine the best features of the original set; these hybrids often have superior value to any of the original alternatives. GM reports that this step routinely doubles the net present value of the decision at hand. Yet the original good options are rejected in favor of the better hybrid.

On a portfolio level, this phenomenon means that there are attractive but unfunded projects waiting for resources to be freed up. This encourages greater flexibility in responding to the natural evolution of research findings: Some currently funded projects will inevitably turn out to be less attractive than originally hoped. Individuals cognizant of the alternative projects will be drawn to those that have better prospects. When the time comes to change funding, there is less resistance to stopping currently funded projects because personnel have already developed interests elsewhere.

Generating alternatives increases the burden on the evaluation process because it must be capable of sorting them out—separating the best from the good. This challenge is typically different for the different types of R&D decisions. For project decisions, it usually means taking the one best direction. For portfolio decisions, it usually means allocating resources to some projects and not others.

Learn How to Create More Value

PHILOSOPHY
The purpose of an organization is to learn continually what creates value and how to deliver it.

PERSONAL PERSPECTIVE
Everyone is excited by learning and growing, and wanting to make their organization the best it can be. They accept criticism and new ideas, see the wisdom in them, and apply what they learn to themselves and their organization.

ORGANIZATION AND CULTURE
Organizational change is viewed as important, energizing, and profitable. Something is always improving somewhere, and change is viewed as routine. Organizational myths and assumptions are questioned. The messenger of "bad" news is welcomed, not strangled; and the news is used to initiate improvements.

SUPPORT SYSTEMS
Formal opportunities and staff are provided for learning and change. Discretionary resources are made available for learning and experimentation.

A great deal has been written over the past decade about the need for organizations to keep learning—about customers, competitors, technologies, and better ways of doing things. We live in an era of "permanent whitewater," according to Marvin Weisbord. "It is the world created by accelerating change, growing uncertainty, increasingly unpredictable global connections of economics, technology, and people. This environment is producing irreversible general change, requiring companies to alter course or face serious disruption."[7] Thus, if there are no permanent solutions, there is only a permanent need: to continue learning what creates value and how to deliver it. This should be a central purpose of any organization.

Xerox's corporation-wide adoption of benchmarking techniques, which saved the company from near certain collapse, illustrates the power of continual learning. In 1981, Xerox discovered that new Japanese competitors were selling photocopying machines in the United States at less than its own cost of production. Initially, Xerox took a defensive stance and accused the Japanese competitors of "dumping," an unfair trade practice. As the pioneer of electronic copying, Xerox thought that no one could make copiers better and cheaper than it could. However, when it talked to its Japanese partner, Xerox discovered that Fuji Xerox could manufacture, ship, and profitably sell a copier in Rochester, New York, at a price lower than Xerox's own production cost in that city!

Fortunately (and painfully), Xerox made the shift to a learning frame. Xerox USA was able to learn the processes of quality manufacturing and design that made both low cost and high quality possible. In the wake of this episode, the company developed structured methods for benchmarking other processes, including those found outside its own industry, and for adapting its findings to improved processes of its own. The Xerox approach to benchmark-based learning is today institutionalized through a corporation-wide system of training, operating procedures, and specialized personnel. Xerox's approach to benchmarking and continual learning became a major driver of the U.S. quality movement.[8]

Removing Barriers

Absence of continual learning creates barriers to best practices in decision making. The absence of this principle is evidenced by a lack of proper skills. Some organizations assume that people will simply pick up things in their "spare" time. By leaving skill acquisition to chance, they unwittingly assure that they will not have the full menu of skills needed to make smart decisions.

The reluctance to change is a deadly trait for any business organization. People and institutions become comfortable with current ways of doing things. And if things are going well, they ask, "Why change?" But technology and customers change. And new competitors appear. People and organizations that fail to change in response to these external developments become irrelevant and ineffective. Continual learning is the best antidote to stasis. By its nature, it encourages people and their institutions to change.

Continual learning lifts the focus from the organization to the outer world, and helps overcome the barrier of internal focus. As Xerox's benchmarking illustrates, too much internal focus can be devastating. The whole premise of benchmarking is to learn from outside the organization. Yet behind this is a deeper issue. Information from the outside can be embarrassing, threatening, or difficult to interpret. People have a natural tendency to react defensively, which drives them to focus internally. In Xerox's case, it was much easier to rally around the idea of unfair dumping than to accept the idea that the Japanese might have found a better way. According to Ed Finein, one of the pioneers of benchmarking, Xerox executives responded to the realization that Fuji Xerox had lower costs by projecting more aggressive annual cost reductions for Xerox USA and showing they would be competitive again in a few years.[9] Only by persevering in learning the full situation did Xerox USA personnel realize that Fuji Xerox was on a totally superior curve—without a dramatic shift, Xerox USA would get farther behind! The principle of Continual Learning means not reacting defensively to dangerous information, and drives people to seek information from the outside. Indeed, the outside may have the best learning opportunities!

The Personal Side of Continual Learning

Learning how to create more value is, at its core, personal, and requires a level of reflection that few achieve. R&D personnel, corporate planners, and managers in general see themselves as natural learners. They are people, after all, who excelled in school; they obviously recognize the importance of learning and know how to go about it. Their particular line of work, in fact, requires them to keep current with their professions. As a group, however, they find it very difficult to learn when learning requires self-assessment and change. As Harvard's Chris Argyris reports:

> Those members of the organization that many assume to be
> the best at learning are, in fact, not very good at it. I am talk-
> ing about the well-educated, high-powered, high-commitment
> professionals who occupy key leadership positions in the
> modern corporation.[10]

Paradoxically, while these individuals are generally among the most enthusiastic about the concept of continuous learning and improvement, they are often the greatest obstacle to its implementation. This paradox stems, according to Argyris, from a tendency to define learning too narrowly—as problem solving. The people we usually think of as good at learning are, indeed, experts at identifying and solving problems in the external environment. They can dispassionately collect and analyze data, identify what is wrong, and what needs to be done. As long as learning is focused on external issues such as the markets, the competition, price levels, and so forth, they do just fine. These issues are not up close and personal.

> But if learning is to persist, managers and employees must also look inward. They need to reflect critically on their own behavior, identify the ways they often inadvertently contribute to the organization's problems, and then change how they act.[11]

This is what most professional managers are *least* good at. Whenever the quest for continuous learning puts their personal behavior or performance in the spotlight, according to Agryris's findings, these professionals react defensively, blaming bad outcomes on customers, coworkers, their managers, anyone but themselves. This defensive behavior is antithetical to learning and continual improvement.

Principles Relating to Understanding the Environment

Organizations face a confusing environment, one that is uncertain and complex, with subtle cause-and-effect relationships and interactions among many players. These uncertainties and complexities play out over time, often in ways that obscure relationships and interactions. Many interpretations of the environment are possible; these lead to ambiguity and confusion.

Understanding the environment means making sense of uncertainty and complexity in ways that facilitate effective decision making. Decision quality requires a strategic perspective that accounts for uncertainty and untangles the subtleties of complex systems. Principle 4, Embracing Uncertainty, is about recognizing what is unknown, and being able to understand, communicate, and manage this lack of knowledge. Principle 5, Outside-In Strategic Perspective, requires creating and validating a strategic interpretation of the environment. Principle 6, Systems Thinking, calls for uncovering complex cause-and-effect relationships, and appreciating the implications of actions and events.

Know What You Do Not Know

PHILOSOPHY People seek to understand all sources of uncertainty and use that knowledge when making decisions. They recognize that decisions can be controlled, although outcomes cannot. They communicate accurately about uncertainty.

PERSONAL PERSPECTIVE People understand uncertainty within their areas of expertise and articulate it in terms of possibilities and probabilities. They know what they can influence and what is beyond their control.

ORGANIZATION AND CULTURE Uncertain information takes the form of ranges or probability distributions. Incentives reward what can be controlled. Forecasts are never turned into commitments. The decision process requires explicit consideration of risk and return.

SUPPORT SYSTEMS Systems and specialized staff help assess and evaluate probability and the effects of uncertainty.

"Our competitors have just acquired Chemical Synthesis, Inc.," said the director of product development. "I figure we have about six months before they get their act together and bring out the next-generation product. If we do not get our next-generation product out before they do, we are going to miss an important window. Can you have a new product ready to go within six months?" He looked toward the project leader and waited for an answer. There was a long pause.

The project leader thought to himself, "Our current plans call for a nine-month development cycle. To deliver on his schedule, we would have to overcome three technical hurdles without delays or unforeseen problems. But beating our competition is important, and my project is key to our success. It is possible we will make it, so I had better show that my team is on board."

"Yes," he finally answered. "We'll have the product ready in six months."

"Good. I'm relying on you," replied the director.

As the project leader left the director's office, he swallowed hard. "I hope things work out," he thought to himself. He briefed the team immediately. "The director needs us to accelerate the schedule. It is crucial to our competitive situation that we succeed. Let's make a big push and get this done."

He knew his team would work hard. Last time the pressure was on, people worked nights and weekends and postponed vacations. They had delivered before, and he hoped they could do it again. Even though it was getting late, he poured himself a cup of coffee and started to work.

Five months later he found himself in the director's office again. "I've got some bad news," the director said. "Our competitors have just announced their new product. They have moved faster than I anticipated and their new product looks good. How long until our product is ready?"

The project leader looked at him glumly, "As you know, we have been working day and night. We have been able to address two critical technical hurdles, but the hardest one, keeping the heat down, still eludes us. We should be ready in another three months."

The director looked surprised. "I thought I could count on you. A product that late is next to useless! You told me you could have it in six months."

"I tried. As you know our original plan was nine months. When you asked me to accelerate product development, I agreed and we worked hard to meet the schedule. You always tell us to have a 'can-do' attitude, so I did not tell you about my uncertainty."

"But now we are stuck without a product," the director responded. "If I had known of your uncertainty, I would have bought a license or allocated more resources to a parallel approach."

Cases like the one just described are common. General managers and R&D executives agree to business plans based on "negotiated" schedules of delivery from R&D. During the planning process, the R&D community often accepts unrealistic goals to show that they are "on board." When they miss these goals, as they do routinely, R&D is perceived by the business community as the cause of great expense and consternation, confirming the R&D community's belief that business managers are unreasonable and do not understand research. Neither business managers nor researchers can learn in this environment, and neither can accept or communicate the reality that the world—especially the world of R&D—is very uncertain.

Organizations are constantly surprised by events that in hindsight they might reasonably have anticipated. Psychological research by Amos Tversky and Daniel Kahnaman has demonstrated that repeatable biases cause people to misconstrue uncertainty or avoid dealing with it. Practical procedures and training are available to overcome these biases and to prepare for uncertain events before they happen.[12]

Organizations must plan for the future, but they must also recognize that *there are no facts about the future*, only uncertainties. A smart organization learns how to work with uncertainty in its decision process, identifying what it knows and does not know. It makes decisions without sweeping uncertainty under the rug. It identifies the key sources of uncertainty, assesses them as well as possible, and then creates strategies with the best balance of risk and return. It recognizes that it can hedge and manage uncertainty, but never eliminate it.

Embracing Uncertainty Leads to Better Results

The principle of Embracing Uncertainty requires that people clearly communicate about uncertainty at all times. Doing so leads to better results. To see how, let us rewrite the case of the project leader and the R&D director that started this section on embracing uncertainty, this time adjusting it for the principle.

"Our competitors have just acquired Chemical Synthesis, Inc.," said the director of product development. "I figure we have about six months before they get their act together and bring out the next-generation product. If we do not get our next-generation product out before they do, we are going to miss an important window. Can you have a new product ready to go within six months?" He looked toward the project leader and waited for an answer. There was a long pause.

The project leader thought to himself, "Our current plans call for a nine-month development cycle. To deliver on his schedule, we would have to overcome three technical hurdles without delays or unforeseen problems. But this is important, and my project is key to our success. It is possible we will make it, but I do not want to mislead the director."

"Yes," he finally answered, "it is possible we could make it. However, there are still three technical hurdles to overcome. To accelerate the project, we will have to take some shortcuts, which puts us at risk. I'd give us about a 70 percent chance of making it within six months."

"Only 70 percent?" the director responded. "I cannot take that level of risk for something this important. It is also possible the competitor will introduce a product sooner, perhaps in four months. Would it help if I gave you more resources?"

"Only a little," replied the project leader. "Testing the design just takes time. More skilled people would help, of course, but bringing them up to speed would take some effort. If you want the product in four months, I'd give us only a 40 percent chance of making it."

"It looks like we had better hedge a bit," concluded the director. "I have an opportunity to license a technology that is not as good as what you're working on, but it will give us a product that responds to the competitive situation. If we beat them with this licensed product and come out with a superior product based on our own technology a few months later, that should keep us ahead of the competition in our customers' eyes. Still, try to complete your project within six months."

The project leader briefed his team immediately. "The director needs us to accelerate the schedule. It is crucial to our competitive situation that we succeed. Let's make a big push and get this done." He knew his team would work hard. They had delivered before, and he hoped they could do it again.

Five months later he found himself in the director's office again. "I've got some bad news," the director said. "Our competitors have just announced their new product. They've moved faster than I anticipated and their new product looks good. Fortunately, we've grabbed some market share with our licensed product and we have a few months maneuvering room. How long until our product is ready?"

The project leader looked disappointed. "As you know, we have been working day and night. We have been able to overcome two critical technical hurdles, but the hardest one, keeping the heat down, still eludes us. We should be ready in another three months—I'd give it a 95 percent chance."

The director shared his disappointment. "I am sorry to hear that it is turning out to be harder than you thought. But things could be much worse. A 95 percent chance of a new product in three months is still a good business bet."

In our example, the willingness of the two parties to communicate about uncertainty has made an important difference in the company's competitive position. It opened up some new options about resources and hedging through licensing that were not previously available. Although the project team worked just as hard and produced exactly the same technical result, the impact on the health of the company was completely different. Communicating about uncertainty turned a major competitive setback into a staged product introduction. Communicating uncertainty, however, requires some shifts in how people establish and maintain credibility, the types of agreements people make, and how people are held accountable.

Credibility

Consider the project leader's first statement of uncertainty: "I'd give us about a 70 percent chance of making it in six months." In the wrong context, this could sound indecisive or unsupportive. In the original dialogue, the project leader's simple "yes" communicated a can-do attitude. But suppose that the director had asked the project leader, "How long will it take you to complete the project?" In a typical organization, the expected response is decisive: six months. Suppose the project leader instead responds, "I'm not sure. Between four months and twelve months." Which sounds more credible—the project leader who gives the point estimate (six months), or the one who has a range of uncertainty? In an organization committed to the principle of Embracing Uncertainty, it is the person who communicates clearly with the range of uncertainty.

Accountability, Decisions, and Outcomes

Embracing uncertainty requires a change in the types of promises that people make. In the first dialogue, the project leader promised to deliver results, which is what the director wanted to hear. But in doing so, he left the company exposed to uncertainty because he promised something that was out of his control. In the second dialogue, he promised to accelerate the program. He promised to do something that was under his control. Although this was not what the director wanted to hear, it forced the director to think about alternatives.

Making this distinction between decisions, which we can control, and outcomes, which we cannot, is crucial to embracing uncertainty. Yet it requires reexamining how people are held accountable. The smart organization upholds accountability, but only for decisions, not for uncontrollable outcomes. It documents decision quality to ensure good decisions at the time they are made and to learn from them later.

One of the purposes of accounting is to track objective measures and see if managers are looking after investors' money prudently. The banker, stock analyst, or shareholder wants to see how much money the company has used, where it has gone, and if it has been managed wisely. If the accounts show that the money has been mismanaged, the investor withdraws his or her money or takes other actions, and in this way the manager is held accountable for the results. This is good as far as it goes.

This tradition often carries over to budgets in an R&D organization. Was the money well spent? Did it achieve the desired results? These are good questions, and management should be held accountable. Yet in situations of uncertainty, this is often carried too far and seriously distorts decision making.

For example, Mark wanted to start an R&D-based spin-off. The core business had developed a new type of chemistry that had applications in other industries. In particular, he thought there were many chemical intermediates that he could develop using this new chemistry. So he went to the CFO to talk about funding. He was given an endowment of a few million dollars and a few years. "After that," the CFO said, "you have to be self-financing. Then we will talk about a spin-off."

After a year, Mark had tried a few compounds and found one that seemed attractive, compound X. Because there were several interested customers, he had to scale up production. The CFO said he could use his endowment to finance the production plant, which he did. Unfortunately for Mark, compound X was found to have limited applicability in the market. It produced a small revenue stream—enough to cover the initial investment, operations, and turn a little profit—but not enough to continue to finance the R&D.

When he asked for more money, the CFO took a hard line: "Before I authorize more money for R&D, I want to see that you have become self-financing with the first endowment." To continue his exploration of compounds, Mark turned to his potential customers for funding. With each one, he cut a cofunding deal. By helping to fund the R&D, they gained rights to use the results. In this way, Mark became self-financing, met his financial targets, and carried on business development.

Although this example sounds like a success story, it is not. To meet his financial goals, Mark gave away much of the new value he was creating to his customers. He was being held accountable to the wrong thing by the parent company. To understand this, let us look at the business proposition again from the perspective of uncertainty.

What Mark saw was the ability to try lots of potential compounds using the new type of chemistry. He could try about fifty applications in five years. Each one had a small chance of working technically. Even if it worked technically, the compound might not be commercially viable. Of those that were commercially viable, most would have limited application, like compound X. What Mark was really hoping for was a blockbuster compound. One blockbuster compound would produce a profit stream almost as large as the core business; two would change that business fundamentally.

Finding a blockbuster compound is an uncertain proposition. Of the fifty compounds Mark thought he could pursue, each one had about a 1 percent chance of becoming a blockbuster. As a portfolio, this amounts to about a 35 percent chance that Mark's course of research would produce a single blockbuster and about a 15 percent chance that it would produce more than one. These possibilities are the true source of value in Mark's enterprise.

By cofunding the development with his customers, Mark had given them most of the upside. Since they owned rights, if the compound was a blockbuster, the customers could simply make it themselves. Had the core business taken more of a venture capital perspective on Mark's proposition, it would have funded the entire project itself. Yet the CFO wanted to hold Mark accountable, and so forced him to seek outside funding. In a project with a 50 percent chance of producing only limited results, this sort of accountability does not make sense. He should have been held accountable to the things that were really under his control—doing a good job developing and commercially testing compounds as rapidly as possible.

This attitude about an entrepreneur's accountability is reflected in some broad cultural trends. In an article about venture capital in Europe versus the United States, *The Economist* noted that Europe's venture capital industry has had limited results, while Silicon Valley has the Midas touch. It attributed some of the differences to the ability to embrace uncertainty. "If you start a company in London or Paris and go bust, you have just ruined your future. Do it in Silicon Valley, and you have just completed your entrepreneurial training."[13] In Silicon Valley, entrepreneurs are judged in part by how well they have tried and by the quality of their decisions. It is recognized that companies sometimes succeed and fail for reasons outside of management's control. There are only two ways to deal with this kind of uncertainty: avoid it by sticking to more certain but less profitable pursuits or embrace it by funding a large enough portfolio of uncertain ventures to ensure good portfolio results.

Implications for the R&D Portfolio

Mark's project represents a miniportfolio of compounds to be tested. The same counterintuitive statistics in Mark's miniportfolio apply to any portfolio of R&D projects. For example, a portfolio of ten R&D projects, each with a 20 percent chance of becoming a winner, has a 90 percent chance of at least one winner. With twenty such projects, the portfolio has a 99 percent chance of at least one winner.

Yet it is impossible to predict which project will produce the winner. People confuse their inability to pick winners with the economic risk of the whole portfolio, which may be very low! A decision process dedicated to picking the winners is wrongheaded. Once projects are screened to a certain level of quality, and a healthy *portfolio* is developed, it is better to embrace the uncertainty than try to control the uncontrollable.

In a portfolio of R&D projects, embracing uncertainty requires that each individual project manager's perspective of risk and reward be the same as the overall company. In the portfolios described above, each project manager faces an 80 percent chance of failure. How the company deals with this risk of failure quite understandably dictates the behavior of its managers. Individual managers should be rewarded for pursuing their projects professionally and their incentives should be tied to portfolio rather than individual results. If individual managers are punished for failure and rewarded for success, they will seek higher probability projects with lower potential value. This will reduce the overall value of the portfolio to the company. In organizations where individuals are rewarded on portfolio results, they can afford to accept higher project risk for higher portfolio return.

Few people in an organization live with as much uncertainty as do R&D workers and managers. For them, it is part of the landscape; it is what makes R&D, R&D! So it is important for them to understand the sources and amounts of uncertainty, to communicate those understandings accurately to others—especially with people in other functions—and to deal explicitly with uncertainty when making decisions. The principle of embracing uncertainty requires building a common language for communicating uncertainty and managing it appropriately.

Seeing and Acting on the Big Picture

PHILOSOPHY	The company understands the dynamics of its industry and customers. It uses this perspective to frame and evaluate strategic decisions at all levels.
PERSONAL PERSPECTIVE	People can distance themselves from their personal circumstances, see the big picture, and appreciate its implications for strategy.
ORGANIZATION AND CULTURE	Outside information is actively sought and used in decision making. Inside-out frameworks are viewed with suspicion.
SUPPORT SYSTEMS	Strategic marketing and competitive intelligence units generate alternative future scenarios based on outside information. Staff members build top-down industry models. This perspective is accessible to everyone in the organization.

A specialized plastics company we benchmarked thought it had found a great new opportunity. Its best customer was developing an important new product and asked the plastics company to formulate a special material for it. Like all suppliers, the plastics company was overjoyed at the prospect of working in partnership with a key customer, and quickly moved to developing the new material. It shifted half of its discretionary R&D investment to the new project, and within eight months had developed a material that met all the technical requirements of its customer.

This story should have a happy ending, but it does not. The customer's new product fizzled in the market, and demand for the new material fizzled with it. Our friends at the plastics company had a new specialized material and the capacity to produce it, but no one to buy it. If they were lucky, someday they would find another application and customer for the material.

An outside-in perspective might have prevented this unhappy outcome. In fact, when he learned the reasons for the product failure, an R&D manager of the plastics company told us:

> If we had only taken our own look at the end customer's situation we would have recognized that the application would not work. We shouldn't have accepted their need for the new compound without developing our own perspective on the final marketplace. In fact, we could have served our largest customer best if we had been able to warn them that their product was likely to fail.

Plan Outside-In, Not Inside-Out

Products (or services) must satisfy end customers, but many organizations are buried so far down in the value chain that they fail to understand what these customers want and need. To be alert to end-customer needs, we must start with them, understand how they are changing, and how the industry that serves their needs is evolving, and then work back through the value chain to understand the basis of competition at each stage. Armed with this perspective, we can appraise our present position, and decide whether we are already well positioned and simply need to continue serving our customers with excellent products, or whether we would create more value by repositioning ourselves in the value chain. If we have enough leverage, we may even be able to take the lead by shifting the basis of competition.[14] A conceptual diagram of such a model is shown in Figure 7-3.

This approach to planning and analysis is almost heretical. Traditional corporate planning begins with the present and extrapolates incrementally into the future. It scans for threats among the field of established competitors. Not surprisingly, the future it forecasts is an extension of the present, with minor variations. And it is almost guaranteed to miss the structural changes that blindside businesses and cause them to miss important opportunities. It fails to note one of industry's most enduring lessons—that business-killing innovations usually come from some as-yet unknown entity operating outside the circle of current competitors.

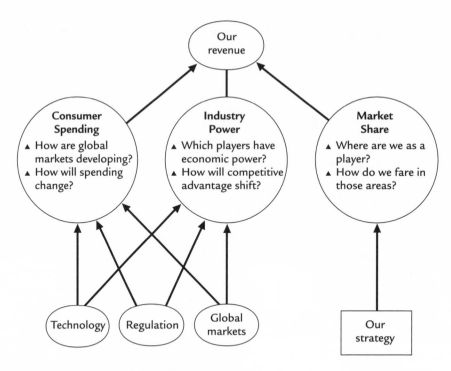

Figure 7-3. *A Typical Outside-In Model*

An outside-in approach gathers external information to form a broad conception of who customers are, how technology and customers' needs are changing, and how the industry and its basis of competition may be altered. It gives us a perspective we can use to position ourselves advantageously and possibly influence competition in our favor.

The outside-in perspective provides a basis for interpreting specific events and framing decisions in the right context. Consider the case of an American company whose major customers were located in Italy. One of these customers had gone to a competitor, and the American company did not want to lose another. In the spirit of "customer intimacy," it formulated a campaign to understand Italian customers better. "Italy First!" became its unofficial corporate slogan. Although the slogan was a great sales motivator, it distracted R&D, which had been charged with developing a next-generation product. The "Italy First" imperative channeled R&D work toward meeting the needs of the company's Italian customers.

An outside-in perspective revealed that Italian customers were not particularly relevant as future buyers. Their plants were based on an old technology that, owing to regulatory constraints, would probably not be rebuilt. In fact, many of the Italian plants would be decommissioned by the time the outputs of R&D were scheduled to come on stream. The company's real future lay elsewhere, in growing Asian markets. R&D should have been focusing on meeting the needs of these new customers with a technology unconstrained by the needs of current customers. Only by developing a strategic outside-in perspective could R&D focus on what really mattered for the future of the company.

Lacking an outside-in perspective, a company will always be a follower, and it will always be surprised by future events. Companies that operate with the outside-in principle constantly sense the external environment for relevant information. One top-drawer global materials company maintains a small but effective competitive intelligence unit in its marketing department. This unit scans continually for changes that could affect its strategic interests: technical breakthroughs, changes in government regulations, initiatives by rival firms, trade agreements, and so forth. Needless to say, this company experiences few strategic surprises.

*Know the Full Implications of Actions
and Events*

PHILOSOPHY   Complex questions are answered by thinking
through cause-and-effect relationships from
the perspective of the whole business. Leverage points, feedback loops, and key factors are
identified.

PERSONAL   People understand how their jobs and their
PERSPECTIVE   actions are part of a larger system, and work
to incorporate multiple and whole-system
perspectives into their thinking.

ORGANIZATION   Decision makers expect people to think
AND CULTURE   through the full implications of their proposals and bring multiple perspectives to every
important choice.

SUPPORT SYSTEMS   Formal models and sensitivity analysis are
routinely used to support business decisions.

Several years ago, we did some work for a company whose main
business was buying and fattening cattle for market. This was a high-
volume, low-margin business whose profitability was tightly bound
up with certain commodity prices: for cattle, feed, and so forth. We
were told that the owner was a major player in the cattle and related
futures markets. Naturally, we expected to find that the owner reduced his risk by actively hedging company profits through futures
contracts on these commodities. We, along with his own top executives, were astonished to find just the opposite: The owner routinely
took unhedged positions worth millions of dollars in either direction. When asked why he risked his profitability on the vagaries of
commodities markets, he replied in effect, "It's not risky for me. I understand what moves these prices."

To prove his point, he took us to an empty room whose walls were filled with current cattle prices, corn and soybean prices, futures prices of various types, and weather data from key agricultural regions of the United States. He explained that as one of the largest companies in his industry, he was supplied with the best data about what was happening with the supply and demand for cattle of various ages, the costs of feed, and other information. Also, as an expert cattle feeder using the latest computerized nutrition models, his company knew just what it cost to bring young cattle to market in six months to a year. Understanding the dynamics of the cattle-raising *system*, he said, made it possible to predict changes in prices that, from his highly educated and informed perspective, were inevitable. This man was a systems thinker and market-maker.

Systems thinking recognizes that everything is fundamentally connected to everything else, and that things we do have far-reaching and often counterintuitive consequences. We need to understand the important aspects of these consequences without becoming mired in endless detail.[15]

Systems thinking requires an agile mind and a keen understanding of how parts of the world (the system) are dynamically linked. It is much simpler to naively assume that certain parts of the system will remain conveniently fixed, even as we change other parts. For example, a company plans to lower its price by 10 percent, thereby taking away its competitor's customers. This, of course, assumes that the competitor will make no change in its own price. Experience tells us that competitors do react, sometimes by matching our price cut, sometimes by increasing advertising, and sometimes by doing things no one would have anticipated.

The case of P&G's development of a new form of cookie in the early 1980s illustrates the importance of systems thinking. Then (as now) Nabisco was the king of bakery products. P&G wanted to enter that market, and thought there was an opportunity because Nabisco seemed complacent. "It was a sleepy oligopoly," said Hugh S. Zurkuhlen, an analyst with Salomon Brothers.[16] P&G figured that it could come in and capture market share. To this end it spent close to $30 million developing a new type of soft cookie that contrasted to Nabisco's traditional hard cookie; it conducted test marketing and a big rollout. The result was P&G's capture of up to 35 percent of cookie sales.[17]

Nabisco's reaction, however, was far from sleepy. It quickly engineered its own soft cookie, rolled it out through its well-established distribution channels, and recaptured most of its lost market.[18] P&G was pushed back, and is no longer in the cookie business. Why? Because it failed to anticipate the counterattack of its strong and entrenched rival.

To be effective systems thinkers, we need to understand our own enterprise, its activities, and the competitive environment as an organic whole. This makes it possible to think through complex cause-and-effect relationships from the perspective of the entire business and to find leverage points for effective action.

Treat Causes, Not Symptoms

Consider the case of the measurement laboratory of a large chemical processing company. In response to customer requests to lower their personnel costs, the laboratory had embarked on an R&D project to develop equipment for automating their processes. Yet early successes did not seem to satisfy the customers. Much to the surprise of the researchers, one customer stopped the implementation of a particular piece of equipment it had requested on the grounds that it added no value. It was not until the researchers took a systems approach that they realized the root of this problem was not the personnel costs, but rather a poorly understood system of cost allocation. In fact, their effort to reduce personnel costs was slowly driving the laboratory out of business.

The initial problem this laboratory faced and tried to solve was the high cost of labor. Figure 7-4 diagrams this situation.

Start with vicious circle number one. Here, the central lab uses allocated costs to charge its customers. The rate for labor reflects the allocations of expensive equipment. The lab is under pressure to reduce its personnel because labor is so expensive. This makes capital investment in automation look attractive. The plus between the two bubbles indicates the nature of the cause-and-effect relationship: the higher the allocated costs, the greater the attractiveness of the investment. Attractive capital investment motivates purchases of equipment to replace personnel. The organization is now left with fewer people and more capital costs, so the allocated costs go up. This increases the attractiveness of more capital investment, and so on. The organization is trapped in a vicious circle. A systems approach

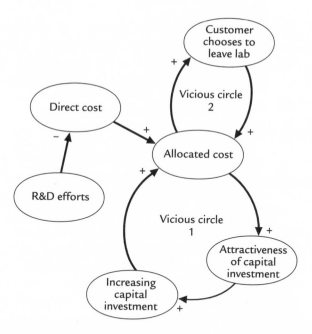

Figure 7-4. *A Systems View of Cost Allocations*

changes our diagnosis of the problem: The cost allocation system is misleading decision makers.

Turn to vicious circle number two. Here, as labor costs rise, customers of the central lab perceive its services as more expensive than those obtainable through outsourcing and win the right to seek new suppliers. As these customers leave and the workload of the lab is further reduced, the same level of overhead is allocated across fewer labor hours. This increases the allocated cost per hour, reinforcing the vicious circle.

This deeper understanding of the system changes our diagnosis again: The allocated cost system is driving the central lab out of business, while at the same time encouraging the company's investment in the lab.

The bubbles on the left side of the diagram represent a major R&D initiative aimed at lowering direct costs. Since the majority of direct costs are personnel-related, most of R&D's efforts focus on reducing the workforce, hence the minus sign between them. This in turn lowers the base for allocations, and so increases the allocated costs.

The long and short of this systems analysis tells us that the R&D initiative is having exactly the opposite of the intended effect! A project intended to reduce costs is raising them for its customers, putting the lab in a no-win situation. To break out of this situation, something has to change, such as the abandoning firm's counterproductive cost allocation system or creating other R&D initiatives that add revenue rather than merely reducing costs.

Removing Barriers

The principle of Systems Thinking can overcome several barriers to implementing best practices. Fundamentally, systems thinking requires people to deepen their diagnosis of a situation and not respond to superficial features. It is consistent with Deming's advice to ask "why" five times to get to the root cause. This deeper understanding overcomes the tendency to oversimplify.

Systems thinking also overcomes perceived difficulties in measurement. People often think that the value of R&D cannot be measured since its value is diffused through the larger economic system. The principle of systems thinking traces particular technical features to what customers value and how products (or services) play in a marketplace. Understanding this sequence of cause and effect makes the measurement of R&D value possible.

Principles Relating to Mobilizing Resources

Organizations consist of specialized, interdependent resources. These include assets, such as cash, buildings, and plant, as well as people. People are highly specialized, with different perspectives and backgrounds: marketing, R&D, financial, and manufacturing. They are all organized through a management hierarchy and both formal and informal interpersonal networks, which must be coordinated and mobilized to create purposeful action.

Mobilizing resources means determining and taking strategic actions to achieve the organization's purpose in the face of a confusing environment. Principle 7, Open Information Flow, provides everyone in the empowered organization with the information needed to make quality decisions. Principle 8, Alignment and Empowerment, is about delegating and harnessing everyone's energy while keeping them focused on strategic values. Finally, Principle 9, Disciplined Decision-Making, triggers strategic decisions at the right times and engages the right people in a dialogue that results in decision quality.

Inform and Be Informed

PHILOSOPHY   Virtually all information is available to
whomever wants it. Information is used in
surprising ways to create value. The flow of information crosses functional boundaries.

PERSONAL   People feel safe in sharing what they know
PERSPECTIVE   and feel obliged to contribute to information-
sharing systems. They are excited about teach-
ing and learning.

ORGANIZATION   Information is routinely captured, packaged,
AND CULTURE   shared, and applied. An ethic of "giving and
getting" supports information sharing and
discourages information hoarding.

SUPPORT SYSTEMS   Formal and informal communications channels are abundant: newsletters, E-mail, group-
ware, workshops, and so on. Networks of people and computers deploy information where
it is needed, even across geographic and functional boundaries.

The marketing department of a pharmaceutical company had a
reputation for jealously guarding its information. We found this out
the hard way. In the course of evaluating a multimillion dollar pharmaceutical R&D project, we called upon the most knowledgeable
person in the marketing department. We asked for specific estimates
of market size and uncertainties, whereupon she replied, "As much as
I personally want to give you those estimates, it is the department's
policy to take questions in writing and provide answers only after approval by the marketing vice president." Deciding that it was best to
play along with departmental policy, we submitted our request in

written form. A week later we were told that the marketing department was "currently too busy" to respond to our request.

It was clear that the person we initially approached had the information we needed. However, her boss, the marketing vice president, used information as a way to exercise personal power. This executive had a habit of sabotaging the R&D department's recommendations by withholding information until the eleventh hour—usually at high-level decision meetings.

Good decisions are rarely made in an information-restricted environment. When an organization aims to create value, everyone needs information to do his or her job effectively. And it is often impossible to know in advance which information is important or how some apparently disconnected piece of information will trigger someone's powerful insight. John Seely Brown, chief scientist for Xerox's PARC lab, once remarked that the most valuable knowledge often resides where we are least able to see or control it: on the front lines, at the periphery, or with the renegades.

Based upon her studies of innovation in the pharmaceutical industry, Rebecca Henderson echoed that sentiment when she reported that "the companies that take advantage of knowledge generated from all areas of the organization are significantly more productive than their rivals." She noted that while rapid change has toppled leading companies in machine tools, steel, xerography, autos, computers, and other industries, the same companies that dominated the pharmaceutical industry during the 1940s and 1950s remain dominant today. "These companies," she wrote,

> have demonstrated an ability to learn and grow that confounds conventional wisdom. Despite their age, size, and success, the best of these companies have found ways to retain the flexibility and responsiveness of companies one-tenth their size and age. And they have already solved some of the competitive challenges in the research arena that companies in other industries are just starting to grapple with.[19]

Henderson and her collaborator, Iain Cockburn of the University of British Columbia, note that the longevity of these companies attests to their ability to foster a high level of specialized knowledge, while preventing that information from becoming embedded in ways that permanently fixes them in the past. Because modern drug discovery requires an integration of knowledge from many disciplines (molecular biology, physiology, biochemistry, synthetic chemistry, and molecular kinetics), success requires a free flow of information within the company and between it and outside sources. "Successful companies must keep abreast of the changes within particular scientific disciplines and successfully integrate this knowledge within and across company boundaries."[20] Her findings suggest that companies that take advantage of knowledge generated from many locations in the organization are significantly more productive than their rivals. The free flow of information across boundaries is fundamental to building this knowledge.

The environment of free-flowing information Henderson describes is quite different from the one that many R&D managers and professionals experience. Too often, they work in isolation from colleagues, without opportunities for cross-pollination among projects. The smart organization encourages the flow of information to all of its parts. Eastman Chemical, for example, enters all information about customer needs into a companywide database, which can be accessed by Eastman's managers and technical professionals worldwide. As Gary McGraw, Eastman vice president of development, stated, "Ideas can come from many different people in the company. We like to keep them all in one place and allow people to browse through them."[21] Following this advice, the division head of another major chemical company placed computer terminals throughout the plant so everyone could look up any and all corporate information.

In the smart company, individuals broadcast requests for specific kinds of information and others try to provide it. Contributing to the information system is seen as part of the payment one made for access to the information contributed by others. The principle of Open Information Flow works especially well in a culture of continual learning and outside-in perspective, and it is demanded by aligned and empowered people. The smart organization actively creates channels for information flow with newsletters, electronic mail, discussion groups, video conferencing, cross-functional forums, and so on.

Secrecy

Achieving this level of information flow may challenge existing operating principles. For example, many organizations operate on the principle of restricting information to those who "need to know" in an attempt to protect almost all information from their competitors.

In our experience, this principle often destroys more value through poor decision making than it creates by the benefits of secrecy. To be sure, there are situations where secrecy is important, such as real trade secrets, privileged information relating to litigation, or personal information held in confidence by an employer.

We often find that the attempts to keep information secret are more damaging than the release of the information. For example, "secret" information is often known already by the competitors and so the need-to-know principle effectively prevents a company's employees from being as well informed as the competitor. Often keeping information secret creates a sort of compartmentalized information structure. Those in the information compartments do not have a broad enough view to make sense of the whole picture. Compartmentalization of information creates cross-boundary conflict and suboptimization. In theory, those at the top can make sense of it all. In practice, top management is too overloaded and cannot be expected to understand enough of the details. We have seen organizations that were effectively immobilized from information compartmentalization, as illustrated in the example of the pharmaceutical company at the beginning of this section.

Secret information also slows cycle time and directly reduces decision quality. In one company, R&D created a cost-reduction project, but was unable to focus it properly because the operational division refused to provide detailed cost information on the grounds that it was secret. The project leader spent eighteen months trying technology push approaches, which the plant always rejected. Eventually, he was able to demonstrate his need to know the cost information, and quickly focused his project on the true needs. Secrecy reduced the quality of the project leader's decisions and delayed cost reductions by at least eighteen months.

Secrecy is often important, but may be more trouble than it is worth. We have a reasonable test of whether information should be kept secret: If the person about to receive the information would agree that it is better that he or she not know it, then it is appropriately a secret. Otherwise, let the information flow.

Removing Barriers

Free-flowing information helps overcome several of the barriers to best practice implementation. For example, many crossfunctional misunderstandings (e.g., between R&D and marketing, or R&D and operations) stem from a lack of shared information. Free-flowing information makes people aware of what is going on in other functions, and creates a basis for meaningful interaction.

One organization we worked with was considering its approach to securing regulatory approval for a new drug. One of the key questions was, Which countries should be pursued for approval, and in what order? In a meeting with the regulatory staff and a marketing representative, we asked the sizes of each market and the commercial implications of accelerating approval in some countries while delaying others. The marketing representative said, "I never realized that you needed information on markets. I thought you just ran the approval process. Would it be helpful if I sent you market information from time to time?" People were amazed that marketing had not recognized the value of this information to them. The response was overwhelming: "Absolutely!" The connection had been made, and the boundaries between the organizations were lowered.

Coordinate Everyone Effectively

PHILOSOPHY
: The organization is guided through a shared understanding of its strategies for creating value. People are empowered and trusted to pursue value creation.

PERSONAL PERSPECTIVE
: People see themselves as part of a corporation-wide team, understand their individual roles and those of others. They feel empowered to act. They take the responsibility both for action and for maintaining a shared sense of purpose.

ORGANIZATION AND CULTURE
: Strategic decisions are made through a participative process. Horizontal and vertical dialogue is used to realign the organization during periods of change.

SUPPORT SYSTEMS
: A decision hierarchy maps decisions at multiple levels and sets coordinated strategic agendas. In the context of each decision area, the system guides management when to communicate about what, and when to take the next "strategic interlude."

Not long ago, a major fine chemicals manufacturer needed to consolidate and modernize its system of seven aging plants. Normally, a high-level task force would have worked slowly through each of the effected units, developed recommendations, and passed them on to top management for a decision. Strong functions and an elaborate internal review would have stretched out this laborious process for almost two years. In this case, however, the company opted to use a crossfunctional team with the authority to make key decisions. To the surprise of just about everyone, all the issues were clarified and the decisions made in four months. Based on these decisions, the company would shut down four plants, modernize two, expand one, and adjust all affected logistics.

The team estimated that, because of the company's no-layoff policy and its traditional careful pace, the first plant could be closed in about one year. However, because these empowered organizations were so aligned on strategy, they managed to find a way to close the worst plant in only three months. Both the speed of the decision and the speed of implementation made it possible for the company to capture the benefits of consolidation and modernization nearly two years sooner, adding millions to the value of the company.

Many companies have taken the view that the traditional top-down, command-and-control model of management and decision making is obsolete. With its requirements for centralized knowledge and authority, command-and-control management is too slow and too removed from the real work of creating products and serving customers to prosper in today's competitive economy. Nor is it acceptable to the growing numbers of highly educated employees who expect to be treated as participants, not as cogs in a large machine.

Simply substituting empowerment for command-and-control, however, is a recipe for disaster, as the experience of one major company makes clear. This company's love affair with empowerment gurus during the 1980s created empowerment without alignment. Project managers for this company thought empowerment meant that they had no one to answer to, and that top management was obligated to support them. When top management questioned their proposals, the too-frequent response was, "You can't question me, I'm empowered. Just approve this expenditure." The result was a great deal of chaotic activity, until top management reasserted its authority. Top management then built alignment through dialogue and then was able to effectively manage an empowered *and* aligned organization. Alignment has been described by George Labovitz and Victor Rosansky as

> a condition in which the key elements of the business—strategy, people, processes, and customer understandings—are brought together in a seamless way with each other and with the competitive marketplace. Alignment is an optimal state in which core business factors, market factors, direction, leadership, and culture are integrated for peak performance.[22]

When an organization is aligned, according to Labovitz and Rosansky, the organization senses change and responds rapidly to it, with a minimum of hierarchy. Employees understand company goals and the parts they, as individuals, are expected to play. Compensation is structured so that what is best for the customer is what is best for both the company and its employees. Processes for satisfying customers are understood by all and are highly efficient.[23]

This description of alignment may sound like a tall order, but it describes the organizational culture in which empowerment is effective. Implicit in this description is an understanding that employees participate at some level in the decisions they are expected to implement. When this is the case, people see themselves as part of an enterprise-wide team, know their roles in value creation, and understand and appreciate the contributions of others.

The Role of Dialogue

At the core of Alignment and Empowerment is an organization-wide understanding of strategic direction. There is only one way to get this understanding, and that is through dialogue, which must occur around each of the following issues:

1. the nature of the problem
2. the process that will be followed in resolving it
3. the inputs to the process
4. the conclusions of the process
5. the implications for the organization and specific course of action

Generally, these issues must be attacked in the order described, as the case of a U.S. computer company trying to fill its R&D pipeline illustrates. This company had two major divisions, one for hardware peripherals and another for software. Both focused heavily on the mainframe business. The software business started as a product tied to hardware sales, but had evolved into the most profitable activity of the company.

Company executives recognized the declining fortunes of the mainframe business and wanted to create an R&D portfolio to renew the business. There were significant differences of opinion, however, about which projects should be funded. Fortunately, this was not the first question addressed by the company.

The first dialogue concerned the nature of the problem. The heads of the major divisions gathered, and their expertise as well as outside perspectives were brought to bear on this problem. People on the hardware side of the company thought it was essential to rebuild that business. To them, it was the neglected "backbone of the company" whose profitability could and should be restored. The software people saw many new opportunities that they felt represented the growth potential of the company. The CEO brought in a stock analyst who reported that the market perceived the firm as a hardware company, despite its booming software sales, and thus valued it at a lower price-to-earnings ratio.

The executives realized that the nature of the problem was different than they had originally thought. They had started with the question of how to develop an R&D portfolio. They now realized that this issue could not be addressed until they had reached agreement on a more fundamental question: What business do we want to be in?

The second dialogue occurred immediately following the first and addressed, What process shall we use? They created two committees. The steering committee consisted of several members of the board and the heads of each division. The working committee consisted of key players in each division and in R&D. In general, this dialogue resolved the questions of who would be involved, the approach, and the major steps that would be taken.

Once they had mutual understanding of the nature of the problem and of the process to be followed, the working committee proceeded to develop the inputs for the decision and the third dialogue on the inputs. For the most part, this was a noncontroversial matter of gathering relevant information. One key area where the company recognized an information gap was in international businesses, so they brought in people who had worked in Europe. The working team also developed several alternative choices of strategic direction and supporting R&D. These covered different emphases on hardware, software, peripherals, installed base compared to potential new customers, and so on. These choices were the most controversial, and through several meetings, the steering committee and working committee came to a mutual understanding of the inputs, especially the alternative strategies. The agreement that each of the alternatives represented a viable way forward was crucial to ultimately achieving true commitment.

With agreement on the inputs, the committees turned their attention to the fourth dialogue, on the conclusions. The working committee conducted an objective evaluation and worked out the logical implications of the inputs. Where necessary, they clarified gaps in information and continued to build a mutual understanding of the evidence. When they met with the steering committee for the fourth dialogue, they had reached a startling conclusion: Get out of the hardware business completely. At first, this was a bit of a surprise. But the case had been built through a series of dialogues, and people were ready to hear and understand the message. Members of both committees recognized that the conclusion was the right one, based on the inputs, and took a tentative decision to divest the company of the hardware business.

The fifth dialogue made this decision real. Both teams worked out the challenges to implementation and the basics of action plans in each major area: software, hardware, and R&D. In a major workshop, the two committees discussed the implications and realized that they were up to the challenges presented by the conclusion. They ratified the decision and proceeded to implement.

Because of the mutual understanding the players in the company had, they were able to implement the decision rapidly . After splitting the company apart, the findings were soon validated. R&D found focus in the new software business, and the stock valuation rose significantly.

Mutual understanding on these five areas creates a high degree of trust so that alignment and empowerment can become a reality. When these agreements are in place, senior management can become advisors, reviewers, and cheerleaders—not micromanagers. They can be confident that the implementors will follow through in the knowledge and spirit of their mutual agreements. The working committee members can proceed to implementation with the ability to make downstream decisions and adjustments to strategy, knowing top management is behind them, supporting their actions.

Higher-Level Decisions Inform Lower-Level Decisions

Alignment dictates that when management makes higher-level decisions, it must guide decisions at lower levels. In the case of our computer company, high-level decisions on corporate and technology strategy naturally guided decisions on R&D portfolio strategy and those of individual projects. The corporate strategy specified that the company would focus on software and divest itself of hardware. The technology strategy, developed simultaneously with corporate strategy, specified the general product areas in which work would be done, the core competencies and technical skills required, and how the company would build a competitive position. These strategic decisions provided the frame for R&D portfolio decisions. The evaluation that had been conducted specified the shareholder value of achieving certain objectives based on which product areas and markets had the most potential to create value.

Out of this strategy, they were able to frame their R&D portfolio needs. Most of their R&D would be directed to product lines, but some general capability in specific kinds of software would cut across product lines. They developed general resource levels commensurate with the potential to create value. At the next level down, they developed goals for each portfolio—the kinds of major software "platforms" they would need to build or acquire and the succession of incremental products they would produce off these platforms. They also designated a central R&D function to develop the common capabilities and to look into new developing technologies that could become new platforms. Resource levels were optimized to produce the most potential value.

Because decision makers at the top had done their homework, it was relatively easy to reach agreement on a set of R&D projects that were consistent with corporate and technology strategy, aligning strategy and the work of individual employees from top to bottom. The R&D community was now empowered to get on with the job of developing products without the need for micromanagement. It could draw on the technology strategy and portfolio strategy to frame its decisions.

Figure 7-5 shows how decisions in the computer company were aligned across levels. Each level is represented as a decision quality chain with the six dimensions of Frame, Alternatives, Information, Values, Logic, and Commitment. The commitment to the technology strategy sets the frame and values for the portfolio strategy, and so on.

When Dialogue Breaks Down

When these dialogues break down, alignment is impossible, empowerment is counterproductive, effort is wasted, and decision making is extremely difficult.

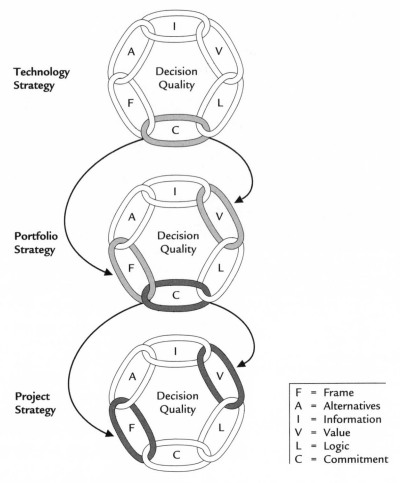

Figure 7-5. *The Chain of Decisions*

A utility company was developing some electronic control equipment for its plants. The engineers were diligently pursuing the published corporate vision, which included a list of specific, measurable objectives. The engineers were using this document to guide their decisions. To frame these decisions, the engineers relied on passages in the document that called for increased communication. They searched for control systems that also allowed increased electronic communication among plants and allowed system status reporting. They measured their decisions against the measures in the corporation's stated vision, and worked hard to figure out the impact on cost, customer service, employee satisfaction, and so on. In the end,

PRINCIPLES

they were able to design a system that increased the measures and moved the company in the general direction of the corporate vision. They achieved a high-quality decision according to the frame (in the vision) and the values (defined by the measurable objectives) they were given.

When they proposed to implement the new control system, they could not get funding. There was no commitment at upper levels to the vision nor to increasing these measures. One senior staff member told one of us privately, "The problem is that you believed our company's corporate b.s." The real problem, however, was that the company's engineers believed it.

This organization failed to achieve Alignment and Empowerment. The engineers had taken initiative and empowered themselves. Yet senior management was not authentically committed to their publicly announced strategy. What was lacking was alignment. The organization did not know what it was committed to. Vertical dialogue had not occurred. The organization missed an opportunity to clarify and increase the mutual understanding of the strategy. The engineers' proposal would have been a good test case: It demonstrably met the guidance from above, but was not funded. Why? An aligned and empowered organization would have initiated a dialogue about the strategy and furthered mutual understanding.

Take Charge of Your Destiny

PHILOSOPHY — A process identifies strategic choices, engages the right people and information, and selects alternatives based on the highest value.

PERSONAL PERSPECTIVE — People understand the philosophy and process of decision quality, and initiate the appropriate process to address strategic decisions.

ORGANIZATION AND CULTURE — A quality decision process is applied to every important decision including portfolio, technology, and R&D project strategy.

SUPPORT SYSTEMS — Process facilitation and analytical assistance are available to support decision making at all levels. A formal process assures that every decision gets the benefit of full scrutiny.

Good companies have well-honed processes for just about everything they do, from invoicing customers to creating and manufacturing new products. Smart organizations have equally developed processes for making strategic decisions. They do not just "wing it," they do not do it differently every time, and they certainly do not allow the people with the loudest voices to direct their futures. Instead, they use a set of objective and logical steps that shift the odds of attaining the highest value in their favor. And they use every opportunity to improve that process.

A culture and a process of disciplined decision making make implementation of best practices much easier. Improvement becomes a matter of changing an explicit routine.

One top-notch R&D organization we benchmarked had an outstanding decision-making process. That process was visibly posted as a diagram indicating how project decisions were to be made. Everyone could see and understand the process, and everyone understood that as long as project teams followed this process, they were empowered to make their own decisions.

This company's decision process was not carved in stone, however, but was open to improvement whenever someone found a better way of doing things. In fact, the nicely printed process diagram we observed was covered with handwritten suggestions and modifications. Anyone could suggest improvements. In this sense, the process enabled empowerment and was periodically invigorated by the empowered.

Individuals at this company could not understand why any organization would have difficulties in adopting a new best practice. In its experience, adopting a best practice simply amounted to discussing it and redrawing the diagram. If the practice worked well in their setting, it became part of the printed process diagram. If it did not, it was modified or dropped. This organization was in control of its future.

A disciplined decision process identifies the decisions that need to be made, resolves them with high quality, and unambiguously communicates the results. Without such a process, it is extremely difficult to mobilize a complex organization toward its desired future.

Faster Time to Market

Good decision processes do more than steer companies in the right directions, they also get them to their destinations faster through cycle time reductions. Marvin Patterson, recently retired Director of Corporate Engineering for Hewlett-Packard, has pointed out that most organizations measure cycle time from project initiation to initial commercialization. However, time spent—and often wasted—in the decision process that precedes project initiation is not counted. Speed and quality in the decision process can thus be a source of competitive advantage.[24]

Expanding the definition of *time to market* to include the decision-making process tremendously increases the leverage an organization has over its future. Historically, companies have focused tremendous effort on reducing cycle time from project initiation to commercialization. This limits management's value added to prioritization and go/no go decisions.

The Benefits of Scrutiny

In our seminars, we often ask for a show of hands of companies that have a clear R&D decision process. Most executives raise their hands. Then we ask what fraction of decisions are actually made with the process. It is surprising how many executives give answers as low as 50 percent. Many projects are treated as special cases: the no-brainers, the strategic projects, the projects championed by powerful individuals. Discipline means that *all* decisions go through the process. This requires that the process be sufficiently robust to handle a wide variety of decisions at different levels of the company.

When we were benchmarking best practices, the R&D head of a very successful company remarked that "executive agreement" was a source of underperformance. This sounded paradoxical at first, so we asked him to explain:

> A few years ago we undertook a study of our failed projects and tried to discover the root causes of failure. Many projects failed for good reasons: The technology didn't work out or the market was smaller than expected. But there was a surprising pattern. The projects we had originally thought were "no-brainers" had a much higher failure rate than those that originally appeared marginal. We asked ourselves, "How could it be that the best projects fail more often than the mediocre ones?"
>
> It took us a long time to figure it out, but it came down to this: When executives disagree about funding a project they require careful analysis and planning as a condition of their approval. This scrutiny actually improves the project's chance of success. The goals are shifted, contingency plans are developed, and so on.
>
> But when they all agree that they're funding a "no brainer," analysis and planning simply go by the boards. With all the best intentions they end up sabotaging our best projects by depriving them of scrutiny. Some of these projects go off the tracks, not because they were bad ideas, but because we didn't give them the attention they needed on the front end.

This executive resolved to give his company's best projects as much scrutiny and deliberation as its marginal ones. The company would have to give up the executive privilege to call the shots in favor of a disciplined process for *all* decisions. The disciplined process simply produced better results.

Keep a Strategic Focus

The proper size chunk for strategic management is a set of tasks that together represent something the company could take to market (or use to improve its processes). Together they represent a coherent set of technical and commercial objectives worth pursuing.

It is important that these chunks be framed at the right level. A good decision process ensures that projects serve larger strategic goals. A common failure is to allow the strategic decision process to degenerate into a glorified task management system. The fundamental question here is, What size "chunk" is suitable for strategic management of R&D? Individual tasks are too small because managers lose sight of larger goals in favor of narrow technical goals. (One client, for example, had many "projects" with the goal of "write a technical report.") Projects that are too large become vague technical capabilities or "motherhood" statements.

One of our client companies started with a list of about 300 projects—a several million dollar budget divided into tiny units of work. After realizing that they had the wrong sized unit for strategic management, they consolidated them. After the first pass, they consolidated to about forty projects and realized they were not done. At the time of this writing, they are making a second pass and expected to end up with around twenty strategic-level projects.

The Strategic Interlude

Many companies lose their strategic focus in the press of carrying out operations and neglect to periodically get their bearings. Strategic decision making is well served by an occasional break—a strategic interlude—in which direction is reassessed.

A stage gate process is one common way to create these strategic interludes: for example at discovery, feasibility, development, scale-up, and commercialization. Pharmaceutical companies have similar phases dictated partially by regulatory requirements. Each gate creates an opportunity to evaluate the project and the decision it is facing in terms of larger strategic goals.

Even though many companies have stage gate processes, not all of them use them to create a disciplined decision process. Many organizations implicitly follow a counterproductive principle: preserving every project as much as possible through resource sharing. It works like this: A portfolio manager gets a new proposal and funds it. But where does he find the funds? He takes just a little bit from every other project—not so much that any will starve, but enough to keep each precious project alive. This approach is quick and expedient, and keeps all projects going. In the long term, however, the effort to save projects is ruinous. Over time, every project becomes improperly funded. The best projects are *under*funded because their resources have been incrementally skimmed off. The worst projects are *over*-funded in the sense that they are failures that should have been axed already.

This undisciplined principle effectively postpones hard decisions and thus minimizes the chance of success. Leigh Thompson, former chief scientific officer (CSO) of Eli Lilly, puts it this way: "Postponing decisions just ensures that many prospects will rot, though at least all the noses will point in the same direction."[25]

Build Quality In

In the "bad old days" before statistical quality control methods, manufacturers employed legions of quality assurance personnel to inspect final output. Items that met specifications went to finished stock, the rest were scrapped or sent back for rework. This practice is now referred to as "inspecting quality in." It is expensive and wasteful. Juran, Deming, and others taught us how to eliminate the need for inspectors—and the 10 to 15 percent of items that ended on the scrap heap—by methods that "build quality in." One of the greatest benefits of a disciplined decision process is its ability to build quality into decision making, assuring us that it was "done right" the first time.

Traditional processes that rely on product champions and managerial review are the decision-making equivalent of "inspecting quality in." The project champion makes a case to someone higher in the organization, who sits in judgment. The judge, or his or her staff, spends time and resources critiquing the case and usually sends it back for rework. This is an extremely inefficient process for making decisions. One of our clients had been reworking a single decision problem for two years!

Building quality in requires new, nonadversarial roles for both those who propose projects and those who approve them. In a disciplined decision process, top executives, who formerly sat in judgment, are brought in at the beginning and at important stages of the

PRINCIPLES

process. The insights of the former "quality inspectors"—representatives of finance, marketing, manufacturing, and other functions—likewise play an integral part in the process. In doing so, these people often become allies to the R&D community.

According to Leigh Thompson, a disciplined decision process results in nothing less than profound knowledge of the business.[26] For every project in Lilly's portfolio, R&D staff and managers carefully gathered knowledge on the costs, commercial potential, timing, and probability of success. They discussed and assessed probability distributions and ranges. They compared and calibrated each project assessment to historical models and to other projects. They aggregated and shared the information. It was a lot of work, and took a lot of discipline. But it was worth it. According to Thompson, "A good portfolio process is like the best truffle sow, able to sniff out valuable assets hidden deeply in a confusing forest floor of fungal flora, and enrich her owners."[27]

Putting Principles to Work

Value Creation Culture. Creating Alternatives. Continual Learning. Embracing Uncertainty. Outside-In Strategic Perspective. Systems Thinking. Open Information Flow. Alignment and Empowerment. Disciplined Decision Making. Years of experience working with hard-headed R&D managers assures us that these are the bedrock values upon which higher-performance R&D is built. When these principles are embedded in the organization's culture, people make good strategic decisions.

CHAPTER 8

ORGANIZATIONAL IQ

> The real voyage of discovery consists not in seeking new land-scapes but in having new eyes.
> *Marcel Proust*

WHEN ORGANIZATIONS TRY to improve their decision processes they almost always encounter barriers to best practice implementation. As discussed earlier, the root causes of many barriers are found in the operating principles of the organization. This chapter will help you identify the root causes in your organization and do something about them. It includes an organizational IQ test that you can take to determine the ability of your organization to routinely achieve high-quality decisions. The text will help you identify the smart principles in your organization and those that are counter-productive.

But first consider the findings of a survey conducted at a meeting of Quality Directors Network of the IRI.[1] Figure 8-1 indicates that most of the participating companies had operationalized only a few smart R&D principles. As the black bars in the figure indicate, only 18 percent of the companies in the survey made Value Creation Culture (VCC) part of their organizational fabric. The most prevalent principle, Open Information Flow (OIF), was followed by only 70 percent of the companies.

Many companies aspire to smart R&D principles, but have poor implementation. For example, the white bars in the figure show that 55 percent of the companies say they adhere to the principle of Outside-In Strategic Perspective (OISP), but that implementation is spotty. Aspirations are ahead of reality.

The tops of the white bars in the figure are high—generally above 60 percent—but the black bars are small, generally 20 percent or less, indicating that while many companies are attempting to live by the principles, few are completely successful.

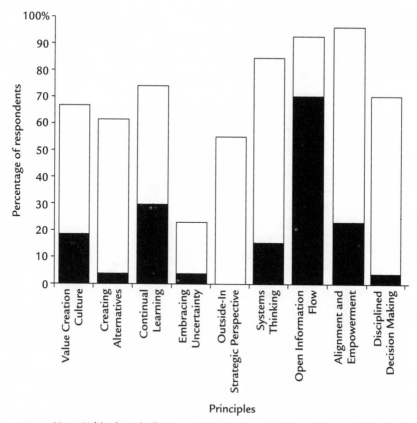

Note: White bars indicate companies who said they adhere to this principle but implementation is spotty; black bars indicate companies who said this principle is part of the fabric/culture/behaviors of their organizations.

Figure 8-1. *Incorporation of Smart R&D Principles*

Most companies that attempt to improve their decision processes encounter barriers. Efforts to improve decision quality are likely to require working at the level of organizational principle. Simply changing the process is likely to raise too many barriers. Which principles is your organization likely to have the greatest problems with?

The IQ Test

We have developed an organizational IQ test for measuring an R&D organization's adherence to each of the nine principles. This test has three basic uses:

1. as a benchmark of organizational intelligence
2. as an indicator of where barriers to decision quality improvements are likely to be encountered
3. to prioritize the principles an organization must focus on to increase its intelligence

The full test is available in appendix B. Take it now and you will get much more out of this chapter. Simply taking the test will deepen your understanding of the principles by forcing you to look at the behavior patterns of your own organization. The practical definitions will help give you a fresh view of your organization. As you take the test, think of a specific organization, subgroup, or level of management you intend to rate, because principles often differ from subunit to subunit.

The test consists of forty-five questions, with five questions on each of the nine principles. It is divided into nine pages, one per practice, with five questions on each page (labeled A through E). A single scoresheet summarizes the results, with a box for each question. Write your score for each principle, using a number from −3 to +3, in each box. For each item a short text characterizes each end of the scale, from +3 for very smart to −3 for the opposite. Score your organization against this scale based on how well it fits. If it has both "smart" and "not-smart" characteristics, give it some intermediate score. If the characteristics are roughly balanced or not present at all, score it as 0.

The Organizational IQ Score

The first result from the test is the organization's overall IQ score. It is a measure of how smart your organization is and a general guide to the difficulty of implementation. To find your IQ score, add up the scores across A through E for each principle. Total the sums for all the principles, and divide this number by nine. The result will be a score between −15 and +15. Use the conversion chart in Figure 8-2 to convert that score to organizational IQ. For example, a score of +5 results in an organizational IQ of about 107. A percentile scale is shown on the right of the graph. An organizational IQ of 130 places an organization in the top 2 percent of companies, indicating that it is smarter than 98 percent of the companies in our database. As with human IQ, 100 is the average (at the 50th percentile), with 15 IQ points per standard deviation.

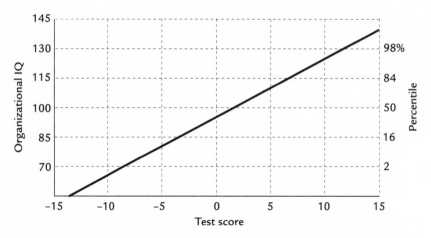

Figure 8-2. *Conversion Chart for Organizational IQ*

An organizational IQ of 100—average—is insufficient for success in a competitive world. Fortunately, organizations are not like human beings. They can improve their intelligence, often dramatically.

The IQ Profile

The IQ profile identifies areas of organizational strength and weakness, and indicates areas for improvement. Answers to the organizational IQ test provide the base data required for the profile. Since most organizations are spotty in their use of principles, this profile diagnoses both positive and negative patterns of behavior. For each principle, then, add the positive scores and the negative scores separately. For example, if your answers for Systems Thinking (ST) are A +1, B −3, C +1, D −2, and E −2, your positive score is +2 and your negative score would be −7. Plot these on the IQ profile. An illustration is shown in Figure 8-3 for the R&D unit of a hypothetical company, AstroTek. Each dot represents the location of a specific practice. For this company, the negative scores for Systems Thinking (score −7) are larger than the positive scores (score +2), so it appears in the lower left-hand corner. Thus, the principles currently operating in Astro-Tek are counterproductive to systems thinking. This is an area for potential improvement, and a likely source of barriers to high decision quality.

Contrast this principle with Continual Learning (CL), which has a

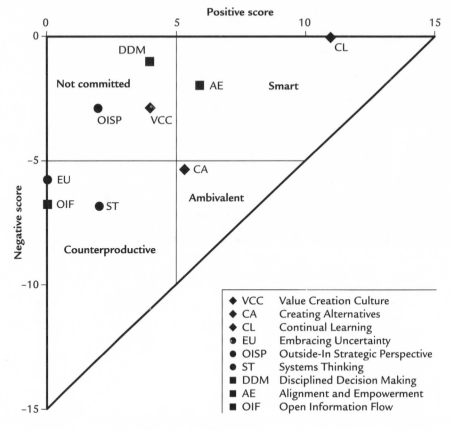

Figure 8-3. *AstroTek's IQ Assessment Profile*

positive score of +11 and a negative score of 0, and appears in the upper right segment. Only strong positive patterns of behavior appear in this area. Since the organization is already smart with respect to Continual Learning, it is unlikely to experience barriers arising from this principle. This principle will be a source of strength as it implements best practices.

The figure plots AstroTek's IQ profile in terms of each of the other nine principles. Together, they create a visual assessment of where this company is weak, strong, or neutral. For instance, AstroTek is smart about two principles, Continual Learning and Alignment and Empowerment, and either *uncommitted, ambivalent,* or *counterproductive* with respect to the others. Uncommitted means that negative and positive patterns are both weak; ambivalent that negative and positive patterns are both strong.

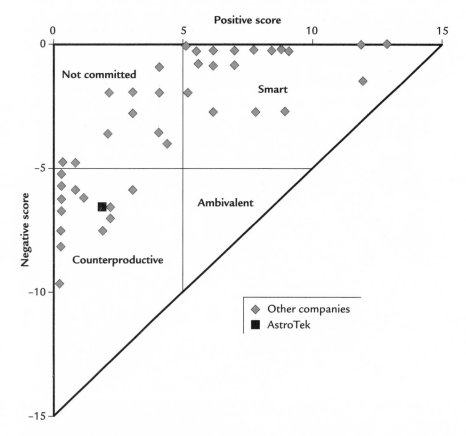

Figure 8-4. *AstroTek's Systems Thinking*

AstroTek has an overall IQ of 95, just a bit below average; it has both strengths and weaknesses. Figure 8-4 shows that its score on Systems Thinking is among the worst in a database of companies. Yet for Continual Learning (not shown), it is among the best.

The principles in which your organization is counterproductive or ambivalent will be the root causes for many barriers to implementation of good decision-making practices and processes.

Getting Smarter

Getting smarter means improving at the level of principle. This section considers areas of assessment in which barriers to being and acting smart are found. Figure 8-5 summarizes steps that can be taken to facilitate improvement.

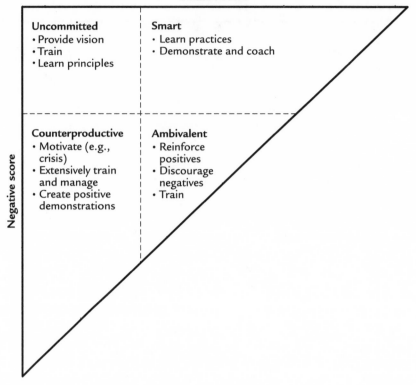

Figure 8-5. *Improving the IQ Assessment*

The easiest two steps for improvement are found in the Smart and Uncommitted areas. Barriers to best practice implementation will not arise as a result of principles in these areas because they contain few negative patterns. If a practice relies primarily on principles in the Smart area, it is just a matter of adopting it. In chapter 7 we discussed the case of an organization that was smart at disciplined decision making: It posted its decision process diagram on a wall where everyone could see it. Trying out a new practice was often just a matter of agreeing to experiment. If a practice relies primarily on principles in the Uncommitted area, then introducing the practice will require learning at the level of principle. But there will be little or no active resistance, and no major barriers.

The real challenges to improvement come from counterproductive and ambivalent principles. Counterproductive behaviors are the greatest challenge to getting smarter because they need to be unlearned before new principles can be learned. These counterproductive behaviors may have been highly functional in the past, which makes unlearning them more difficult. Or they may be rewarded by the organization, in which case the system of rewards and punishments needs to be examined and changed before any lasting progress can be made.

A big challenge in the case of counterproductive areas is creating positive demonstrations of what is possible. In chapter 5 we introduced the example of a project leader who would not mention the possibility of technical failure to her boss for fear of appearing disloyal. It was not until we demonstrated that embracing uncertainty improved the project's prospects that the project leader and her boss even realized that there was a better way.

In the case of principles about which an organization is ambivalent, both positive and negative patterns of behavior are present. Here the challenge is to build on positive patterns and discourage negative ones. One organization we worked with had experienced a major financial crisis and was in the late stages of a financial and cultural turnaround. The cultural change had been driven by a new decision process. When we presented the early results of our research, a key participant in the turnaround exclaimed, "Now I have words to describe what we actually did. We changed the principles for strategic decisions."

We asked him how it happened. He explained that his organization had discovered an evolutionary approach to large-scale change. It has all the elements of Darwin's theory: variation, selection, and retention. To understand how it worked, think of the principles like organizational genes, and individuals and subgroups as carriers of these genes.

When he started improving the decision process, he faced considerable barriers because the patterns in the organization were largely negative. But he was able to get the first project off the ground, partly due to the magnitude of the crisis. It attracted the interest of people who aspired to a smart principle. The first project developed a critical mass of people who already had nascent smart principles. This is the first element of evolution, variation.

One specific principle at the root of many of the barriers was creating alternatives. Historically, the organization operated by having strong champions pitch their ideas to senior management. Senior management employed a stable of staff to review the recommendations and inspect quality in. The new decision process created several alternatives at the beginning and discussed them openly. The old guard resisted strongly. They thought the alternatives were creating confusion, that they would never be able to sort them all out, and that it was unwise to go before senior management before you knew what you wanted. The old guard distanced themselves from the project and its results.

Others in the organization enjoyed talking about alternatives. They felt they were finally getting a chance to apply their creativity in a constructive way. They saw that behind each alternative was the germ of a good idea and a perspective they had not understood before.

In the end, the project was extremely successful. It demonstrated compelling conclusions and had found a significantly better alternative than what had been proposed previously. In spite of the resistance, the project was recognized as a success. This is the second element of evolution, selection.

In the end, the naysayers were wrong. The new decision process produced an unambiguous decision to pursue a demonstrably superior product. Creating options and exploring them through a structured decision process simply produced better results—and everyone knew it. The people associated with the new process received praise from senior management and important new assignments. Those who fought it began to reconsider.

As a result of this success, those associated with the project rose in stature and power slightly. Those who had opposed it dropped slightly. Next, two projects were kicked off using the new decision process. This is the third element of evolution, retention.

Other applications of the new process followed, and soon there was a large and growing group of employees who embodied the principles of smart R&D. They formed a critical mass around which the rest of the organization oriented itself. Transformation had begun, and the organization was on its way to becoming smarter in its approach to R&D decisions. After several years, few people who held the counterproductive principles remained. The visible successes of the new process simply could not be ignored. The people who were truly incorrigible had been so reduced in stature that they were ineffective. The people who were slow adopters started to change and gave up their old ways of doing things.

A large oil company discovered a slightly different mechanism for change. It sowed a great many seeds through a four-day training program for about 2,000 middle managers and staff. Some of these individuals held principles close to those of smart R&D. Many major decisions were made in the new way as executives began using new kinds of information to support their decisions. The new way of making decisions stuck and became the appropriate way to do business.

Undoubtedly there are other mechanisms for major organizational change at the level of principle. The evolutionary mechanism and the seed-sowing mechanism are only two. Each organization must find its own way. But the central challenge of improving principles will remain: build positive patterns (possibly for the first time) and discourage negative patterns in the hearts and minds of many individuals.

Where to Start

A journey of a thousand miles truly begins with a single step. Although the nine principles and organizational IQ provide a good framework for understanding the desired changes to improve strategic decisions, real change is brought about by dealing with specific situations, individuals, and groups.

Some companies begin their journey with a diagnostic demonstration project. They select a high-profile and difficult decision, and address it in a new way. It is not a study; it is not an exercise; it is a real decision. A real problem brings out the best and worst in people and reveals an organization's patterns of behavior. From diagnosis involving the actual participants in the process, an appropriate prescription can be determined. Chapter 5 described a case of long-range planning process that had failed to produce valuable alternatives. When the CEO realized that it was his own behavior that had prevented the results he wanted, the organization had an opportunity to move forward at the level of principle. This experience created new insight about why things were not working.

Some Generalizations

Some principles are more commonly in need of improvement than others. Typically, organizations have a lot to gain from Creating Alternatives, Disciplined Decision Making, and Embracing Uncer-

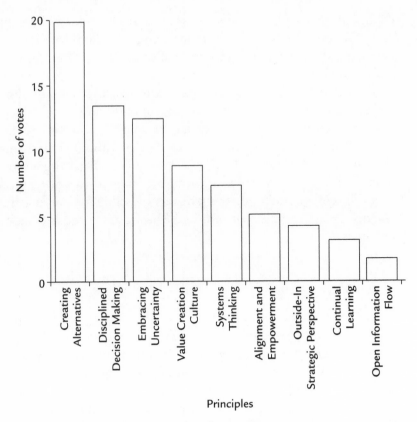

Figure 8-6. *The Most Important Principles to Improve*

tainty, as shown in the results of polls conducted at R&D executive meetings by SDG in Figure 8-6.

One of the poll participants represented a Baldridge Award–winning company. He commented that his organization was pretty good at most principles, but that Creating Alternatives was a real blind spot. He went back to work on it. Even excellent companies have room to raise their organizational IQs.

PART IV

PROCESSES

CHAPTER 9

TECHNOLOGY STRATEGY

> When schemes are laid in
> advance, it is surprising how
> often circumstances fit in with
> them. *Otto von Bismarck*

THIS CHAPTER FOCUSES on making high-quality technology decisions. However, as we discussed in the previous chapter, technology strategy is only meaningful as an integral part of business strategy. For most technology-based businesses, business strategy is
inadequate if it does not address how technology will support and
renew the business on a sustained basis. So the processes for addressing the level of technology strategy in decision making are essentially
the same as those used in any other high-level strategic decision
making.

An interesting example of the technology/business strategy connection is the midsized computer hardware and software firm discussed in chapters 3 and 7. This company had grown on the basis of
scattered initiatives that had produced a wide spectrum of products.
Acquisitions had further broadened its product line, and international distribution channels had evolved from opportunities to sell
existing products to foreign customers. The company's head of R&D
had been charged with organizing a retreat to set better companywide priorities for technology. This executive was concerned that
R&D efforts, although competent and imaginative, were too scattered. Top management concurred and wanted to develop a technology strategy to focus these efforts. The retreat would bring together
all key R&D executives, most project leaders, and a few major shareholders. One of the authors was invited to the retreat to assist in sorting out R&D priorities.

Preparation for the retreat revealed that the company's underlying
problem was its lack of a good business strategy. In the absence of

such a strategy, time spent in sorting out existing technology plans and capabilities would be wasted. The company desperately needed to rationalize its entire business and to decide how to position itself for sustainable advantage. Technology capabilities would be only one important factor in the total equation.

The retreat began with a presentation that described R&D work across the company. Clearly, there was no rhyme or reason to the portfolio. Most projects were incremental developments designed to keep abreast of the competition. There were a few innovative undertakings, but even they aimed at capturing some share of existing markets. The company had no strategies for positioning generations of products in market segments; nor was there an overall strategy for bridging into new markets. For example, foreign markets were seen as opportunities to increase revenue. Such sales, however, would have to be captured with products designed for U.S. customers. The company had no real understanding of the unique needs of foreign customers, nor did it have the research capabilities to discover them.

The company was also falling behind in important technical competencies. For example, it was only dabbling with structured computer programming (C++) at a time when C++ was being widely adopted in the software industry.

The weekend retreat provided in important wake-up call for the company. With the agreement of the CEO and the top management team, a six-month effort to develop a business strategy was undertaken; this of necessity included a high-level role for technology. The strategy that emerged from this effort called for two things: the sale of the company's hardware businesses, and reorganization and repositioning of the remaining businesses. Only after this overarching strategy was established could the company move down the decision hierarchy to the portfolio and project decisions that the weekend retreat had naively expected to make.

The Role of Technology Strategy

As this example indicates, technology strategy is meaningless in isolation. It makes sense only as an element of business strategy that has determined how technology will be used to renew and expand the business.

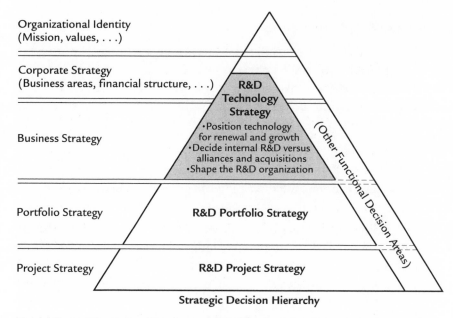

Figure 9-1. *The Role of Business and Technology Strategy*

Figure 9-1 describes the relationship of business and technology strategy to the hierarchy of strategic decisions and lists a few key elements of technology strategy decisions. The biggest decision is how technology will be used to support the renewal and growth of the organization. Here the organization must determine:

▲ what technological mastery it needs today and in the future

▲ which technological assets will give it competitive differentiation

▲ the extent to which it is counting on R&D versus acquisitions for a continuing pipeline of products and processes, or to break into whole new areas

Given an understanding of these issues, what shape and size organization best serves the company's purpose? Is it better to centralize, decentralize, or both? How much basic discovery should be pursued, if any, and in which areas? Whom should be hired? What kind of applied R&D programs support strategic business plans?

To have a long-term business strategy, answers to these questions are essential. The answers provide the guidance to recruit appropriate R&D staff, form alliances, balance the portfolio, and optimize specific projects.

Decision Process Design

Clearly the choice of business and technology strategy is not an isolated matter to be resolved by the technical staff alone, but is among the most important decisions of the organization. A decision of this magnitude cannot be made haphazardly, but requires a process that is disciplined, powerful, and robust. This process must:

▲ develop intellectually correct conclusions

▲ build a commitment to action

▲ align and empower diverse implementors to act in harmony with a minimum of micromanagement.

Building on the decision quality chain, the best practices, and the nine principles of smart R&D, Strategic Decisions Group designed such a process in 1981. Since then, that process has been used, tested, and refined by our firm and its clients in hundreds of strategy development applications that span most major industries. One major adopter of the process is General Motors, which has been using and adapting this process for both technology and business strategy for about ten years. A summary of its experience has been published in Vince Barabba's book, *Meeting of the Minds*, which introduces the term *dialogue decision process*, which we adopt here.[1] The beauty of the process is that it provides the foundation for similar, principle-based approaches to strategy at all levels and across all business areas.

Process Phases

The decision process has six major phases, each designed to add decision quality (see Figure 9-2). The process does not end with the decision, but is carried through planning and implementation. This gives the strategy every chance of avoiding the pitfalls that undermine implementation of many otherwise good decisions. Effective planning and implementation often take as long or longer than making the decision itself.

Process Dialogue

To achieve an intellectually *correct* decision, a process needs input from everyone who has something to contribute. This includes both people in the organization and selected outsiders (other divisions, customers, experts, and so forth). In order to reach a decision with *commitment*, and to achieve alignment and empowerment for imple-

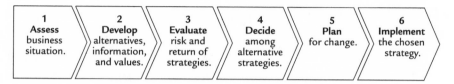

| 1
Assess
business
situation. | 2
Develop
alternatives,
information,
and values. | 3
Evaluate
risk and
return of
strategies. | 4
Decide
among
alternative
strategies. | 5
Plan
for change. | 6
Implement
the chosen
strategy. |

Figure 9-2. *The Phases of Strategy Development and Implementation*

mentation, the decision process must involve both decision makers and implementors. Both groups need to understand the basis for the selected strategy; and each must have sufficient confidence in the other to get through the tough job of implementation. The best way to achieve this is to have them develop the strategy together through a process of dialogue.

This process design stands in sharp contrast to the champion or bottom-up recommendation process. We have mentioned that executives cannot be expected to "inspect quality in." In fact, they have the most to contribute at the beginning of the process in ensuring the situation is framed correctly, selecting the right experts and information sources, and contributing their experience and creativity in designing good strategic alternatives to test in the evaluation phase.

Teams

We usually organize process participants into two teams: a decision team and a strategy team. The decision team—sometimes called the steering committee or review board—is composed of individuals with sufficient stature and authority *to make the decision stick.* In the case of high-level decisions, decision team members tend to be senior executives: the CEO, division general managers, technical executives representing R&D, and marketing, finance, and manufacturing managers. In the case of lower-level decisions, these teams may include middle managers.

The decision team is involved from the very beginning, chartering the mission of the strategy development project, reviewing progress, and making its own contribution at least once during each phase. It also ensures that decisions are actually implemented.

The strategy team—sometimes called a working group or core team—carries out the strategy development and evaluation process described in this chapter. The strategy team is usually a crossfunc-

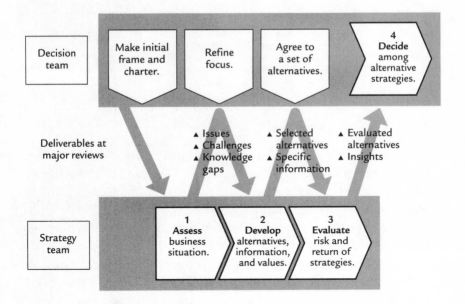

Figure 9-3. *The Dialogue Decision Process: Deciding*

tional group of people who have a wealth of relevant information and who will later act as implementation leaders. This may include managers from areas represented on the decision team, as well as staff experts in market research, R&D, and so forth. These team members are usually expected to dedicate 25 percent to 100 percent of their time to the task. Others may be enlisted for more limited roles on the strategy team: as advisors and helpers, as participants in key meetings, or as task force members. Together these people should have a broad understanding of the issues, know where to go for information, and have high credibility in the organization. The job of the strategy team is to carry out the process steps and to engage the decision team in useful dialogue.

The Dialogue Decision Process

In order to use these teams to achieve effective communication and organization of the process, they need to interact. In Figures 9-3 and 9-4 this added dimension is represented by vertical arrows that show the key points of interaction between the two teams. Here, staffing the process, educating participants for their roles, setting schedules

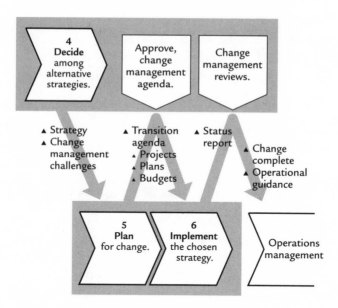

Figure 9-4. *The Dialogue Decision: Implementing*

and expectations, and defining the initial framework of the project might be considered phase zero.

We call our process the *dialogue decision process (DDP)* because it supports a decision-focused dialogue among knowledgeable parties who represent many perspectives and responsibilities. The key phases in this process are outlined in bold in the figures. The delivery of specific results at the end of each phase keeps the process on track and builds shared understanding and "buy-in" among participants. Experience has shown it to be an effective method for enlisting the best sources of information, knowledge, and creative thinking. It is also a powerful format for applying analytical tools and for dealing explicitly with uncertainty. It is effective in:

▲ exposing strategy proposals to the light of rational discussion
▲ requiring that alternatives be sought and weighed
▲ creating new alternatives that are often superior to original concepts
▲ eliminating power plays and personal agendas by key managers and executives
▲ enriching the decision with the insights of many parties
▲ laying a solid foundation for implementation

Naturally, the DDP is only effective when the participants are dedicated to optimizing the decision at hand. Using this process does not guarantee that decisions will prove out in the long run. But it does increase the probabilities of success in favor of the organization.

The principles of smart R&D establish the foundation and organizational habits that ensure that the DDP produces high-quality, value-creating decisions. The decision quality chain guides the development of content throughout the process.

The Dialogue Decision Process in Action: A Case Study

We illustrate the dialogue decision process with a disguised case of a major electronics company that was concerned about slipping behind in television and related technology. This company was a major manufacturer of TV sets and had a full line of consumer electronics and electronic components including video and audio equipment, computers and peripherals, professional products, and industrial components such as picture tubes, video display components, and integrated circuits.

Senior managers of the company were motivated to try DDP because their television business was maturing, margins were eroding, and competitors were gaining leadership in the next generation of television. The Japanese had already developed a high-definition television (HDTV) standard, which they were broadcasting in Japan, and which they were pressing the rest of the world to adopt. The company had a normal smorgasbord of new features and product improvements in the pipeline, but realized that only a change in broadcast standards held a realistic prospect for revitalizing their business. In the face of eroding profits and globally strategic competition, this company decided it was time to develop a strategy focused on the high-end television business. To develop that strategy, it needed to determine how to support the evolution of TV, which competing technologies to support, and whether to lead or follow. Whatever the strategy, it would require most of the R&D personnel and enormous capital investment to implement.

Phase Zero: Frame and Charter

The dialogue decision process was chartered by the decision team selected by the CEO and his key executives. That team bore responsibility for the initial framing of the problem. Getting everyone to operate within a common frame is critically important but does not come naturally. To understand this, consider the different people involved and their backgrounds. In most cases they will represent very different areas of specialized training and experience, and each sees the world—and the problem—in a different way. As the saying goes, "If you are a hammer, everything looks like a nail." People who work every day on marketing issues usually have a much better grasp of customer requirements than anyone else, but R&D and manufacturing issues are not part of their normal conversations or concerns. In contrast, the financial manager looks at the same problem in terms of revenues, costs, tax consequences, and capital requirements. The R&D experts see new technologies to meet new needs. Bringing individuals with these different perspectives together provides some assurance that all relevant business and technical issues will be represented in the decision process.

These different perspectives are a two-edged sword: They contribute to the robustness of our understanding of the problem; but they create the danger of never achieving a common understanding of the problem. In the worst cases, the different functional areas are either hostile to one another or have conflicting understandings or agendas. The challenge to the decision team is to be sure these different perspectives are focused on the same problem. While the initial framing gets the project off to a good start, it should not be held sacred. At every stage the frame should be questioned and refined, especially after major new information or insights are developed.

The decision team that framed the issues for our electronics company was chaired by the head of Display Products and included executive members from Research, the Integrated Circuits and Display Components business units, Product Development, Broadcasting, and Finance. The CEO chose not to become a member of this team because he was too focused on other critical corporate issues and was willing to rely on this group to make the decision. In this he was clearly delegating and *not* reserving judgment for later.

Phase 1: Assess

Once the problem is properly framed and understood by members of both teams, project team members can begin assessing its dimensions. This involves collecting relevant information, understanding important issues and challenges, examining values, scoping the range of possible actions, and making a work plan to fill potential gaps in the next phase. The goal at this stage is to understand the drivers of the problem, rather than to define its solution.

Assessment includes developing external understandings of the problem, attaining an outside-in perspective, and applying good systems thinking to the drivers of consumer and industry change. Business enterprises too often think that they are fairly closed systems and forget that there is a much larger, more complex system outside their corporate boundaries. That external system includes customers, suppliers, competitors, university technologists, regulators, and others. Depending on the enterprise, the boundaries between these two systems may be sharply delineated or open and fuzzy. Whichever the case, the assessment activity must gain external understanding about:

▲ relevant technologies

▲ competitors' capabilities and plans

▲ evolving technical standards

▲ customers' preferences

▲ new methods of manufacturing and distribution

During the assessment phase, the electronics company articulated many major concerns and issues:

1. While we paint high-tech visions of a distant future, competitors will improve the current standard and run away with the business.

2. Information and entertainment will merge, therefore we should devote our limited R&D resources to developing *digital* high-definition television.

3. HDTV will require an enormous investment. Can we afford it?

4. If we do not offer an alternative as soon as possible, the Japanese will destroy us.

5. These HDTV sets will be very expensive. Who will be able to afford them?

Because HDTV is totally incompatible with today's TV sets and broadcasting infrastructure, many speculated as to which industry player would initiate the cycle of conversion to HDTV. Would it be the broadcasters or the equipment providers? The last major innovation in American television had been the introduction of color broadcasting, which had two things going for it: (1) color broadcasts were compatible with black and white sets—only the broadcasters had to buy new equipment; and (2) RCA was the leader in TV sets and broadcast equipment, and owned NBC—factors that put RCA in a unique position to call the shots. Today, no one has that much market power (except possibly Sony in Japan), so HDTV would require a cooperative effort.

The team explored these and many other issues that we will not delve into here. However we will give an overview of a framework developed by the strategy team in the assessment phase and refined through the rest of the process.

The Influence Diagram

The influence diagram is a useful tool for assessing the business dimensions of any particular problem. Figure 9-5 is a simplified version of an influence diagram used in the electronics company problem. Shapes and arrows represent the decisions, uncertainties, and results of a given situation, and shows how each element influences the others. For example, technical standards for HDTV were highly uncertain at that time. Japanese competitors were already developing their own standards, and it was not certain if the European Union (EU) would accept the Japanese standard or back a unique European standard. Depending on the standard that prevailed, both TV programming and the time to market of equipment would be affected. Likewise, the company's own choice of a technology strategy would be expected to impact technical standards, the likelihood of technical success, R&D costs, and subsequent decisions about alliances and acquisitions.

Developing an influence diagram has a useful effect: It makes each team member acutely aware of the role his or her function plays in the overall scheme. Engineers understand how their choices of technology will impact R&D costs and the probabilities of technical success. Marketing members of the team have a visual image of the many factors that influence market share and their own role in creating value.

Sometimes the influence diagram remains only a graphic tool in the assessment stage. In other cases it is the basis for back-of-the-envelope calculations on how the project might fare. This and other tools drive the assessment phase to its conclusion, which has the following deliverables to the decision team:

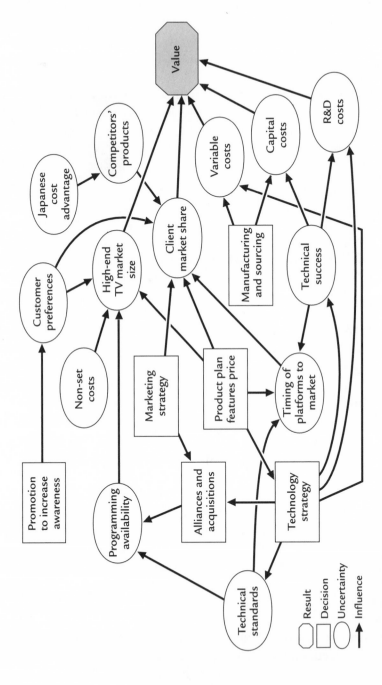

Figure 9-5. *Influence Diagram: HDTV*

1. understanding of the business situation
2. the key challenges to an excellent strategy
3. a clear plan for filling the gaps in the three decision bases: information, alternatives, and values

Phase 2: Develop

One of the most common failures is acceptance of an unsatisfactory set of alternatives. Before the development of artificial sweeteners, consumers could have low calories *or* a sweet taste. Before the quality movement, manufacturers and consumers saw their choices as *either* high-quality products *or* low-cost products. In each of these cases, the alternatives were viewed as mutually exclusive and, for most, unsatisfactory. Eventually, someone recognized these as inadequate choice sets, started thinking "outside the box," and created new and more satisfying alternatives.

The dialogue decision process is unique in formally developing a set of creative but doable alternatives that are good contenders for producing value for the firm and its customers, before they are evaluated. Given an opportunity and some encouragement, a creative group of individuals can produce many alternative solutions to any problem. They can make decision team members earn every cent of their paychecks by requiring them to choose among a number of excellent alternatives. This is only possible, however, when the decision process *demands* excellent alternatives and not simply one clear choice among several "straw men."

The Strategy Table

No organization has the resources to evaluate dozens of alternatives in a timely manner. Thus, once a set of reasonable alternatives has been put forth, the team must narrow it down to those having the greatest practical potential. One tool we recommend for both generating alternatives and selecting a manageable set of good candidates for evaluation is *the strategy table*. The strategy table is a matrix that casts alternative strategies against the decisions that would logically flow from them. For example, the electronics firm confronting the issue of developing high-definition television created several strategies, some of which are listed in the first column of Figure 9-6.

Key Decisions

Strategy Theme	Platform Introductions	Feature Introductions	Feature Development Capability	Display Development	Alliances and Cooperation	Manufacturing
Aggressive Analog	Improved conventional (1995); HD analog (2001)	Reserve all for HDTV introduction	Lead (develop IC design capability)	Focus on large CRT	Take leadership of EC/industry HD project	Enhance large CRT capability and quality control
Evolutionary Improvement	HD analog (1995)	Sequential annual introduction in conventional standard 16:9 aspect ratio (1992); CD audio (1993); Comb filter (1994); 100 Hz progressive scan (1995)	Follow (purchase ICs)	Emphasize projection LCD	Strong role in conventional standard council	Source initially from alliance partner
Information Age	Improved conventional (1993); HD digital (2003)		Negotiate for exclusive IC rights with supplier	Switch resources to digital mirror device projection	Join U.S. HDTV consortium	Build pilot LCD projection plant
VCR–The shortest road	HD digital (1998)	Sequential annual introduction conventional TV; CD audio (1992); Comb filter (1993); 100 Hz progressive scan (1994); 16:9 aspect ratio (1995)	Co-develop key ICs with competitor	Concentrate on large flat panel advances	Passive participation	. . .
Conventional plus						
. . .						

Figure 9-6. *Strategy Table: HDTV*

Of the many strategy themes defined, the following three turned out to be key:

▲ *Aggressive analog strategy.* Lead a coalition of government and industry to aggressively promote a unique analog (versus digital) high-definition standard.

▲ *Evolutionary improvement strategy.* Continue improvement of the conventional analog TV system. Take a neutral approach to HDTV, and let the technology and market develop before making a major move.

▲ *Information age strategy.* Make a clean break with analog systems; instead, focus on digital technology.

In the remaining columns of the table, the project team listed the major decision areas the company would need to address to flesh out these strategies. The heading of each column describes the decision area and the entries under it represent strategic options in that area. A complete strategic alternative (or strategy) was specified by selecting one option from each column and connecting them to make a path from the theme through their choices in each column, as shown in Figure 9-7. Over the course of several weeks the team came up with new strategy themes, defined them carefully by making the appropriate choices in each column, adding columns for new decision areas or new options within decision areas, compared them, and then boiled them down to a small set. The final set of strategic alternatives was selected to define several significantly different strategic visions of how to manage the overall business. After approval of the entire set by the decision team, each strategy was slated for evaluation in the next phase of the DDP.

The actual development of a strategy table does not always follow the linear explanation given above. For example, people usually have opinions about what choices they want to make in each column and only afterwards do they name their set of choices with a strategy theme. Also, initial strategy tables are often missing columns and entries that are added as the discussion evolves. Developing actionable alternatives is a very creative process that in the end produces a small set of creative and significantly different alternatives out of the overwhelming multitude of possibilities that could be imagined.

The ultimate test of a strategy table is straightforward: A person familiar with the situation should be able to define and manage implementation of the strategy according to the table. If major issues are unclear, then more columns need to be added until all of the key

Key Decisions

Strategy Theme	Platform Introductions	Feature Introductions	Feature Development Capability	Display Development	Alliances and Cooperation	Manufacturing
Aggressive Analog	Improved conventional (1995); HD analog (2001)	Reserve all for HDTV introduction	Lead (develop IC design capability)	Focus on large CRT	Take leadership of EC/industry HD project	Enhance large CRT capability and quality control
Evolutionary Improvement		Sequential annual introduction in conventional standard 16:9 aspect ratio	Follow (purchase ICs)	Emphasize projection LCD	Strong role in conventional standard council	Source initially from alliance partner
Information Age	HD analog (1995)	CD audio (1993); Comb filter (1994); 100 Hz progressive scan (1995)	Negotiate for exclusive IC rights with supplier	Switch resources to digital mirror device projection	Join U.S. HDTV consortium	Build pilot LCD projection plant
VCR–The shortest road	Improved conventional (1993); HD digital (2003)		Co-develop key ICs with competitor	Concentrate on large flat panel advances	Passive participation	
Conventional plus	HD digital (1998)	Sequential annual introduction conventional TV; CD audio (1992); Comb filter (1993); 100 Hz progressive scan (1994); 16:9 aspect ratio (1995)				

Figure 9-7. *Three Key Alternatives Defined*

variables have been captured. Realistic strategy tables for a complex situation occasionally have as many as fifty columns. Such tables are usually broken into a set of several logical subtables that define the columns of the high-level table with more clarity and specificity. However, a strategy table does not define implementation completely, only to the level of specificity necessary to get strategic insight and to evaluate which strategy is best.

Once the best strategy has been selected, its implementation path needs to be fleshed out in detail. In the context of this overall strategy, many more important decisions will require implementation. That is why using the DDP to gain alignment and empowerment is so important.

Other Developmental Tasks

In addition to this unique approach to generating alternatives, the development phase spends considerable effort filling in gaps of information identified in the assessment phase. Also, if values and trade-offs are critical, time is dedicated to understanding them further and to preparing for discussions with the decision team. For example, we have commented (in chapter 3) that companies often impose inappropriately high discount rates on long-term R&D. Discussion to gain concurrence for a more appropriate rate would begin here.

At the end of the development phase, the strategy team reports to the decision team with:

1. a set of alternative strategies to be evaluated
2. better information and insight about the business situation
3. clarification of value issues

The primary aim of the review meeting associated with this phase is to agree on a small set of alternatives to be evaluated. This set should be broad enough to cover the range of strategic possibilities while excluding the far-fetched and the straw men. The decision team should agree that, for each alternative, if evaluation showed it to be the one that would create the most value, it would be possible for the organization to undertake it.

Phase 3: Evaluation

During the evaluation phase, the strategy team determines how much value each alternative might produce, the key drivers of that value, and the degree of uncertainty associated with each. The first step in making these determinations is to build a quantitative business model such as the one shown in Figure 9-8.

On the left are the uncertainties that are thought to have potentially significant impact on market success and business results. At the bottom are the selected strategy alternatives. These are characterized in sufficient detail to estimate their costs and to project their influence on business results. The business and market models, typically captured on a computer spreadsheet, determine the cash flow results of any specified combination of uncertainties and choice of strategy. The value model deals with discounting to NPV as the summary measure of shareholder value added. As you will see at the end of this step, when the uncertainties are captured as probability distributions, the model calculates the resulting uncertainty in that NPV, and portrays it, for example, in terms of a probability distribution on NPV as well as expected NPV.[2]

As the influence diagram made clear to the electronics company, television market share is subject to competitive forces and customer preferences, which were very uncertain at the time of the strategic decision. In fact, uncertainties are usually so numerous that we must narrow them down to the key ones before we can do probabilistic analysis.

Sensitivity Analysis

At this stage, we use a technique called *sensitivity analysis* to identify the uncertainties that most significantly affect the value of each strategic alternative. Sensitivity analysis determines the impact of each uncertainty on the NPV of an alternative. Figure 9-9 indicates how NPV for one of the HDTV alternatives—the evolutionary improvement strategy—could be affected by key uncertainties. In this method, we follow these steps:

1. Identify each of the significant variables associated with the strategy and assess the range of uncertainty. We usually estimate three values: a low value at the 10th percentile (a 1 in 10 chance the variable will fall below this value), a high value at the 90th percentile (a 1 in 10 chance the variable will fall above this value), and a medium (or base case) value at the 50th percentile (an equal chance the variable will be above or below this value).

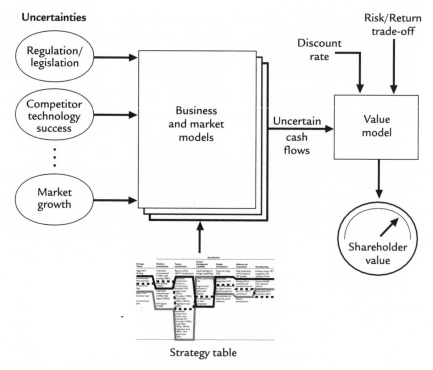

Figure 9-8. *Key Elements of a Strategic Business Model*

2. For each uncertainty, we use the decision model to determine the NPV impact of this range of uncertainty. By definition, the range of outcomes between the low and high values will contain 80 percent of the probable outcomes.[3]

3. Rank the NPV ranges of these uncertainties in descending order of impact and plot them as shown in Figure 9-9. The resulting shape suggests the popular name for this method—the "tornado diagram."

Many decision makers worry about strategically unimportant uncertainties while ignoring the ones that could have tremendous impact on NPV, depending on how the future unfolds. The tornado diagram helps solve this problem. One glance at a tornado diagram will tell decision makers which uncertainties are worth losing sleep over and which are not. As in the HDTV illustration, the top five or so variables usually contribute the most uncertainty to the bottom line. Other variables may be uncertain, and we may be curious about how they will unfold, but the real economic impact is found in the top few

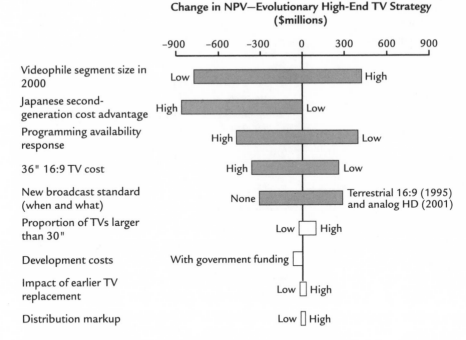

Change in NPV—Evolutionary High-End TV Strategy ($millions)

Figure 9-9. *Sensitivity Analysis: Evolutionary HDTV Improvement*

variables.[4] Since greater information often tends to reduce the range of any particular uncertainty, it indicates where additional time and effort have the greatest potential return.

Clearly, each of the top five uncertainties in Figure 9-9 could alter returns from this strategy significantly. The strategy team may find it advisable to get more information about each of these to establish better ranges of uncertainty.[5] In contrast, the bottom four uncertainties in the chart appear to have little impact on the actual outcome. If decision makers are focusing on these, they need some redirection. In many real cases we find that the least significant uncertainties monopolize executive attention while some of those at the top of the chart are neglected. Sensitivity analysis directs attention to the most important issues.

Other Tools

The strategy team for the electronics firm found that each of its three selected alternatives would be subject to large uncertainties with respect to market size, technology standards, program availability, competition from Japanese rivals, and so forth. These are indicated in the influence diagram, which evolves as deeper understandings are used to revise and augment its structure and as sensitivity analysis is used to simplify it. In the end, the influence diagram should contain only the key decisions and the crucial uncertainties, as measured by their ability to impact potential value creation. For each of these crucial variables, the team went back to the experts and more carefully developed a complete probability distribution, rather than just a range, to more fully and accurately describe the nature of the uncertainty. Then they made a decision tree to map out which combinations of these crucial variables (or scenarios) might occur, which is given in abbreviated form in Figure 9-10.

The decision tree is made of a series of nodes. A decision node is represented by the small square at the left; chance nodes are represented by the small circles across the page. Flowing from each node are branches that represent alternative choices for decision nodes and possible resolutions of uncertainty for chance nodes. The number of branches at each node determines the amount of detail in the tree.[6] A selection of one branch at each node gives one scenario, which is run through the business model to calculate its NPV. Multiplying the probabilities along the path that defines the scenario determines the probability of that scenario and, hence, for its NPV. By running each scenario through the business model we can calculate the full range and probability of results for each alternative strategy. Calculating these financial results and probabilities for each scenario in the tree allows us to plot the risk/return relationship of each alternative strategy, as shown in Figure 9-11.

How should we interpret these curves? First, curves to the right, having higher NPV values, are better. Therefore, Aggressive Analog is dominated by the other two strategies. To see this, take any probability level, say 0.6, and trace it through all three curves. It intersects Aggressive Analog at about $1,900 million, which means this strategy has a 60 percent chance of falling below this value and a 40 percent chance of exceeding this value. It intersects the other curves farther to the right, at $2,400 million for Evolutionary Improvement, and $2,900 million for Information Age. These alternatives, then, have a 40 percent chance of exceeding these higher values. This is true for any probability level, so Aggressive Analog is inferior to both other strategies.

Another way to come to the same conclusion is to target an NPV

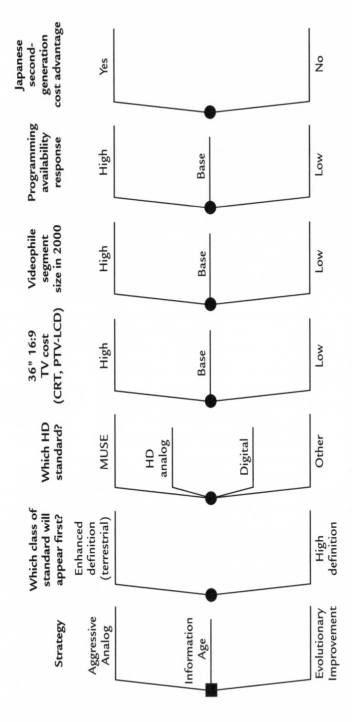

Figure 9-10. *Decision Tree Analysis: Three HDTV Strategies*

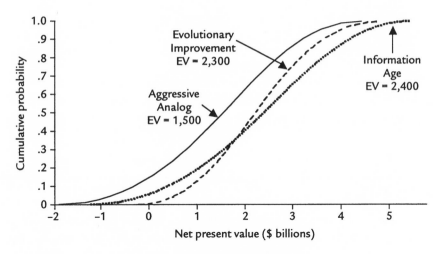

Figure 9-11. *Evaluation of Three Strategy Alternatives*

result, say $3,000 million, and trace it vertically through the three curves. These points are about 0.85 probability for Aggressive Analog, 0.75 for Evolutionary Improvement, and 0.65 for Information Age. Since these numbers represent the probability of falling below $3,000 million, Aggressive Analog is clearly inferior. And this is true over the whole curve.

However, comparing Evolutionary Improvement and Information Age is not so simple, since they cross at an NPV of $1,800 million and a probability of about 0.36. Below these values Evolutionary Improvement is better (to the right) and above these values Information Age is better. If we study these curves, we see that this occurs because the Information Age curve is broader, representing more uncertainty or risk. At the same time, Information Age has the higher expected NPV of $2,400 million versus $2,300 million—or $100 million more than Evolutionary Improvement.

Thus, Information Age has both higher return and higher risk. A very large firm, one that could easily absorb this uncertainty, would simply pick Information Age because it has the highest value. A smaller firm might be tempted to choose Evolutionary Improvement, giving up $100 million in expected NPV in order to have a little more certainty of results. But both courses of action are still very uncertain, with ranges of uncertainty in excess of $3 billion!

At the end of this evaluation phase, the strategy team delivers a recommendation and all of the insight it can derive from its efforts. Specific deliverables are:

1. fully evaluated alternatives
2. quantification of value measures: expected profitability, uncertainty, and risk
3. insight into critical factors, sensitivity analysis, and implementation challenges

Phase 4: Decide

The decision phase usually begins with a presentation and discussion of the findings by the two teams. Although one might think that this would lead to a quick decision, this is not usually the case. The executives on the decision team want to understand completely the recommendations and insights. They, after all, will have to justify the decision to top management, the board, or even the shareholders, as well as live with the uncertainties they are being asked to embrace. The decision phase is usually one of final iteration and generation of insights.

In the HDTV case, top management pressed to find a new strategy—one that achieved most of the upside of the Information Age strategy with the limited downside of the Evolutionary Improvement strategy. A creative discussion ensued and lasted well beyond the scheduled ending time of the meeting. This discussion could not have occurred, nor would it have been so productive, had the dialogue decision process not already built a foundation of personal trust and a comprehensive shared understanding of the technical and business issues. The best contributions of each team were played out during what proved to be a long but exciting exchange of ideas. The meeting ended with a number of excellent ideas for building a still better strategy. The strategy team was charged with bringing their collective ideas together into a new alternative that could be subjected to the same rigorous evaluation.

In less than three weeks the strategy team had come up with a much better hybrid strategy—dubbed Sooner and Later—that focused on feature leadership in conventional TV, dropped analog HDTV entirely, and devoted substantial resources to an alliance-based, but slower approach to a common American- and European-driven digital development. The results of the final evaluation are portrayed in Figure 9-12.

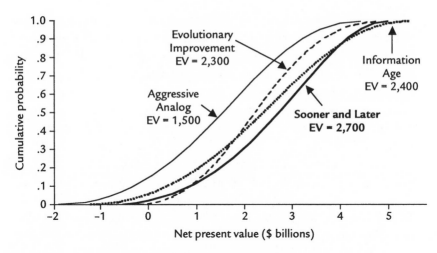

Figure 9-12. *Evaluation of the New Hybrid Strategy*

Sooner and Later dominated all strategies—it had both higher return and lower risk. (Sooner and Later shows insignificantly more downside risk than Evolutionary Improvement, given the degree of imprecision of the model and its inputs.) Its potential shareholder value exceeded the value of the Aggressive Analog strategy by about $1,200 million. In truth, any of these strategies would have improved the prospects of the electronics company, which had no coherent, up-to-date strategy before this decision process was initiated. Its plans were uncoordinated and often counterproductive. Even a well-aligned and empowered Aggressive Analog strategy would have provided much more value than the company's initial situation.

At the end of the decision phase, the process should achieve:

1. clear choice of a strategic direction that creates high value
2. commitment of resources
3. assignment of responsibility

Phase 5: Plan

Clearly, developing and evaluating a high-level business and technology strategy, like the one involving HDTV, requires a much higher level of aggregation than the typical long-range planning process. And once the decision is made, and the strategy has been selected, the strategy team is augmented with additional members who will work toward successful planning and implementation. Budget-focused planners often begin to address strategic problems at this point, mistakenly thinking they are developing strategy. Detailed planning should begin only after a clear strategy is in place.

Often the team organizes implementation task forces for each affected area. Besides planning and budgeting, these teams build an understanding of the uncertainty being faced and put strategic intelligence and contingency plans in place to obtain early warning and manage risk, thereby embracing uncertainty in their implementation plans. The dialogue process continues to aid team members—building true understanding of the challenges and a strong commitment to making the strategy successful. The end of this phase should deliver clear plans including:

1. design for a transition to new strategy
2. detailed implementation plans: business, functional and project plans; contingency plans
3. organization and responsibilities: incentives, monitoring and control systems

We cannot go into the methods for smart implementation in this volume. However, the principles of smart R&D and the Dialogue Decision Process do set the stage for effective action. The electronics company in this chapter successfully implemented its new strategy for the TV business. It was invigorated with a new and shared understanding of the business and its customer. It harnessed the energy of all of its divisions to pull together and make the new strategy a reality. And it is a key player in the unfolding digital and high-definition industry today.

When properly executed, the DDP increases the odds that a decision will have a favorable outcome. The future is always uncertain, and so there can be no guarantees. But, this process brings out the facts, quantifies the return potential, and identifies and measures the uncertainties. Equally important, the dialogue decision process is a powerful antidote for the many organizational behaviors that lead to poor decisions.

CHAPTER 10

R&D PORTFOLIO STRATEGY

> God is in the details.
> *Ludwig Mies van der Rohe*

S OME ORGANIZATIONS SEE the portfolio as a top-down statement of aspirations, allocating resources to broad categories. For others, the portfolio is merely a bottom-up accumulation of available projects. The place where top-down aspirations meet bottom-up realities is where the details of portfolio decisions come into play. As in architecture, portfolio strategy is a meeting of the power of the imagination and the reality of materials and construction.

Several years ago we helped a large conglomerate do a quick evaluation of a divisional R&D portfolio. This organization had, over the previous few years, acquired substantial pharmaceutical R&D capabilities. The division in question had a handful of existing products, and generous R&D funding, and aimed to be a major pharmaceutical entity.

Quantitative analysis of about twenty major projects, using portfolio tools described in this chapter, indicated that most of the division's R&D efforts were being spent on incremental and "me-too" products. Why? We were told that management did not want to burden R&D with both establishment of a new laboratory and an attack on difficult markets.

Unfortunately, this strategy guaranteed that the division would not become a pharmaceutical major. With the high development expenses and long lead times of this industry, the only way to put this division on the map would be to gain strategic advantage in new markets. Management saw the point, and within a few months redirected most of its work toward revolutionary objectives. Only time would tell if they would make the hoped-for breakthroughs. However, the division's initial portfolio strategy had not had a chance to accomplish the company's larger business strategy.

The objective of good portfolio strategy is creating the most value—the same as the objective of technology strategy. R&D port-

Figure 10-1. *The Role of R&D Portfolio Strategy*

folio strategy, however, is a balancing act (see Figure 10-1). It must reconcile the intent of business and technology strategy with a set of existing projects and new opportunities. Portfolio strategy represents a company's choice as to which set of projects balances the potential delivery of R&D results over time. It indicates how much to focus on various segments of the portfolio (business units, technologies, markets, etc.). Ultimately portfolio strategy determines which R&D projects should be funded and at what levels.

One of the most difficult aspects of portfolio strategy is striking the right balance between innovative but risky projects and incremental projects with more certain returns. Operational business managers usually cast their votes for projects with greater certainty and more immediate returns, and R&D managers like to please them. This may explain why laboratories established to do innovative R&D quickly become the servants of short-term business needs, with the result that real innovation must be sought through acquisition.

The forces favoring incremental, short-term, high-probability projects are indeed strong, especially when the operational culture punishes failure, and when discount rates applied to R&D are inappropriately high. Ironically, the same managers who push R&D in the direction of incrementalism look to it for their company's next blockbuster.

PROCESSES

Portfolio strategy must ensure that all funded projects receive the resources they need to be successful. If sufficient resources are not available, either more must be obtained or some projects must be eliminated or postponed to allow full resourcing to others. Cutting resources to all projects to meet budget constraints usually destroys value because *all* projects accomplish too little or arrive too late to market.

Portfolio decisions are best made with a dialogue decision process similar to the one discussed in the previous chapter for technology strategy. However the requirements are different and the process needs more custom tailoring. Some of the design issues are:

1. How should we aggregate our opportunities into manageable strategic projects?

2. Who is the overall process owner and who will facilitate the analytical process?

3. How do we guarantee a level playing field and sufficient credibility that top management and project leadership will believe the results and stand behind the recommendations?

4. How will we respond to the results of a portfolio assessment? Do we simply want to prioritize the projects on the basis of value creation potential given the organization's strategic direction? If the portfolio results have significant strategic implications, how will we initiate discussions of new direction and subsequent implementation?

5. How will business and marketing units interact in the process? Should we use one cross-functional decision team for the whole portfolio, divide responsibilities by business or technical areas, or use a multilevel review structure?

6. How will we keep the portfolio strategy evergreen?

If the process is annual, steps are usually taken at the beginning to ensure that all projects are treated appropriately, but not necessarily equally. For example, one would not demand the same scrutiny of a small project as of a large one. Also there is often provision for one or more sessions of peer or management review to crosscheck the quality of inputs for consistency. For example, one peer group might review all of the regulatory approval assessments across the portfolio, while another one might review all market assessments.

If the portfolio process is tied to stage gate reviews of individual projects, these reviews can be set against the backdrop of the entire portfolio. For example, the chief technology office of a major biotechnology company refuses to review any project on a stand-alone basis. He always considers project decisions in the context of adjustments to the overall divisional portfolio.

Some organizations use a combination of the two processes, individual project reviews when they pass stage gates and an annual portfolio review, with updates to projects that have not been reviewed during the past year.

Understanding Project Differences: The R&D Grid

Most R&D organizations spend only a small portion of their budgets, generally 5 percent to 15 percent, on very early stage discovery research. This kind of work takes place at the leading edge of science, where the commercial possibilities of new discoveries is largely unknown. This research supports high-level business and technology strategy decisions and develops technology and capabilities that will create project opportunities to support existing businesses or establish new ones.

The bulk of R&D budgets, the remaining 85 percent to 95 percent, is directed toward projects with identifiable paths to commercialization and value creation. Yet these have differences. Some are shorter term, others longer term. Some are more uncertain; some are less uncertain. Some constituencies favor the short-term and less uncertain projects; others favor the long-term and more uncertain projects. Achieving the mutual understanding required by alignment and empowerment requires a common process framework for comparison and discussion.

The R&D grid (Figure 10-2) shows how these different projects contribute differently to their portfolios. It is an important part of a process for reaching mutual understanding about the appropriate balance of risk and return. This grid measures projects in terms of technical difficulty and commercial potential. In our lexicon, projects are either bread and butter, pearls, oysters, or white elephants, according to their characteristics.

The grid has four quadrants, each with different project characteristics. The vertical axis reflects a project's probability of success in overcoming all hurdles (technical, financial, regulatory, etc.). The horizontal axis reflects potential commercial value. We measure this value in terms of the expected net present value of cash flows. This axis represents the magnitude of potential value creation. Roughly

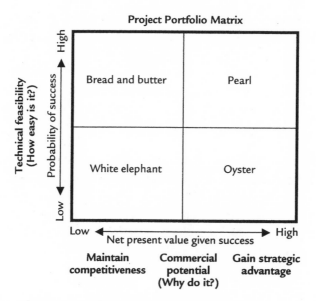

Figure 10-2. *The R&D Grid: Project Portfolio Matrix*

speaking, projects that produce results on the left end of this axis maintain competitiveness in existing businesses. Projects on the right create new strategic advantage, either by revolutionizing existing businesses or by creating new ones.

To use this grid, we need reliable quantitative measurements for all projects in the portfolio. It is tempting to use this grid as a qualitative focus of discussion, with project leaders simply placing their projects where they think they belong on the grid.[1] This approach violates several principles. For example, Embracing Uncertainty requires more than a quick judgment of risk; it requires understanding the sources of technical uncertainty. Top-of-the-head estimates, and others infected by bias or wishful thinking, will not do.

Bread-and-Butter Projects

The upper left quadrant represents projects with high probabilities of success and good commercial value. These projects usually focus on evolutionary improvements to current products and processes in existing business areas. They are also characterized by modest extensions of existing technology or their applications. Bread-and-butter projects fulfill the need to produce regular results for existing business units and to support shorter-term profit objectives. Some examples include:

- ▲ a new form of insulin
- ▲ upgraded software tools with new features and ease of use
- ▲ product extension of an antiparasitic drug
- ▲ manufacturing cost reduction program
- ▲ one-pass truck for garbage collection and recycling

Pearls

The upper right quadrant contains projects with the greatest potential for *both* commercial and technical success. Pearls address revolutionary commercial applications, and they deal with proven technical advances. Ideally, R&D portfolios contain dozens of pearls, each one poised to produce long-term competitive advantage. In nature, a pearl is a rare thing and is only found by opening a great number of oysters. The same applies in the field of R&D. Examples include:

- ▲ subsurface imaging to locate oil and gas
- ▲ next-generation IC chip
- ▲ artificial heart
- ▲ phase III drug for an unmet medical need
- ▲ replacement for silver in offset printing

Oysters

The lower right quadrant of the R&D grid represents early stage projects designed to produce new strategic advantage. They have blockbuster potential but breakthroughs are needed to unlock this potential. Here, the potential payoff is very high but the probability of success is initially low. The majority of projects in this quadrant, in fact, are expected to fail. (In the cultured pearl business, seeded oysters have only about a 5 percent chance of producing a marketable pearl.) But those that do succeed should win big.

Over time, the uncertainties surrounding both the commercial potential of these projects and the likelihood of technical success diminish. As this happens, these projects can shift to other quadrants. For example, as the technical barriers to success of a particular "oyster" project are overcome, that project may shift to the pearl quadrant unless its commercial potential has eroded to divert it into the bread-and-butter quadrant. Some examples of oyster projects are:

- ▲ new approach to pain control
- ▲ optical computing

- ▲ technology for high-definition displays
- ▲ intelligent packaging materials
- ▲ catalyst improvements for refineries
- ▲ new kinds of plastics

White Elephants

According to legend, the king of Siam gave white elephants to his troublesome underlords. These rare animals were regarded as sacred and so required lavish care and feeding, and could not be required to work. Instead, they consumed many of their masters' resources and reduced the underlords' ability to create mischief in the kingdom.

Projects in the lower left quadrant of the grid are like the king's white elephants: They consume resources, displace more promising projects, and are unlikely to enjoy technical success or produce substantial commercial value. Obviously, no rational person would select one of these beasts for his firm's portfolio—and few would claim credit for their inceptions. But almost all companies have them. Invariably, white elephants begin life as oyster or bread-and-butter projects, but become white elephants as commercial or technical defects emerge. Examples of white elephants include:

- ▲ videotape rental vending machine as prices dropped
- ▲ immunochemistry product for a saturated market
- ▲ innovative approach to cancer that was potent but too toxic
- ▲ technical approach to match competitor's actions
- ▲ too small an investment in microelectronics
- ▲ demonstration pollution test site that was politically correct but used obsolete technology

To executives brave enough to admit the existence of white elephants at their companies, we ask, Why haven't you killed them? These are the typical answers:

- ▲ There is nothing else to work on.
- ▲ We are not willing to give up our sunk costs.
- ▲ They have influential backers (often a customer).
- ▲ We are unwilling to pay the costs (real and political) of shutting down.
- ▲ Hope springs eternal.

The final problem is the lack of a disciplined process to evaluate all projects and find out where the white elephants are hiding.

Managing across the Grid

We encourage our clients to do three things with the R&D grid:

1. Assign each R&D project to an appropriate quadrant based upon quantitative evaluation of the project opportunity.
2. Capitalize on pearls, eliminate or reposition white elephants, and balance the resources devoted to bread-and-butter and oyster projects to achieve alignment with overall strategy.
3. Use their understanding of grid quadrants to shape the way they manage individual projects.

Items 1 and 2 makes it possible to see at a glance how risks and potential returns are being balanced (or not balanced) in the portfolio. Item 3 helps us to make the most of the entire portfolio.

Although projects on the grid are defined *quantitatively*, projects in each quadrant are *qualitatively* different, and should be managed differently. Bread-and-butter projects are usually part of a pipeline of incremental products and processes needed to generate near-term results. They need to be managed to deliver results on time, on specification, and on budget. Personnel involved with these projects should have incentives for results and conformance to goals.

Pearls are even more valuable as projects, but managing them for short-term deliverables is usually inappropriate. Pearls represent potential breakthroughs that should be exploited in many ways and for multiple generations—often in ways that we cannot understand in advance. Thus, pearls should be managed to encourage entrepreneurship and tolerate the circumvention of rules and systems that stifle value creation.

Uncertainty is the key issue in managing oysters. Since few oyster projects are expected to succeed, it is a mistake to reward success and punish the failure to produce results. Doing so simply encourages people to drag out project time in the vain hope of producing positive results or, worse, to avoid the consequences of impending project failure. Instead, people should be encouraged to determine quickly which oysters contain pearls and which are empty and should be eliminated. This means working on the most challenging technical hurdles first. If a project team cannot find a way over its greatest hurdle, there is little point in working on the others. And failing fast minimizes resources spent on failure, which allows the project team to pursue another opportunity.

Not all white elephants should be killed—at least not immediately.

Once identified, white elephants should be examined rapidly to see how they might be redirected. If a project is technically difficult and aimed at a small market, a simpler technical approach to the same market might turn the white elephant into a bread-and-butter project. For example, researchers might be applying their favorite high-tech solution to a market that cannot afford it, when a lower-tech solution would address most of the market needs. Likewise, that same technically difficult project might be moved over to the oyster quadrant if there is some possibility of addressing the needs of a broader market. For example, researchers might be aiming high-tech solutions at easy market targets either out of the false conservatism of addressing a well-known market or out of ignorance of what the true market could be. If neither of these avenues appears promising, the white elephant project should be terminated, or possibly sold or licensed to someone else who can make better use of the technology.

Balancing Risk

The easy portfolio decisions involve capitalizing on pearls and repositioning or terminating white elephants. The more difficult decisions are found among the bread-and-butter and oyster projects. As described earlier, business pressures tend to favor bread-and-butter projects. It is rare that a manager has lost either job or bonus by supporting incremental R&D for established products—the politically safe thing to do. But incremental R&D does not sustain competitiveness over time. The groundbreaking work associated with oyster projects is needed to renew the business in the long run.

The recent history of the Swiss watch industry provides a clear example of the limits of bread-and-butter R&D. Swiss companies dominated the world watch business for generations and continued to make incremental improvements to their timepieces. They broke new ground in the 1960s with their development of quartz technology, then settled back into their traditional pattern of incremental improvement.

Asian watchmakers, primarily in Japan, adopted quartz technology, and incorporated it into families of inexpensive watches that offered superb quality and customer-pleasing features at prices the Swiss could not match. All through the 1970s, the Swiss conceded one market tier after another, beginning with the low-priced mass market. By the late 1970s, Swiss producers—now clinging to small luxury niches—could lay claim to only 44 percent of the North American and European market, down from 80 percent. Even in these high-priced enclaves their dominance was threatened.

No amount of bread-and-butter R&D could have reversed this situation for the Swiss. What did reverse it was R&D conducted by ETA S.A., a subsidiary of Société Micromécanique et Horlogère (SMH), an entity into which two failing Swiss watch companies had been merged. ETA developed a simple and reliable product platform with fewer than half the number of parts used in comparable Asian quartz models. This platform was capable of supporting tremendous product variation. A parallel R&D effort created breakthrough molding and assembly processes for low-cost mass production of this platform and the entire watch assembly.

The outcome of these R&D efforts was the Swatch Watch, a product family that returned industry dominance to the Swiss.[2] High-risk R&D projects, like the one that produced the Swatch Watch, are required for long-term competitiveness, but need to be balanced with incremental R&D.

Understanding the Risk of Oysters

People misperceive the uncertainty of a well-diversified set of oyster projects. A portfolio of sixteen projects that each have a 25 percent chance of success is expected to produce four successful projects, and there is only about a 1 percent chance that all will fail. These numbers should be reassuring to even the most risk-averse, but one annoying uncertainty remains: We cannot identify in advance which four or so will be the winners.

People confuse their inability to pick winners with financial risk. Embracing uncertainty in this context means being able to live with not knowing which projects will succeed because you are quite certain that the portfolio will have a sufficient number of successes to pay off well.

A Case of Too Few Oysters

The core business of a Fortune 500 manufacturing company was under siege from worldwide overcapacity, foreign competition, and technology substitution. The company's centralized R&D laboratory served several business areas and pursued many new technologies.

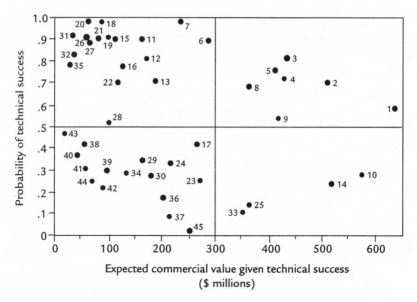

Figure 10-3. *Portfolio with Too Few Oysters*

Given its situation, top management favored allocation of resources to new high-growth businesses, and R&D was expected to
follow this strategic shift. To do this, the company's entire R&D portfolio (over $100 million annually) was analyzed to determine how
portfolio decisions, and budgetary reallocations, could improve future R&D results. One of our colleagues was asked to help with this
challenging undertaking.

Over a period of six months, each of the firm's forty-five major
projects or programs was examined. This work included quantitative
evaluation of the probability of overcoming each technical hurdle. In
addition, commercialization paths were identified for each project
and estimates of customer, industry, and market conditions were incorporated into NPV estimates that would follow in the wake of technical success. The result of this analysis was displayed in a portfolio
grid like the one in Figure 10-3.

This portfolio contained many projects of strategic importance
and good expected value. But the grid made clear at a glance that it
contained too few high-risk/high-potential return projects to generate and sustain long-term growth.

Figure 10-3 indicates several interesting findings. First, the portfolio has seven pearls, which should lead to long-term value creation.

This number, however, is surprising in view of the fact that there are only four oysters! Since many oysters are needed to produce a single pearl, we have to ask ourselves two questions: Where did the seven pearls come from, and what will be the sources of future pearls? We would not expect this portfolio to renew its supply of pearls from so few oysters. There seemed to be a lack of systems thinking about the current portfolio.

Looking elsewhere on the grid, we observe a reasonable set of bread-and-butter projects, enough to deliver results to the business units in the near term. But why are there so many low-value, low-probability white elephants?

We eventually found answers to our questions about the odd shape of this portfolio by digging into the history of the company's R&D establishment. It had been headed by an individual who understood uncertainty and the dynamics of R&D investments and had aggressively funded oyster projects. These projects produced the pearls we later observed. However, when this individual retired, the company directed his successor to reorient the department to the short-term R&D demanded by the business units. The principle of systems thinking about R&D was not broad based.

Under its new head, the R&D organization did, indeed, redirect its focus. However, its tradition of technical excellence was so ingrained that it could not let go of its many technically interesting projects. R&D lacked a value creation culture. Almost all of the former oysters migrated into white elephant territory. Despite the limited commercial potential of these projects, R&D personnel worked diligently at solving their technical challenges. They transformed a few into bread-and-butter projects, and a few were redirected in other useful ways. But most former oysters simply absorbed staff time and money without producing tangible results.

The better way to reorient the R&D effort toward short-term results would have been to eliminate most of the technically difficult work! Of course this would have meant dismantling a technical capability it took decades to build.

By not understanding the dynamics of R&D, and by succumbing to the short-term business pressure, this company's management had destroyed much of the value of its excellent laboratory. In the process they created an ineffective mix of bread-and-butter and white elephant projects, and had almost eliminated the company's potential for future renewal through R&D.

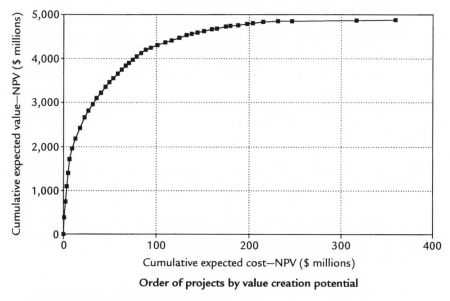

Figure 10-4. *R&D Productivity Curve*

The R&D Productivity Curve

Part of the problem was R&D's lack of a value creation culture. This had led management to tighten the reins and focus on short-term projects. This organization had no way to obtain mutual understanding among employees about what created value for the organization. The R&D productivity curve, illustrated in Figure 10-4, moved their discussion to a new level and focused both sides on value creation from R&D. This curve measures cumulative R&D contributions to firm value (in terms of net present value) as a function of cumulative expected remaining R&D costs. It is a measure of the incremental productivity of R&D investment. To create this curve, first order projects by the ratio of expected value to expected cost, starting with the highest ratio. Beginning at the origin, each point of the plot adds these two components for the next most productive project in the portfolio.

The curve in Figure 10-4 shows a typical case of diminishing returns for increasing R&D investment. It follows the usual 80/20 rule: 80 percent of the value of the lab is produced by about 20 percent of the R&D investment. And the last few projects are costly and barely produce a one-for-one discounted return. These projects are mostly the big white elephants from the R&D grid.

For the company in our case, the challenge is clear; many of its projects are contributing very little. How can this lab revise or trade the projects on the right side of its grid for ones more like the projects on the left? Step one is to provide a wake-up call about many of these nonperforming projects.

Reallocating Resources

Further analysis of segments of the portfolio showed that projects dedicated to applying new technology to existing markets—a favorite focus of R&D work in this company—had an average productivity of 2:1, while finding new markets for existing technology had an average productivity of 14:1. Other similar insights were generated. These insights guided the reallocation of scarce resources to projects with high productivity. Laboratory management eliminated some of the projects and reallocated resources to new projects that, according to their own evaluation, resulted in a 30 percent increase in the total expected return from R&D, which translates (at an average 3:1 productivity ratio) into $90 million in extra value creation per year from the same $100 million annual R&D budget.

One important result of these strategic reallocations was that top management gained confidence in the R&D laboratory and, at a time when most other functions were suffering deep cutbacks, increased its overall budget by 40 percent over two years. The process helped the entire organization toward the principles of smart R&D: alignment and empowerment through mutual understanding of choices, embracing the uncertainty in the R&D portfolio, a systems understanding of the long- and short-term impact of R&D, and a focus on value creation.

Maximizing Portfolio Value Creation

Managing R&D in support of both short-term needs and long-term competitiveness is one part of the portfolio balancing act, but finding completely new value is another.

The pharmaceutical industry is increasingly aware of the importance of portfolio management. Several majors have embarked on multi-year efforts to learn better methods for managing their global R&D portfolios for maximum value creation. This case, based on a composite representative "company," demonstrates the typical increase of about 30 percent in R&D return.

This company wanted to go beyond making yes/no decisions about each project in the portfolio to considering reallocation of resources among all of its existing and potential projects. Some skeptics felt that each project was highly constrained by technical considerations. Others thought that additional resources applied to some projects, and programs would generate far more value than the cost of taking these resources away from other projects. To make these kinds of comparisons in a geographically and culturally diverse organization would require building high credibility in the treatment of each project and fair comparisons of the value-generating potential across projects. That is, there had to be a "level playing field."

This company sought alternative ways of carrying out each project, and then optimized the overall portfolio by optimizing the resourcing of each project for maximum incremental returns. To do this in a credible way, the R&D staff designed a dialogue decision process tailored to gain understanding and buy-in from different therapeutic areas and from top management (Figure 10-5). The process meets the dual needs of top management and each therapeutic area to be part of the portfolio decision process and committed to its results. By establishing an effective and credible process at the beginning, they laid the groundwork for powerful strategic decisions at the end, with the commitment to make them stick.

In the first month of the project, therapeutic area and project leaders were asked to respond to the following questions:

▲ What are your current development plans and what are the resources required to carry them out?

▲ If you were given a significant budget increase (say 25%–50%), how would you use the added funds to get the most additional value out of your project?

▲ If your budget were significantly decreased, how would you cut back your project while preserving as much value as possible?

▲ What budget would be required to terminate your project while still capturing its "salvage value" (e.g., through out-licensing partially developed work)?

Answering these questions forced managers to think deeply and creatively about their projects, and to develop explicit alternatives for both increased and decreased funding. Table 10-1 is a sample of

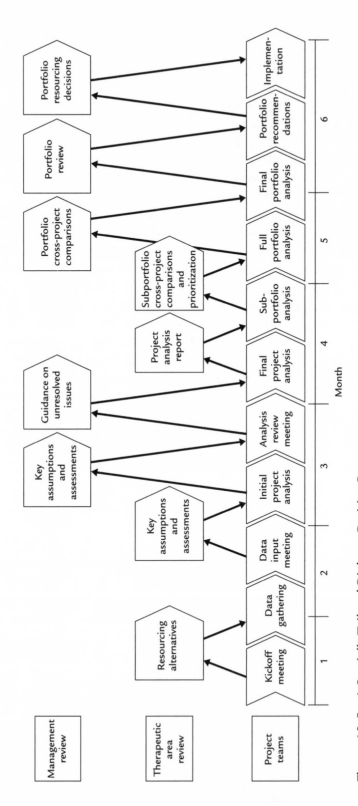

Figure 10-5. *A Specially Tailored Dialogue Decision Process*

Table 10-1. *A Sample of Alternatives with Different Levels of Funding*

COMPOUND	CURRENT	EXPANDED	REDUCED	MINIMAL
Alpha	▲ Target launch for hypertension ▲ Initiate long-term outcome study in Phase IIIb ▲ Conduct Phase IIIb comparator studies	▲ In addition to Current, two alternatives: (A) Pursue PLE with patent extension (B) Accelerate NDA filing	▲ Current, but eliminate Phase IIIb long-term outcome study	▲ Stop all development activity after Phase IIb ▲ Pursue license-out opportunity
Beta	▲ Target launch for prostate cancer in U.S. and Europe 3Q99 ▲ Start a comparator study vs. major competitor (not to be included in regulatory file)	▲ Current, but add mortality study	▲ Not applicable	▲ Stop all development activity ▲ Pursue license-out opportunity
Gamma	▲ Target file date for Alzheimer's: Sept. 1998 ▲ Pursue seven Phase IIIa studies in parallel ▲ Pursue one comparator study	▲ In addition to Current, three alternatives: (A) Perform two disease modification studies starting Jan. 1997 (B) Perform two disease modification studies starting Oct. 1997 (C) Perform two disease modification studies starting April 1998	▲ Two alternatives: (A) Current, but perform two fewer Phase IIIa studies (B) Current, but drop comparator study	▲ Stop all development activity after Phase II ▲ Pursue license-out opportunity

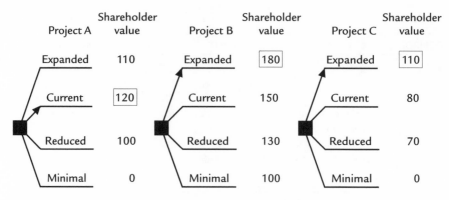

Figure 10-6. *Identifying Highest Values across Projects and Funding Levels (in millions)*

the kinds of alternatives created for three projects (compounds), indicating how they could be changed according to different levels of funding.

Each project was then analyzed and reviewed through the dialogue decision process. In the end, the shareholder value (SHV) potential was established as estimated by the net present value of increased cash flows (net of investment) for each project and each alternative, as shown in Figure 10-6. These values indicated, in the absence of resource constraints, how each project could be funded to achieve optimal performance. For example, the SHV of project Alpha is optimized at current budget levels. In contrast, SHV for projects Beta and Gamma improve measurably with expanded funding. To maximize shareholder value, an organization should be prepared to fund the best alternative for each project as long as its shareholder value is positive.

Using the R&D Productivity Curve

The next step in the pharmaceutical company's process was to determine the extent to which optimizing increments of project funding across the entire portfolio would increase portfolio productivity and value creation. As a baseline, a productivity curve was developed assuming all projects are funded at the current levels (Figure 10-7). Overall the current portfolio was expected to generate high shareholder value, achieving over $8 billion in SHV on some $200 million in incremental investment (that is, not counting the many years of sunk costs it took to arrive at this enviable position). However, as we

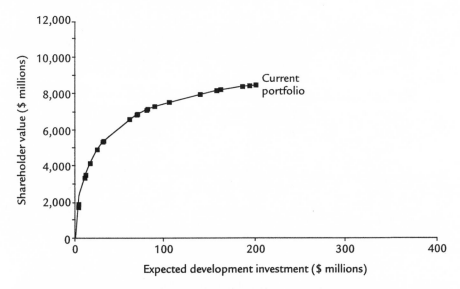

Figure 10-7. *Base Case Productivity Curve*

might expect, the 80/20 rule appears to be at work. That is, most of the value appears to be generated by a minority of projects.

But appearances are not always reality—a systems thinking approach is required to understand where the value is really coming from. Projects on the steep side of the curve are often close to reaching the market; the projects on the shallow side may be early stage projects, some of which will eventually migrate to the steeper side over time. Simply cutting all of these less productive projects would endanger the future.[3] Deeper analysis is required to draw firm conclusions about whether some of the projects on the shallow side of the curve are the oysters that could turn into the next-generation pearls.

The next step was to build a new curve based on all possible combinations of funding levels for every project in the portfolio. Unfortunately there are about 10^{12} (one quadrillion) possible combinations. However, there are mathematical methods for determining the optimal set of combinations for any resource level (called *the efficient frontier* in investment portfolio theory). Figure 10-8 plots the optimal set—considering shareholder value versus costs—for the company's total R&D portfolio.

Shown against the base case productivity curve, adoption of the optimal combination of project funding levels would produce an

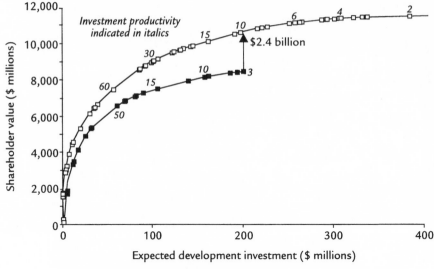

Note: Solid squares ■ represent the current portfolio; open squares □ represent the highest value portfolio.

Figure 10-8. *The Optimal Productivity Curve*

additional $2.4 billion in shareholder value, a 30 percent increase, for the same total R&D investment. This optimization depends on the ability to generate and evaluate multiple alternatives. When this is done, the optimization is a straightforward task.

To implement these recommendations, we would have to assure ourselves that we have the right kind of staff, availability of facilities, and so forth. With a little fine tuning, most of this value should be achievable. So far this approach answers the question of how to allocate resources to create maximum value within the financial constraints.

The Case for Increased Funding

One and a half billion dollars in added value is a very good return on the cost of doing one's homework. But for our pharmaceutical company, the story did not end there. The expanded set of project alternatives generated through the study indicated additional high-return possibilities if more development resources could be released. In the months that followed, the organization considered the implications of adding these potential projects and requested an increase in R&D

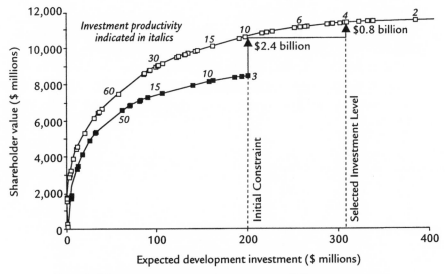

Note: Solid squares ■ represent the current portfolio; open squares □ represent the highest value portfolio.

Figure 10-9. *The Slope of the Productivity Curve at Different Points*

funding to pursue them. The discipline of the portfolio process focused attention on where it belonged: Why were there constraints in the face of excellent prospects for value? A value creation culture works to remove the constraints.

To appreciate the logic of this proposed funding increase, take a systems perspective on the entire enterprise and ask what returns are offered by incremental investment in R&D compared to other areas of the company. Figure 10-9 shows the level of returns offered by R&D. It shows the slope of the productivity curve (i.e., the ratio of incremental SHV to incremental investment) at several points along each curve. In the current portfolio curve, the lowest incremental productivity is 3:1; this occurs at the $200 million investment level. The optimized portfolio curve indicates incremental productivity of 10:1 at this same investment level. This suggests that additional funds could be productively invested in the optimized curve, perhaps up to the original 3:1 level, which would occur at the $310 million level. The fundamental value creation question is, Does the firm have other opportunities that have (long-term) returns of this magnitude? If not, R&D is the highest and best use of incremental resources.

"No way!" was top management's initial response to R&D's request for added funding. A major product was going off patent and management did not want to consider anything that would increase pressure on current earnings. The stock analysts had already been assured that there would be no drop in earnings. Management preferred the plan to hold the budget constant and pick up an added $2.4 billion in NPV through portfolio optimization. To them, it was a "free lunch."

Debate on this issue—which pitted short-term concerns against long-term competitiveness and shareholder value—continued for several months. It is the same debate that takes place in virtually every company that relies heavily on R&D. In the end, the long view prevailed—they expanded the funding level by over 50 percent, which created another $0.8 billion of shareholder value. Management recognized that its obligation to shareholders required added R&D funding. In fact, they held special meetings with the stock analysts to explain the value hidden in their R&D portfolio and their obligation to the shareholders to increase funding. Withholding investment from such excellent R&D opportunities, they concluded, would actually *destroy* shareholder value.

This new way of managing the R&D portfolio did more than simply rationalize the portfolio and increase its funding. The process helped everyone to think deeply about value and the way it is created. It required everyone to find and evaluate alternatives. It gave many individuals the opportunity to gain experience using a rational decision process and tools such as SHV. And it required top management to come to grips in a systematic way with the perennial tension between the present and the future. In making the difficult choice between long-term value and short-term results, top management affirmed value creation as the most important organizational imperative.

Many industries are coming to realize that smart strategic management of their R&D portfolios is their only hope for long-term renewal and strategic success in their base business. It has become obvious that taking calculated risk is the basis of successful competition; companies that fail to learn will fall by the wayside. Successful companies have recognized the need to develop a common approach across global organizations with diverse histories and cultures.

CHAPTER 11

PROJECT STRATEGY

> A lot of things are technologi-
> cally possible, but only the
> economically feasible products
> will become a reality.
> *Robert Noyce*

A EUROPEAN PHARMACEUTICAL COMPANY had a new drug application but was unsure of how best to pursue it. Should it pursue rapid introduction by seeking regulatory approval in one or two European countries? Would it be best to seek approvals on a Europe-wide basis, even if doing so would delay introduction? Should it develop two main compounds for this indication simultaneously—one as a back-up—or should development resources be concentrated on a single compound?

An electronics firm had developed the basic technology for a new flat screen display for laptop computers and similar devices, but was unsure whether to develop this technology through high-resolution color or a low-resolution format.

A materials engineering firm had developed a new process for mold-ing a widely used form of plastic. The market opportunities for the new process were bound to be considerable. Should it pursue these opportunities directly, or would a licensing arrangement with lead-ing process equipment firms create the most value for shareholders?

Each of the situations described above is one in which fundamen-tal technological strategy decisions have already been made. Each firm knows that it is onto something important and is committed to pursuing it. The unanswered question is, Which is the best way? We answer this question through R&D project strategy and its attendant decisions.

Recall our pyramid of strategic R&D decisions (Figure 11-1), which indicates the role of project strategy in smart R&D. Project

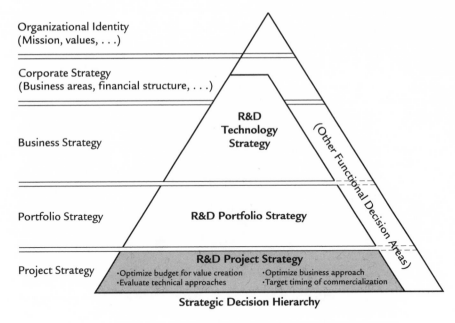

Figure 11-1. *R&D Project Strategy Supports Higher-Level Strategies*

strategy supports higher level decisions about business/technology strategy and portfolio strategy. At the project level, decisions largely revolve around budgets, different technical approaches to the same end, emphasis in project objectives, time to market, other market issues, and commercialization. In general, project strategy has the following characteristics:

▲ *Organizational simplicity.* The people involved in a project are well identified, and the decision makers are fairly clear. Fewer people are involved in discussion and decision making. The dialogue among these individuals is very abbreviated compared to the DDP for technology or portfolio strategy decisions.

▲ *Problems are better framed than technology strategy problems.* Though they may differ on which direction to take, most participants understand the strategic setting of the problem. For example, "We know that this is a good idea, but we need to determine if we should out-license our new process or commercialize it ourselves." Blind spots in the frame are usually rooted in lack of a good perspective on the market and competition.

▲ *Projects have both technical and market uncertainties.* The major challenge is to reveal the extent of these uncertainties, determine their

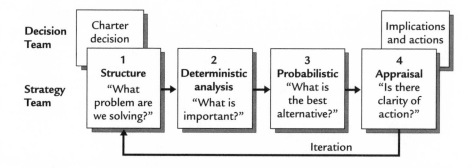

Figure 11-2. *Project Strategy through a Four-Step Decision Process*

impacts on technical and commercial success, and trace these results through to ultimate value creation.

The Process

The way to determine the best strategy for a particular project is through an abbreviated version of the dialogue decision process first described in chapter 9. In this process, we rationally structure alternative courses of action and evaluate them using business models and proven decision tools. This approach has helped R&D managers discover that project strategies they would otherwise have discarded (or have never considered) contain far greater value than their favored alternatives.

Figure 11-2 is a simple rendering of the four-step decision process for project strategy:

1. Structure the problem in terms of what needs to be solved to make a quality decision. This step usually requires dialogue between the decision team and the project team.
2. Move from opinion to real evidence and determine which aspects of the problem are likely to have the greatest impact on the outcome.
3. Apply probabilistic evaluation to a set of alternative project strategies to answer the question, Which is the best option, given what we know?
4. Appraise the results. The key question here is, Have we done enough to be clear about which is the best course of action? This step also requires dialogue between a decision team and the project team.

The final step of the process is the point at which managers ask themselves, Do we now understand enough to commit ourselves to action? In some cases, the answer is "no." We may feel that it is worth taking the time to gather more key information or that we can pause to create better alternatives. In these cases, we recycle the process, focusing this time on aspects of the decision that require greater attention. Most R&D projects can be resolved in one or two iterations.

PolyChem's Project Dilemma

PolyChem was a leading maker of bulk chemicals, mostly polyolefins, a family of chemicals used in plastic cases for computer equipment, carpeting, and other items. This was a commodity business that commanded low profit margins. The company's fortunes rose and fell with the general business cycle and with current levels of industry capacity—neither of which it could control. PolyChem's senior executives wanted to escape from this situation. To do so, they committed the firm to a technology strategy aimed at creating unique, high-margin chemicals. The stated goal of this strategy was to derive 30 percent of the company's revenues from such products within five years.

With the backing of senior management and substantial R&D investments, PolyChem's laboratory scientists made notable progress in developing a revolutionary process for creating a high-performance material, which we will call HPM. This material had electromagnetic properties that were more readily alterable than other compounds, a characteristic with important ramifications for designing the color and brittleness of final products.

The R&D team working on HPM was excited about its potential, even though progress in solving a set of technical problems was slower than anticipated. They already had a working lab model of the process and were eager to move toward commercialization. To that end, the R&D team developed an HPM business plan and sought approval to build a pilot production plant. The president of the Chemicals Division liked what he saw and backed the plan. To him and to several other managers, HPM had much going for it:

▲ It would give PolyChem leadership in the technology.
▲ It fit with the strategic goal of 30 percent of future revenues from specialty chemicals.
▲ It addressed a potentially huge demand for a material that could be altered electromagnetically.

This made development of HPM a very interesting proposition, but not everyone in the organization shared the R&D team's enthusiasm. "This thing still has technical problems to be worked out, and that should be done in the lab, not in production," said the production VP. "The business plan is neither realistic nor practical," complained the marketing VP. "We know very little about the market for this stuff." "Let's stick to a business we understand," counselled others.

The VP of finance was the least convinced of HPM's merits. By his reckoning, the R&D team had already spent a great deal of money and *still* faced costly technical hurdles. He was in a camp that advocated out-licensing the technology already developed.

To further complicate this situation, a competitor was lurking in the background. PolyChem understood that another firm was conducting similar research with a different process, a process that had already received initial regulatory approval. The existence of this competitor evoked different responses, depending on one's faith or lack of faith in HPM. For HPM adherents, the presence of a credible competitor simply confirmed the wisdom of moving boldly into pilot production; for disbelievers, it was all the more reason to be cautious.

In traditional settings, this kind of organizational dissonance would be resolved in traditional ways: People would form into opposing camps and argue based upon assumptions that supported their different views. "Dialogue" would be little more than unproductive advocacy with little or no revelation of useful information.

PolyChem, however, applied a dialogue decision process to the issue. Two teams were set up to evaluate the R&D team's proposal: a high-level decision team to give direction and make the ultimate decisions about the project, and a strategy team to carry out a careful evaluation.

The division president and his VPs of project management, R&D, production, finance, and marketing all formed the steering committee. Their job was to properly frame the issues and certify the quality of the inputs and analysis on which decisions would be made. The strategy team included the HPM project leader and a crossfunctional group of individuals closely associated with the project. Their responsibilities were to:

- ▲ develop alternatives
- ▲ gather information
- ▲ identify the key uncertainties
- ▲ structure dialogue among participants

- ▲ analyze data
- ▲ develop insight

This teaming approach moved the decision situation forward. Designed around dialogue, it is based on the principle of alignment and empowerment. The process steps gave discipline to the decision and set up the teams for success in building a quality decision.

Structuring the Problem

As one might imagine, the dialogue between these two groups could have opened the floodgates to dozens of important questions relative to HPM: Does the company really belong in the specialty chemicals business? Does it have the marketing and manufacturing capabilities to support movement into that area? Should it go into the business alone or through a joint venture? Is the corporation properly organized to undertake specialty chemicals?

The decision team accepted strategic decisions already reached at the technology strategy level, such as the decision to venture into specialty chemicals. Implementation decisions were deferred. For example, the details of a licensing agreement would only need to be studied if they decided to halt further R&D on HPM. This focused the teams on answering the key questions about whether HPM should be pursued, and if so, in what way.

Identifying the Uncertainties

One root of the conflict was perspective on the uncertainties. One camp saw the technical factors as manageable; the other saw them as a major potential showstopper. The principle of Embracing Uncertainty requires communicating clearly about these uncertainties. PolyChem developed an influence diagram to describe what Poly-Chem did not know but needed to understand to make a decision. This was a useful instrument for identifying the uncertainties that must be thought through and for indicating how different factors influence others in the business.

For example, in Figure 11-3, HPM value, the expected SHV contributed by HPM, is the unknown that the team needed to understand above all others. The principle of Value Creation Culture was in operation. This recognition, that they all agreed that SHV was the ul-

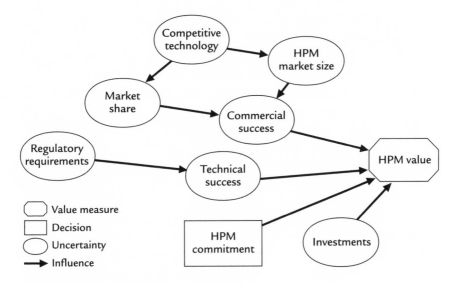

Figure 11-3. *The HPM Influence Diagram*

timate objective, made a major step in bringing the teams to mutual understanding. The teams started to realize that the different camps were built around honest differences of perspective, not political rhetoric.

The camps also agreed on the major factors influencing value: the level of commercial success (as well as the level of investment and technical success), which in turn is influenced by market share and the size of the market, both of which are influenced by competitive technology. Making uncertainties and influences explicit helped team members determine which uncertainties were worth discussing and assessing further.

Defining Alternatives as Decisions

"Let's sell the rights to what we've developed so far," suggested the marketing VP. "We just don't know enough about the market for HPM to make further commitments. I have no idea what level of revenue to forecast from this project."

The financial VP concurred, "Granted, HPM might be a good bet in the long run. But there are lots of technical uncertainties remaining. The investment needed to get the business off the ground could be huge. On the other hand, we've estimated that we could sell the rights now for $25 million. That would recoup our current investment in HPM and earn us a small profit."

But the project leader and his camp stuck with their initial position. "Yes, there are risks, but HPM is as good a project as we're likely to see for some time to support our strategy of moving into specialty chemicals. And in case anyone has forgotten, that's what senior management has told us to do. Let's reaffirm our commitment to HPM by building a pilot plant now. Once it's up and running, we can finalize the blend and validate its properties. The technical and marketing issues can be solved as we move ahead. It's up to the marketing staff to find potential customers for the full range of applications of this material." (Henceforth, we refer to this approach as the "conventional" strategy.)

This conflict was productively moved forward by appealing to the principle of Creating Alternatives. Each view was developed into a coherent alternative for PolyChem. This shifted the perspective away from arguments about which position was best. The conventional strategy (build a pilot plant now) was listed as one alternative. The proposal offered by HPM's opponents, the "sell-the-technology" strategy, defined a second alternative. Participants were challenged to come up with other significantly different alternatives. Extensive debate led to a third alternative that no one really advocated, but which both camps agreed deserved consideration, the "streamlined approach."

The streamlined approach called for the installation of a "bench-scale screw" capable of producing 20 tons of HPM per year and for outsourcing base polymer production. This facility would produce moderate quantities of the material and provide an opportunity to work out technical problems at a reduced level of investment. A mini production plant could be built later. Rather than targeting all possible applications, development would focus on selected market applications aimed at enhancing PolyChem's core business in polyolefins. Figure 11-4 describes the time line of activities in the conventional and streamlined strategies.

Like many middle-ground alternatives, the streamlined strategy satisfied some objections of both camps while gaining the immediate backing of neither. Simply creating it, however, served a useful purpose: Individual members of the opposing camps had to consider alternatives to their current positions—an important step in breaking out of a counterproductive advocacy process.

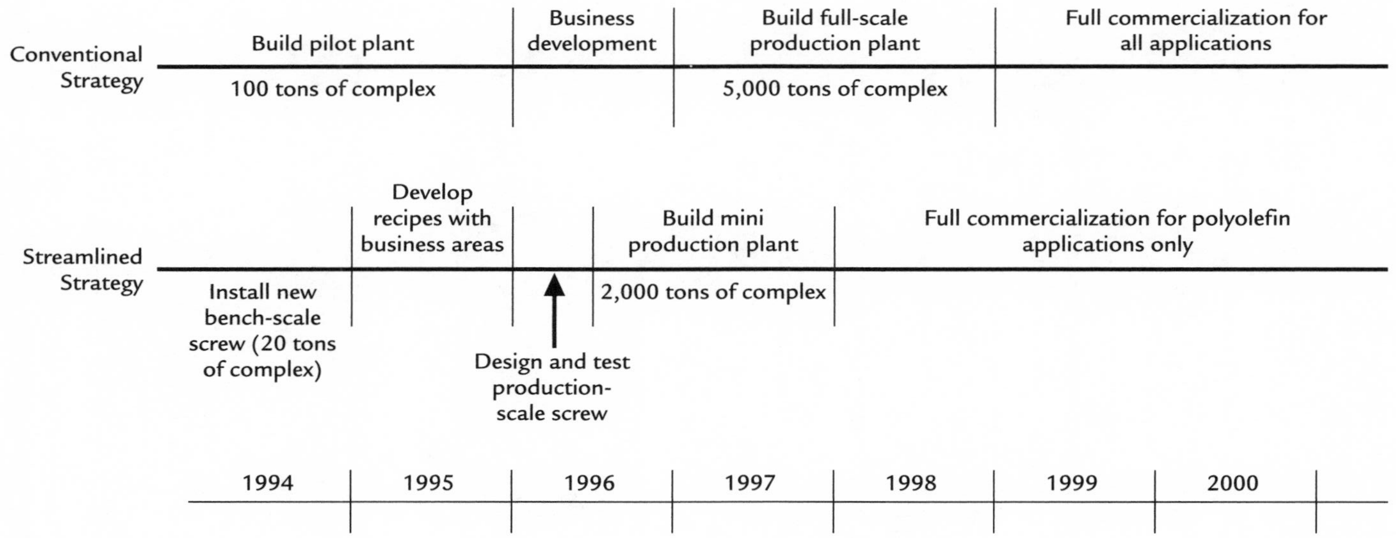

Figure 11-4. *Time Lines for the Conventional and Streamlined Strategies*

Deterministic Analysis

Once the team had three project alternatives on the table—conventional strategy, streamlined strategy, and sell-the-rights—the strategy team went after the details. Its goal was to understand what was really important in determining the value of each alternative.

Everyone agreed that the value of each alternative would be affected by a number of factors: the discount rate applied to projected cash flows, various costs, revenues, and so forth. These factors would be affected by yet other factors. Revenues, for example, would be affected by the size of the HPM market, pricing, and PolyChem's share of the market. A spreadsheet (Figure 11-5) representing this complex of factors was developed by several team members with the values of each linked dynamically to a calculation of overall value. Each alternative was modeled in this fashion.

In agreeing to evaluate the alternatives in this fashion, the teams were using the principle of Systems Thinking. They agreed that it was too complex to intuit the implications of each alternative for value creation, and so chose to work through the chain of cause and effect.

The sell-the-rights alternative was relatively straightforward, but the other two involved a high level of modeling complexity *and* a number of important assessments of uncertain inputs to the model, an activity requiring both systems thinking and embracing uncertainty. One could say, in fact, that the assessments would be the key determinants of value. To ensure a level playing field, team members enforced a critical discipline: They made sure that all alternatives (and different scenarios under these alternatives) adhered to the same assessments. For instance, the median assessment for HPM market size in the year 2000—for both the conventional and streamlined strategy—was 10,000 tons. Likewise, both alternatives assessed that the next generation of technology was most likely to enter the market in 2009. Assessments about factors that would naturally vary with alternatives (capital investments, annual R&D costs, variable costs, etc.) were allowed to vary in the spreadsheet. These combined to make what we call a *base case scenario* for how the world might turn out.

The spreadsheet was used to project cash flows and calculate NPV, as an estimate of shareholder value, looking out over seven years of actual production. For the base case scenario, the graph of Figure 11-6 shows that the conventional strategy appeared to be the superior alternative. But was it?

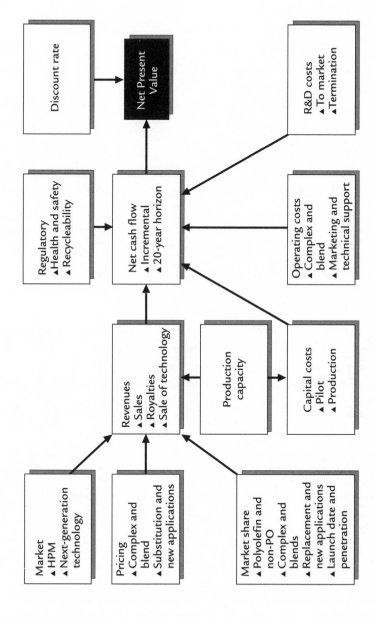

Figure 11-5. *A Dynamically Linked Model for HPM Value*

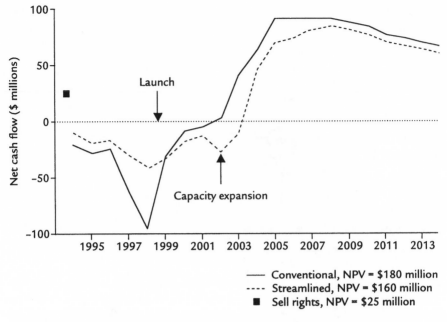

Figure 11-6. *Project Cash Flows Using the Base Case Scenario*

At this point, everyone on the team could testify that the HPM strategy had *already* been given greater systematic scrutiny than had any past project strategy; and some team members were inclined to go ahead with the conventional strategy. It was the best strategy *if* the base case assessments were realized and *if* everything worked as planned. The financial VP objected to pursuing the conventional strategy. "You've assumed technical success," he complained. "Of course it looks like a good strategy. My point is that the new material is not likely to work!"

He was right in the sense that not a single base case assessment was certain. Instead, they were simply point estimates in a *range* of possible outcomes. Consider the conventional strategy's base case that the market for its HPM would be 10,000 tons in the year 2000. This was the median case, but other outcomes were possible. Further analysis indicated a 10 percent chance that the total HPM market in that year could be less than 2 thousand tons and a 90 percent chance that demand could be as high as 20,000 tons. The base production launch date, which was given as 1999, had a 10 percent chance of occurring before 1998 and a significant chance of being delayed past the year

2000. The impact of these unforeseen outcomes on calculated NPV could be dramatic. Imagine the negative impact if the plant opening were delayed by a full year, or if market demand for HPM were only half of the base case. On the other hand, total market demand of 20,000 tons would make NPV extremely high!

To visualize how these uncertainties might impact the value of each strategy, team members conducted sensitivity analysis. They varied each of the inputs over its assessed range of uncertainty and determined the corresponding range of uncertainty of the NPV. Then they constructed a bar graph of these NPV ranges for each input, rank ordering them by their potential impact. Figure 11-7 is the resulting tornado chart for the conventional strategy (the chart for the streamlined strategy was similar). It indicated the most important uncertainties at a glance.

Along the top is a scale of NPV. The center line, at $180 million, is the value of the conventional strategy if every uncertainty is at its base case value: market size at 10,000 tons, base pricing, 50 percent polyolefin share, health and safety approvals obtained, and so on. The horizontal bars show the impact of varying the uncertainty from its base case. For example, if the market size turned out to be only 2,000 tons, the value of the conventional strategy would drop to about *minus* $250 million. On the other hand, if it turned out to be 20,000 tons, the value would increase to about *plus* $600 million. This uncertainty has the largest impact on the value of HPM and is therefore the most important item for further discussion.

The potential impact of uncertain market demand underscores the marketing VP's initial concerns about the project. Pricing can also swing the value substantially, but all possible price levels still result in a positive value.

On the other hand, the financial VP's concerns over capital investments were clearly misplaced. Capital spending on either the low end or high end of the range would have negligible impact on the project's value. This occurs over and over again in project strategies: Variables crucial to profitable operations, such as capital cost, sometimes have little impact on overall value from a strategic perspective. This does not mean they should be neglected operationally, but only that further refinement should be delayed until implementation.

The tornado chart made very clear the impact of what PolyChem did *not* know and told team members which uncertainties had to be discussed further. The principles of Embracing Uncertainty and Sys-

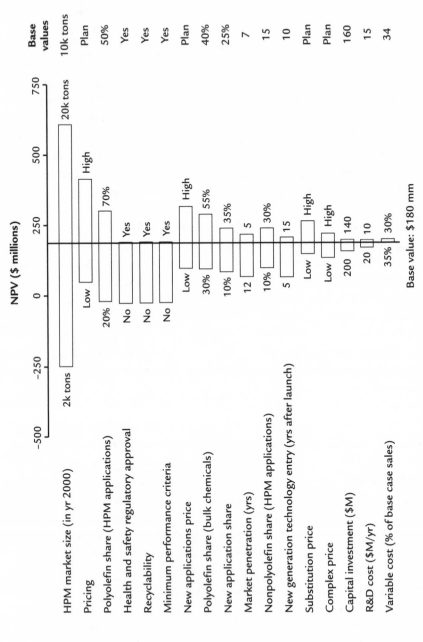

Figure 11-7. *The Most Important Uncertainties for HPM*

tems Thinking had helped them focus on the few factors that were very important to the decision. Companies that fail to practice this type of sensitivity analysis often lapse into lengthy debates about the least relevant issues. For example, in the absence of sensitivity analysis, the financial VP might have diverted efforts into a lengthy reestimation of each alternative's capital requirements. Greater precision in this area, however, would have added little value to the *strategic* decision.

The tornado charts were eye-openers for many on the project team and motivated them to proceed with the next step of the decision process: probabilistic evaluation.

Probabilistic Evaluation

Probabilistic evaluation is the third step in the four-step model. It helped the teams understand the risks and returns of each course of action by identifying the most important sources of uncertainty, assigning probabilities to a range of potential outcomes, and calculating the impact of hundreds or thousands of potential scenarios. Doing this improved their understanding of which is the best alternative. To simplify discussion of the application of this step to the PolyChem case, we only discuss two areas of uncertainty here. The first involves market demand; the second considers regulatory approvals.

PolyChem's biggest range of uncertainty was in its assessment of total market demand for HPM. Lacking hard numbers, the project team decided to develop scenarios within which certain levels of demand would appear. Table 11-1 describes their findings. Here, the optimistic scenario of 20,000 tons is associated with a combination of market-stimulating factors. The likelihood of this optimistic scenario was assessed to be 25 percent. Scenarios for the base case and for low-end levels of demand were developed in the same way.

Assessing the probability of regulatory approval required understanding the various technical hurdles. Four different approvals were required for a material like HPM: the base polymer, the active complex, additives, and recyclability. Knowledgeable individuals were queried as to the probability of approval for each—given current information and requirements. Then these individual probabilities were multiplied together to obtain an overall probability of approval

Table 11-1. *Total HPM Market Demand under Different Scenarios*

	WORLDWIDE HPM MARKET SIZE IN YEAR 2000	SCENARIO
High (25%)	20,000	▲ Price-performance advantages superior to competition for current applications ▲ Significant processing advantages ▲ Unique new applications found in all areas
Base (50%)	10,000	▲ Some price-performance advantages over competition for current applications ▲ Tailorable electromagnetic properties
Low (25%)	2,000	▲ No advantages over competition for current applications ▲ Only advantage is tailorable electromagnetic properties

(Table 11-2). Market constraints played a part in determining probabilities. That is, R&D personnel had to assess probabilities against a backdrop of processes and materials whose costs and availabilities would support a marketable product.

This level of understanding settled a long-standing debate between the project leader and the VP of finance. The VP of finance had been saying, "There are so many obstacles to getting the product on the market that we will never make it. There is no point in throwing good money after bad." The project leader had countered, "Of course the project is uncertain but we can overcome every single hurdle." One of the values of measuring potential success in terms of probability is that probability is a universal language that both lab scientists and nontechnical business managers can understand. The chance of passing *each* hurdle was 90 percent or greater, but the chance of passing *all* of the hurdles was only 77 percent. With this new understanding, the VP of finance backed off a bit from his conclusion that proceeding would throw good money after bad. If the probability of success can be established with some confidence, discussion is more productive.

Table 11-2. *Understanding the Probability of Regulatory Approval*

COMPONENT	PROBABILITY OF APPROVAL
Base polymer	1.0
Active complex	0.95
Other additives	0.9
Recyclability	0.9
Overall	0.77

Base polymer approval has already been obtained by a competitor.
Active complex (with a different dopant) has already been listed by the competitor.
Success of active complex and plasticiser assumes it is at a cost that still allows a
 competitively priced product.
The base polymer may not be recyclable due to emission of potential noxious gas.

Considering All Scenarios

Once they had assessed the probabilities associated with each uncertainty, the project team prepared to look at the full risk and return of
each alternative.

The tornado diagram considered many scenarios, but the team
only looked at varying one uncertainty at a time. For example, "What
would happen if the market size were 20,000 tons?" Understanding
the full range of possibilities requires consideration of combination
scenarios as well. "What happens if market size is 20,000 tons and the
price is low?"

Based on combinations of the most important uncertainties, the
team identified 493 scenarios that needed evaluation. These scenarios are shown schematically in Figure 11-8. Following the conventional strategy, the first uncertainty in need of resolution is health
and safety approval. If R&D fails at this point, PolyChem experiences
a relatively small loss. If it succeeds, the next uncertainty is achieving
the minimum performance criteria. Failure at this later point means
a larger loss.[1] On the other hand, consider success at this point in the
tree. As the product is commercialized the real money kicks in!

The next string of uncertainties describes levels of the commercial
success: market size, pricing, share, and so on. If all were to combine
in PolyChem's favor (20,000 ton market size, high prices, 70 percent
share, etc.), then the business would be worth $1,500 million in NPV.
This scenario, unfortunately, was not very likely. If all the factors
combined against PolyChem (2,000 ton market size, low prices, 20

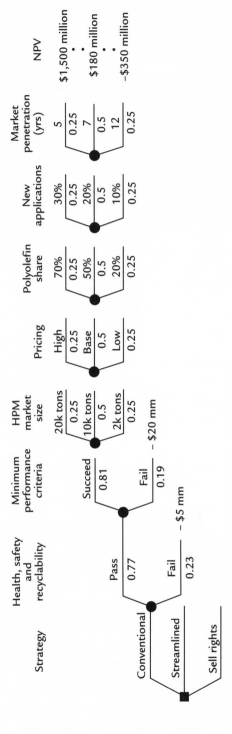

Figure 11-8. *Decision Tree for the Conventional Strategy*

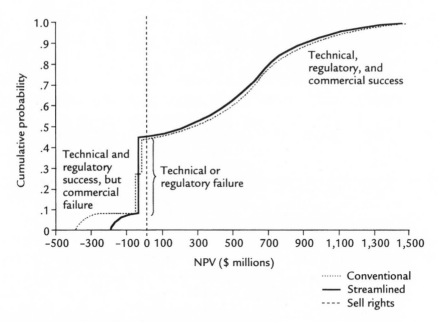

Figure 11-9. *The Risk and Return of Each Strategy*

percent share, etc.), then the company would face a loss of $350 million. Fortunately, this scenario was not very likely either. The base case scenario, with each uncertainty at its middle value, resulted in $180 million of value. Values near this amount were more likely than near the extremes.

Since this product could vary from blockbuster to expensive failure in the marketplace, the real question was, How to balance the upside against the downside? Is pursuing it a wise calculated risk?[2]

Now Which Looks Best?

The PolyChem team produced a set of curves indicating the cumulative probability of NPV for the three strategies, shown in Figure 11-9. These curves were calculated by finding the NPV implied by each scenario and the probability that it would occur. The scenarios were then sorted from worst to best and plotted on a cumulative basis.

To read the graph, pick a target NPV, say the $180 million level for the base case of the conventional strategy. Go up from $180 million to the curve; it intersects the probability axis at approximately 55 percent. This means that the probability of getting $180 million *or less* is

55 percent—the scenarios that have lower NPVs add up to this probability. This means the probability of *exceeding* $180 million in value is 45 percent.

The sell-the-rights strategy is straightforward. Its curve is a dashed vertical line. Its outcome is $25 million and has a probability of 100 percent.

To appreciate the differences among strategies consider three parts of the curve: upside, technical failure, and downside.[3]

The length of the curve to the right of $0 NPV is the *upside*, where on a discounted basis the results create more than enough value to cover the costs. Here, technical and regulatory issues have been overcome, and commercial challenges have generally worked out favorably. If every commercial factor turned out in the company's favor, it would be in the upper-right corner at $1,500 million NPV. Consider a point on the curve where NPV is $500 million. Here, the company has enjoyed technical and regulatory success, and many commercial possibilities have worked in its favor. Note that both streamlined and conventional strategy have similar curves in the upside region. This means that the potential for return from both projects is about the same.

The vertical drop in both curves shows the possibility of *technical failure*. If either project alternative fails to reach the market, Poly-Chem stands to lose a modest R&D investment. Again, these lines are more or less on top of each other. The loss is about the same, and the probability of technical failure is about the same. Both lines drop from about 47 percent to about 7 percent, for a probability of technical failure of about 40 percent. In terms of risk of technical failure, both projects are about the same.

The *downside* part of the curve (to the left of the vertical drop) represents technical and regulatory success, but commercial failure. This is the worst possible outcome, because the R&D and capital expenses of getting the process approved and launched have already been incurred. Here the conventional and streamlined strategies part company, with conventional—because of its larger capital investment—resulting in the greater loss. The two strategies differ only in their downside potential, with the conventional strategy risking larger losses.

Which strategy looks better now? At this point the decision team and strategy team were in a far superior position to make a decision. With the greater insights of probability-based valuation, they could

Table 11-3. *Comparison of Strategies by Shareholder Value Strategy*

STRATEGY	SHAREHOLDER VALUE
Conventional	$110 million
Streamlined	$125 million
Sell rights	$25 million

see that the conventional and streamlined strategies produced no materially different values under conditions of technical, regulatory, and commercial success. In the event of commercial failure, however, the streamlined strategy would produce a much smaller loss to Poly-Chem.

To make a final comparison of the ability of each alternative to create shareholder value, the team used a probability-weighted average NPV, or expected NPV. In situations where the size of the project is small relative to the size of the company, that is the best number valuation of the entire probability distribution.[4] Table 11-3 shows the numbers the decision makers had to consider.

This table verifies the insights: The streamlined strategy is better than the conventional strategy (by $15 million). And both of them are substantially better than selling the rights now, which would result in a loss of $100 million in shareholder value relative to the streamlined strategy.

Appraisal

The final step of the project decision process is to ask, Do we know enough to move to a decision? For most members of the PolyChem team, the answer was now "yes." But there were two important hold-outs. The first was the HPM project leader. She had been working on the underlying technology of this material for a number of years and was committed to making HPM a major new business. For her, the streamlined strategy felt like a half-measure and a signal that the corporation was not entirely committed to her project. The second hold-out was the financial VP, who still could not see HPM as an important new source of value for the corporation. To him it was a risky venture with little likelihood of real success. He continued to favor the sure thing—selling the rights.

Other members of the team respected the concerns of their two colleagues, but believed those concerns were misplaced. Rather than outvote them, and risk alienating them from the future course of action, they decided to provide each with a different perspective on the data. They developed a summary table (Table 11-4) that indicated *what would have to be true* for each strategy to be the best alternative. We call this *robustness analysis.*

The VP of R&D explained the table to the two dissenters. "If you look at the base case, in which everything is set at its median value, the best strategy is the streamlined approach (the middle column under Best Strategy). If you knew for sure that the market size would be only 2,000 tons per year—the low end of our probability distribution—then selling the rights would make sense. Similarly, if you believed that prices would be low, the share would be low, or there were limited new applications, then the best strategy would be to sell the rights. On the other hand, if you knew for sure that the market size would be 20,000 tons per year—the other extreme—the conventional strategy would be best. In fact, that would be the *only* situation under which the conventional strategy would be superior."

Looking the project leader in the eye, he continued: "If you really believe that the market will be 20,000 tons, then show us the evidence. If you can't, you're not holding a sustainable position."

The project leader was a tough-minded scientist who understood the numbers and was honest enough to recognize when her feelings were getting in the way of her judgment. "No, I don't have the evidence," she conceded, "just a strong belief in HPM and the people who are working on it. In fact, I do not have a full perspective on the market. Since the VP of marketing came up with the probability distribution, it is a better assessment than I could make myself. I'll accept the streamlined strategy."

The financial VP also relented. "If I really believed the market was going to be 2 thousand tons, I should change jobs. I'm not a marketing expert, so I cannot say with any certainty that the HPM market won't develop. I guess I was just trying to be conservative in looking after our money." He understood that if the company wanted to generate higher returns for its shareholders, it would have to take calculated risks.

The result of this process was complete consensus and alignment around the new strategy, which no one had favored initially. Everyone enthusiastically supported a strategy none of them liked at the

Table 11-4. Robustness Analysis for HPM

KEY UNCERTAINTY	UNCERTAIN RESULT			BEST STRATEGY		
	Low (1/10)	Medium (50/50)	High(1/10)	Low (1/10)	Medium (50/50)	High (1/10)
(Tons/yr) HPM market size in year 2000	2,000	10,000	20,000	Sell rights	Streamlined	Conventional
HPM prices	Low (−35%)	Base	High (+50%)	Sell rights	Streamlined	Streamlined
Share in Polyolefin applications	20%	50%	70%	Sell rights	Streamlined	Streamlined
New applications	10%	25%	35%	Sell rights	Streamlined	Streamlined
Market penetration rate	5	7	12	Streamlined	Streamlined	Streamlined
Minimum performance criteria probability	60%	81%	95%	Streamlined	Streamlined	Streamlined
Conventional capital investment ($ M)	140	160	200	Streamlined	Streamlined	Streamlined
R&D cost ($ M/yr)	10	15	20	Streamlined	Streamlined	Streamlined

beginning when the streamlined strategy was introduced as a poor compromise. In the end, overwhelming evidence pointed to it as the best option for the corporation.

Situations like PolyChem's are commonplace. Wherever R&D is conducted, decision makers find themselves confronted with different approaches to the same project—different approaches whose values and risks are unclear. It is equally common for people to form opposing camps, each bent on single-mindedly advancing their own approach. Lines are drawn, and each camp advocates for a decision in its favor.

As shown in this chapter, there are practical methods for making project decisions in situations of uncertainty that embody the principles of smart R&D—methods that are far superior to advocacy.

PART V

BEYOND R&D

CHAPTER 12

THE SMART ORGANIZATION

> If you want to change the culture
> of an organization, change the
> way it makes decisions. The rest
> will follow. *Vince Barabba*

P REVIOUS CHAPTERS of this book have drawn on R&D cases and examples to explain quality decision making. This chapter makes the case that the principles, practices, and processes that ensure decision quality in R&D can do the same elsewhere in the enterprise—at any level—creating the "smart organization." Indeed, quality in *any* decision contributes to overall performance, whether that decision involves a merger, capital spending, the choice of distribution channels, joint ventures, or anything else of strategic significance. All quality decisions shift the odds of success in favor of the enterprise.

William K. Linvill, the founder of the Engineering-Economics Department of Stanford University, was dedicated to searching for "portable concepts," powerful concepts that could cut across many different situations. We have come to appreciate the principles of the smart organization as portable concepts. If understood and properly applied, they can motivate and generate high-quality strategic decisions in any setting. Anyone who consistently applies these principles will uncover best practices and be drawn to tools that effectively support strategic decision processes. In working with these principles, we have learned how to cut through situations that stifle decision making in any area in many organizations. They provide a practical road map to what is needed and what might be going wrong. We have even found them helpful in personal decisions![1]

Competitive Bidding

To appreciate the universality of decision quality concepts, consider an example far removed from the field of R&D: competitive bidding.

The following case illustrates what can go wrong without the principles of Embracing Uncertainty and Outside-In Strategic Perspective.

In the early 1990s, a South American country was privatizing its state-owned steel plants through a complex bidding system. The major player in that country, which we will call SA Steel, saw in this an opportunity to significantly expand its production capacity. In preparing its bid, SA executives had to answer a key question, What was the value of these plants? Their value would guide SA's bidding. The executives knew there would be serious competition for the plants and wanted to avoid overpaying.

In assisting SA Steel we worked with Stephan, the senior staff member responsible for estimating the value of the state-owned plants. Stephan had built a quantitative model of the steel industry and of SA Steel's anticipated role in its future. He ran simulations of this projected future with SA Steel owning and not owning the plants now on the auction block. Using the difference in valuation between these two cases, he could estimate the value of the plants to SA Steel.

Stephan's approach to the problem was genuine and thoughtful, but there was a systematic bias in his assumptions. The case based on *not* owning the plants was based on SA's carefully developed current business plans. The case based on SA's plant acquisitions, however, was based on a long string of highly conservative assumptions about how the market would develop and about SA Steel's ability to capitalize on its new assets. This case did not embrace uncertainty.

We worked with Stephan and his group for several days, trying to improve their thinking on the uncertainties associated with the plant purchases. In the end, we produced a probability distribution of potential values. Stephan's initial estimate was at about the twentieth percentile. In other words, most scenarios indicated that the value of the plants to SA Steel were far higher than his conservative estimate. Even so, Stephan interpreted this as validating his conservative assumptions and his strategy of bidding low to avoid overpaying.

Several weeks later, SA Steel submitted its bid to the government, as did several other industrial companies. We got a call from Stephan shortly thereafter. He was in shock. SA Steel had come out of the bidding empty-handed. It had been the low bidder, and by a wide margin. The next bid was over three times higher than his and the winning bid was still higher. By failing to embrace the uncertainty in the valuation, Stephan had lost a major opportunity.

Stephan's problem was not simply his approach to uncertainty.

His model compared what SA Steel could do with the plants compared to its current business plan: an inside-out perspective. He
should have started with an outside-in perspective, considering what
would happen if a major competitor acquired the state-owned plants.
Stephan's biggest fear was that SA Steel would overpay. He should
have feared the consequences of a major competitor entering its markets with these plants—which is what happened!

Picking Winners in Hollywood

Motion picture production decisions are far removed from the usual
world of R&D. But they do require the same smart principles, including Disciplined Decision Making, Systems Thinking, and Embracing
Uncertainty, as the following case indicates.

One of the major motion picture companies found itself in a crisis.
It had lost heavily on a number of expensive, star-studded releases,
and its creative staff had been unable to propose a solid slate of films
for the coming year. Its "green light" decisions—decisions to fund
particular movies—were a mess, characterized by high-paid executives
trying to pick winners by second-guessing casting choices and quib-
bling with scriptwriters. Hit-and-miss results had caused 100 percent
turnover in the top management team over the past few years.

In analyzing this situation for the studio, we found that its decision makers were following counterproductive principles. Like other
movie studios, they reviewed thousands of scripts each year. From
these they would select about twenty for production. You would
think that this winnowing process by experienced movie executives
would considerably reduce the risk in the handful of projects that got
the green light. But the data tells a different story. The selected film
projects were full of uncertainty! About 5 percent of all major films
become big money-makers. About 50 percent are money-losers, and
the remaining 45 percent yield a small profit.

Our movie moguls were, in effect, presiding over a portfolio of potential pearls, oysters, and white elephants with different return and
uncertainty characteristics, but they didn't behave like portfolio
managers. Instead, studio executives relied on a presumptive sixth
sense for picking winners. Unfortunately, their intuitive ability was
unsupported by statistical evidence.

Embracing uncertainty in this case meant managing the film portfolio. The studio could have anticipated losing money on most films.

By managing the portfolio well, however, it could have raised the chances that one or more films would be the blockbusters that would pay for all the losses and still produce a profit.

In the strange world of Hollywood, however, the term *portfolio management* is not a familiar phrase. Movie executives desperately try to pick winners, often doubling their bets by spending up to $20 million on one of the few stars they think will draw people to the box office. These high costs in turn undermine the ability of the small number of successful films to generate sufficient profits to cover the losses of other studio films. The big winners in this situation seem to be a handful of film stars and their agents.

Capital Investment

A manufacturer was about to invest in a large new plant. All signs were favorable: Demand was robust and growing, and prices were high. The decision seemed obvious. But if things went wrong, the investment level could nearly bankrupt the company. So management went to great lengths to avoid a mistake. It commissioned a process to create a quality decision. Crucial insights for this process came from systems thinking and an outside-in strategic perspective.

As part of the assessment, the working team built a dynamic supply and demand model for the product to be manufactured in the new plant. Recognizing that competitors had new plants in the planning stage, the team factored in the probability of their actual construction, and their effect on supply, demand, and pricing. They also realized that some of these competitors, particularly in southeast Asia, were going to build these plants whether profitable or not, because the governments of those countries wanted to industrialize. The model predicted, under a very wide range of scenarios, a significant price drop in the near future.

Based on this analysis, management decided against plant construction and directed its resources to a more promising alternative investment. Within less than a year—well before the time the new plant would have gone on line—prices dropped, and the firm's competitors began taking losses with no end in sight.

Institutionalizing Decision Quality

We have found opportunities for applying the principles and practices of the smart organization in virtually every industry and in many kinds of decision situations. In every case in which management has heeded their conclusions, these applications have improved the outcome of strategic decisions. Their greatest value is not found in individual decisions but in the *sum* of an organization's collective decisions. It is usually far better to make quality decisions routinely than make one or two of them well. This can only happen to the extent that organizations institutionalize the principles and practices of decision quality. This is a major challenge, because it requires substantial change in organizational culture and the attitudes of managers and employees. This is never easy, but there is a proven way forward.

It is difficult if not impossible to change an entire large organization in a single stroke. In fact, we are hard pressed to think of a single example of sustained success. Besides the magnitude of the task, attempting a massive "rollout" invites chaos and provides naysayers with opportunities for resistance. Organizational change by degrees, beginning in narrow areas, is more likely to succeed. Obstacles can be understood, the plan can be adjusted based on lessons learned, and early successes convert doubters to supporters. Successful change in narrow areas can then be rolled out to successively larger corporate arenas.

For most situations, application of the dialogue decision process to important but circumscribed strategy decisions is an effective method for initiating organizational change. As people become more adept in use of the DDP and its methods, and as its value becomes broadly recognized, its use can be extended to larger and more diverse decision situations.

Transforming General Motors

One striking example of the institutionalization of decision quality—and of the DDP in particular—can be found at General Motors Corporation (GM), where it has revolutionized decision making over the last decade.

The broad application of decision quality at GM roughly coincides with the hiring of Vincent P. Barabba in 1985 as director of market research and planning. Barabba, a nationally known figure in market research and a former director of the U.S. Census Bureau, was one of several high-level individuals brought on-board during the mid-1980s to help the giant auto maker reform itself. GM was facing enormous competitive challenges at the time, and its tradition-breaking search for outside talent reflected the magnitude of its concern. GM executives knew that the company had to change, and were searching for outside ideas. They gave Barabba a charter to intervene in the decision process and supported his efforts.

Barabba had come from Eastman Kodak where he had learned about our approach to decision quality first hand. At GM, he assembled a team of people with backgrounds in decision analysis and brought in the decision quality advisors he had met while at Eastman Kodak. Together, they held a series of seminars to familiarize their GM colleagues with decision quality concepts. These seminars convinced a broad set of influential GM managers that decision quality had potential value and, with their cooperation, several projects were identified as subjects for its application.

Using a small staff organized into a strategic decision center, and supported by outside consultants, the DDP was applied to several decisions. The first application was not fully successful; it was simply too big for the embryonic group to handle. This was an important lesson. Barabba later conceded that he had learned the principle of Continual Learning: "We made mistakes, but we learned from them, and several people saw merit in the new approach."

Fortunately, Barabba had a mandate to keep trying, and successful applications followed. These included product development leading to the 1997 Buick Park Avenue model, and a portfolio of advanced research developments in product engineering. These early successes were greatly facilitated by the presence of several knowledgeable people on the review boards.

Building Quality In

At the time of Barabba's arrival from Eastman Kodak, General Motors was a functionally organized company with a command-and-control approach to management. Strategic and product decisions were generally made in a courtroom-like atmosphere, where contending parties advanced their proposals. "People saw their jobs as bringing their own ideas forward and getting them approved," according to Barabba. "It was someone else's job to shoot them down." To be precise, it was the job of decision makers and the company's thousands of staff analysts to challenge these proposals and determine which were valid and superior. This approach had its analogy in the quality assurance programs practiced by GM and other industrial companies prior to the 1980s. In these programs, quality was "inspected in." Products coming off the assembly line were examined by teams of inspectors to determine whether they met specifications. Those that did were shipped; those that did not were scrapped or reworked. The same method was being applied to decision making.

Modern quality methods, however, have eliminated the need for inspectors by creating processes that make products right *the first time*. What Barabba and his colleagues sought was a process that would ensure that proposals brought to the firm's decision forums would, like its products, meet quality standards the first time. In fact, they had little choice: Between 1986 and 1996, the ranks of GM's corporate staff analysts—the quality inspectors—were slated for dramatic reductions. Most of them soon would be gone.

To change this culture into one that supported seeking alternatives to create more value, Barabba and his colleagues created the analogy of a "test well." Initial ideas (alternatives) were like test wells used to explore the territory and gain insight into where greatest value might be. There was no expectation that the site of this test well was the best place to drill. After sinking a number of these test wells (i.e., after putting forth a number of alternatives), GM teams evaluated them. In the process they gained insights for hybrid "production wells" that captured the most value. These hybrid solutions usually proved to be more powerful than the initial proposals.

The ethic of seeking alternatives has now become so grounded at GM that when someone presents an idea, he or she is always asked, "What else have you considered?" In the new GM culture, alternatives must be considered and evaluated. Paradoxically, this new habit has *shortened* GM's product development time. The old process of sending project proposals back for rework had been terribly time consuming, giving GM the slowest product cycle time in the industry. "We didn't understand until later," Barabba explained, "how the old product champion system had forced design and manufacturing to make time-consuming mistakes."

> Now when someone asks, "Did you consider x?" or "Did you run the numbers this way?" the answer is "Yes!" We don't have to keep reworking the problem. With the dialogue decision process cycle time has improved, and the process continues to

work well after the corporate staff has been downsized to fewer than one thousand.

GM also learned to involve resource allocators from the beginning. Using the DDP, these decision makers learned to ask questions such as:

▲ Did we get the right frame?

▲ Did we cover all the alternatives that could create value?

▲ Did we do the analysis in a way that demonstrates that we understood the situation?

▲ Do we agree?

At the end of this decision process, executives "nod" and resources are allocated. GM decision team members typically take part in about four half-day DDP meetings. The process starts slowly but ends fast, because, to quote Barabba, "When it's done it's done. There is no 're-work' of the final decision."

Analytical and People Power

General Motors initially thought the greatest value of the dialogue decision process would be its analytical methods of evaluation. These have, indeed, proven their power. For example, the tornado sensitivity diagram indicates sources of risk that the old ways hid. The estimates given by project advocates were invariably on the optimistic side of the range, leaving all the risk on the downside. In the old system "deception" was the only way to leap over unrealistically high financial hurdles.

However the real breakthrough for the new process came when a strategy team recommended acceptance of a project with a base case that did not meet the old financial hurdles. A lively and informative discussion ensued, during which mutual understanding of the risks and return of the project was developed. In the end, the executive decision team approved the project and gave up their old unrealistic financial hurdles.

Despite the power of the DDP's analytical tools, even greater value has been generated on the people side by bringing together the right people on important decisions, breaking down functional "silos," and obtaining agreement on action—a solid case of alignment and empowerment!

New Value of GM Stakeholders

Over time, more and more managers and engineers were familiarized with the new decision process, its unique vocabulary and technical tools. The process itself was applied to an expanding set of situations across GM's many operating units. By fall of 1996, over 100 applications of the DDP had been made, including every new product introduction. Today, every product decision goes through this process, which has been introduced to nearly every functional area of the company and in every region in which the company does business. Though the DDP was initially resisted by some overseas units as a "North American solution," these now see its usefulness and several recent applications have been made to global decisions.

How much value has this process created for the giant auto maker? Barabba will not be pinned down to hard numbers, but has benchmarked the process against the "momentum" strategies—those the company would most likely have followed in the absence of the process. For "small" vehicle programs—those spending $200–$400 million—the differences, according to his estimates, run in the range of $10 million to $50 million of shareholder value, as measured by the net present value of incremental cash flow. For major strategies, the difference was measured in billions. To be sure, much of this value potential has yet to be realized in shareholder value as the outside world sees tangible results from excellent implementation.

The Road Ahead

The dialogue decision process is now "in the DNA" of some parts of GM, where it supports disciplined decision making. The vehicle development program, for example, has written it into its manuals. The vehicle launch unit has developed its own customized version called, aptly, The Launch Process. A strategic decision center staffed with full-time decision specialists is available to help these and other GM units with the process.

The Least Painful Way to Change Corporate Culture

Much has been said and written about the need to change the culture of an organization to make it more agile and effective in competing in the global economy. Indeed, our own "principles" indicate the need for a value-creating business culture. Reorganization has been the tool of choice in transforming culture. In recent years, many companies have reorganized around essential processes—product development, customer fulfillment, and so forth—as a way to break apart powerful "silos" and connect more solidly with customers. Indeed, during the early 1990s the concept of "horizontal organization" gained great popularity.

Although reorganizing can improve operations, it is expensive and leaves many employees shell-shocked. Even worse, reorganizing does little to alter patterns of behavior. The old approaches to decision making survive and sprout anew in the reorganized company.

We contend that the processes and principles that support decision quality can be more effective than reorganization in reshaping the culture of the enterprise. Based upon his experience at GM, Vince Barabba contends that the most effective way to change the culture of an organization is to change the way it makes decisions. "The rest," he says, "will follow." This is happening today at General Motors.

Syncrude Canada

An example of another company in a different industry parallels the experience of General Motors in institutionalizing decision quality principles.[2]

Syncrude Canada is a unique organization—an oil producer owned by several oil companies. It produces crude oil from oil sands in Alberta's Fort McMurray area, where its leases hold 20 percent more oil than all of Saudi Arabia. To recover this oil Syncrude must mine the sands, often under harsh conditions, and turn it into crude through complex processing technology. This operation must run twenty-four hours a day, every day, to squeeze a return from the company's immense capital investments.

In 1989 Syncrude faced a daunting array of technical and political decisions. Its capital- and labor-intensive cost structure forced it to keep pushing the technological envelope to improve operating efficiency and profit margins. This brought it face to face with a number of strategic decisions: Which were the best mining and extraction technologies to pursue? How large did Syncrude want to become, and how much were its current (or new) owners willing to invest?

What royalty and tax terms would apply to new project investments? What environmental challenges were posed by expanding Syncrude's vast surface mining operations?

Decisions in these important areas were made more difficult by a strategic compass that pointed in many directions at once. Syncrude's different owners had different objectives for the company. As Eric Newell, new CEO at that time recounts, "We had a very complex and cluttered strategic agenda. In fact it was worse than that. We had four owners wanting to harvest the business and four owners wanting to grow it. So we had no consensus on what path we should be on." Further disagreements on whether to grow the business or milk the existing investment festered for lack of a strategic dialogue. Crucial planning information and assumptions were deemed too sensitive for each owner to share openly.

Syncrude needed to unblock its strategic agenda and begin developing the value potential of the business. Phil Lachambre, CFO and Vice President of Business and Corporate Affairs, describes how this belief drove the search for a solution:

> We had a shared belief among all our owners that there was value in this business if we could get at the right levers on the technology front, the cost front, and marketing. There was enough of a belief in the future potential of this industry that everyone was willing to work the strategic process in earnest, even though we were running at close to break-even in those days.

They did agree on a major principle; Syncrude desperately needed to create more value. But how could these different parties reach agreement on important strategic issues?

The DDP to the Rescue

The dialogue decision process offered Syncrude a new paradigm for strategic management. Its multilevel, multistage collaborative approach would ensure that people from the management committee down to the technical line managers would contribute their best knowledge and insight to the process in a disciplined way. It seemed to be what Syncrude and its joint venture owners needed.

A joint Syncrude/consultant team embarked on an ambitious effort in the winter of 1989–1990 to complete a full (albeit pilot) cycle of the DDP. The complexity of their decisions became clear as work on strategic issues progressed. Operations were very capital intensive, and the intricate relationships that made the entire techno-economic system work made it easy to err in assessing the consequences of decisions. Decisions had to be made despite a lag of up to six years before results would be seen. Systems thinking was fundamental to the strategy. A commodity oil price environment subject to substantial periodic swings added yet another element of uncertainty to future planning, an uncertainty that had to be embraced.

As the process moved forward, the owners began to feel that they were at last getting at the long-elusive strategic issues. The strategy team used its time with the management committee to identify and prioritize a strategic agenda and to demonstrate how the dialogue decision process could systematically address the owners' concerns while driving to high-quality strategic decisions. According to the COO, Jim Carter, "The discipline of the process focused the board and senior management on the longer-term strategic issues and on building a better understanding of the overall business. We were more productive and really focused on strategy."

Into High Gear

The implementation team shifted into high gear in October 1990. Issues and alternatives were defined. A careful analysis of potential synergies was made. Key levers for setting strategic direction were identified including governance options, plant capacity, ownership structure, community relations, and options for technology, environmental management, marketing, and crude oil quality. These were organized onto a strategy table and further developed into a small set of coherent and promising alternative strategies. The strategy team then applied analytic tools to model the impact of each alternative on Syncrude's ultimate value (as measured by discounted net cash flow). The results were quantified with probability distributions.

The results created a sea change in the shared vision for the business. As CFO Phil Lachambre relates:

> We shifted our business focus from maintaining the status
> quo, minimal capital investment, with a "fence around two
> leases" to a regional development role. We went from a linear,
> one-product couple-of-lease business system to acquiring ad-
> ditional leases and developing plans for remote mine/extrac-
> tion operations and multiple product marketing.

The first cycle of the dialogue decision process played out over nine months. We reached crucial agreements that defined our execution agenda for the next year and a half. Our organization also made tremendous strides in improving its operations. The owners developed a new vision and mission statement for the stakeholders—not just shareholders, as used to be the case. We are now planning on about $3 billion in capital investment over the next seven to ten years to create an expanded, regional, multi-product operation.

In five years, Syncrude managed to increase the value of its business by 40 percent, and looked ahead to similar growth over the next five years. Table 12-1 illustrates the magnitude of value creation this new vision was able to achieve.

Future Opportunities

The Syncrude story is still being written. Participants at its 1995 strategy session came up with new strategy tables to guide future strategic decisions. As described by Lachambre:

Those strategy tables are ripe with new opportunities to create value and grow the business. There are new market opportunities and levers to further increase volume and product quality. There are new mining and extraction technologies, including a new vision of how to use technology to gain competitive advantage, a cunningly simple idea called hydrotransport [which] has staggering potential for Syncrude. . . . Hydrotransport will transform Syncrude's business and cost structure.

Table 12-1. *Syncrude's Value Creation*

VALUE MEASURE	1989	1995	CHANGE (%)
Crude oil production	54 MBbls	74 MBbls	+37
Full production cost	$15.42/Bbl	$13.69/Bbl	−11
Work force	4,670	3,672	−21
Productivity	11,700 Bbl/person	20,000 Bbl/person	+71
Operating cash flow	$247 million	$614 million	+148
Earnings (pro forma)	$52 million	$265 million	+410
Return on capital employed	3.1%	8.9%	+187

Note: Bbl means barrels of oil; MBbl means millions of barrels of oil.

And it is now a lever for Syncrude to pull because exploring its potential was a decision reached in the 1991/92 round of the dialogue decision process.

The hydrotransport technology Lachambre refers to may triple the current output of the oil sands industry over the next twenty years to 1.2 million barrels per day. That would represent half of Canada's crude oil production.

The head of the Syncrude consulting team throughout this period of strategic decision making later reflected on the transformation process and the effectiveness of the decision process:

> There was a huge shift from 1989 to now in adopting a value-creation mind-set. In 1989, no one could agree on how to even measure value. Today, everybody uses the same language to describe and measure it.
>
> We constantly had to reinforce and shift the process to keep building a strategic culture and not fall back to advocacy-based decision making or to operational tactics. There was a need for constant renewal of the process, especially as new owners entered the group. . . . By now, the management committee plus Syncrude's top management naturally use these tools in a way that shows strategic excellence has become a part of their culture.

CEO Eric Newell summarized the value of the DDP as follows:

> Today we have ten owners who have very different situations, and we have the strongest consensus we've ever had in terms of our business plan and the strategic direction for the future. The discipline of the dialogue decision process enables us to work through the many strategic issues in front of us and, in the end, to develop a very strong consensus amongst all of our owners about what is the right path and the right strategy for Syncrude to pursue. That is the tremendous value of our strategic planning process.

Smart Decision Making

As in the GM example, the Syncrude case demonstrates the ability of a principles-based decision process to transform the culture of a complex organization. These two organizations faced quite different

Figure 12-1. *Nine Principles of the Smart Organization*

circumstances, but both were able to adapt the dialogue decision process—and the organizational principles that support it—to their needs.

Our experience with these and other firms confirms the ability of smart principles, processes, and practices to improve decision quality across the entire organization. We have observed applications resulting in strategic choices that create millions to billions of dollars of new value. These large figures are dwarfed, however, by the value that could be created if *all* strategic decisions met the standards of decision quality. The principles of the smart organization point the way (Figure 12-1). By becoming a smart organization, every enterprise—including yours—can create this greater value.

Appendix A

Participants in SDG's Benchmark Study

A.T. Cross Company
ABB, Inc. (Asea Brown Boveri Inc.)
Abbott Laboratories Diagnostic
    Division
Abbott Laboratories
Accuride Corporation
Advanced Cardiovascular Systems Inc.
AKZO
Allied-Signal Inc.
Aluminum Company of America
American Cyanamid Company,
    Chemicals Division
American Home Products
    Corporation
Ameritech Services, Inc.
Amoco Chemical
Amoco EPTG
Amoco Technology Company
Apple Computer Inc. Mac Systems
    Division
Asahi Glass Company Ltd. Central
    Research Center
Ascom Tech
Ashland Chemical, Incorporated
    Company
AT&T Corporation
AT&T Bell Laboratories
AT&T Global Business Communi-
    cations Systems
AT&T Global Public Network
    Platforms
AT&T Network Systems
AT&T Operating Systems Bus. Unit
Atlantic Energy Inc.
Atlantic Richfield Company
Avery-Dennison Corporation
B.F. Goodrich Company

Baxter Pharmaseal Inc.
Bayer Corporation, Pharmaceutical
    Division
Becton Dickinson & Company
Bell Canada Corporation
Bellcore
Berlex Laboratories Inc.
Bethlehem Steel Corporation
BHP Steel
BICC PLC
Binney & Smith Inc.
Black & Decker Corporation
Boeing Commercial Airplane Group
Bristol-Meyers Squibb Company
British Gas PLC
British Nuclear Fuels
Bull Worldwide Information Systems
Campbell Soup Company
Chevron Corporation
Chevron Chemical Company
Chevron Oil Field Research Company
Chevron Research and Technology
Ciba-Geigy Corporation
CLARCOR Inc.
Clorox Company
Coca-Cola Company
Compaq Computer Corporation
Compaq Computer Corporate
    Development
Compaq PC Product Development
Conoco, Inc.
Control Data System, Inc.
Corning, Inc.
CPC International, Inc.
ABB Daimler-Benz Transportation
Daimler-Benz Aktiengesellschaft
Danfoss Inc.

Deere & Company
Dow Chemical Company
Dow Chemical North America
DuPont Central R&D
DuPont Chemicals
DuPont Merck Pharmaceutical
  Company Project Management
  Group
Dynamet, Incorporated
Dynatech Corporation
Eastman Chemical Company
Eastman Chemical Development
Eastman Chemical Research
Eaton Corporation
Electric Power Research Institute
Electronic Data Systems Corporation
Elf Atochem North America, Inc.
Eli Lilly and Company
Ethyl Corporation
Ethyl Corporation Petroleum
  Additives Division
Eveready Battery Company
Exxon Corporation
Federal Highway Administration
Ferro Corporation
Florida Power and Light
FMC Corporation
Ford Motor Company
Franklin Oil Corporation
Freeport Research & Engineering
Gas Research Institute
Gates Rubber Company
GE Aircraft Engines
GE Corporate Research and
  Development
GE Silicones Division
Gencorp Inc.
Genentech Discovery Research
Genentech Product Development
General Motors Corporation
Georgia Power Company
Gillette Corporate R&D
Gillette Research Institute
Glaxo Wellcome
Glidden Company

Grumman Aerospace & Electronics
  Group
Halliburton Company
Harris Corporation
Helene Curtis Industries,
  Incorporated
Henkel Corporation
Hewlett-Packard Company
Hewlett-Packard Company Corporate
  Engineering
Hewlett-Packard Company, Systems
  Support Division
Hoechst Celanese Corporation
Hoechst Marion Roussel,
  Incorporated
Hoffmann-La Roche Inc.
Honeywell Inc., MICRO SWITCH
  Division
Hydro Québec
IBM Applications Development
ICI Chemicals & Polymers
ICI Paints
Ingersoll-Rand
Institute of Paper Science &
  Technology
Intel Corporation
International Paper Company
Jefferson Smurfit
Johnson & Johnson
Johnson & Johnson Medical,
  Incorporated
Johnson & Johnson Pharmaceutical
  Research Institute
Kaiser Aluminum
Kirin Brewery Company Ltd.
Knauf Fiber Glass
Kraft General Foods, Inc. USA
Lockheed Martin Missiles and Space
  Company
Lonza, Inc.
Lord Corporation
Lubrizol Corporation
Matsushita Electric Industrial
  Company Central Research
  Laboratories

Matsushita Electric Industrial
Company Tokyo Research Institute
Maxwell Laboratories Incorporated
McDermott International
McDonnell Douglas Corporation
McDonnell Douglas Helicopter
Company
McDonnell Douglas Research
Laboratories
Mead Corporation
Merck & Company, Incorporated
Merck Project Management Group
Merck Regulatory Affairs Group
Microsoft Corporation Development
Microsoft Corporation Research
Mitsubishi Chemical America Inc.
Mitsubishi Electric Corporation
Research Laboratory
Mobil Chemical Company Inc.
Mobil Research and Development
Corporation
Monsanto Company
Monsanto Agricultural
Monsanto Company Chemical Group
Motorola Inc. Automotive and
Industrial Electronics Group
Motorola Inc. Semiconductor
Products Division
Motorola T&Q
Roche
Niagara Mohawk Power Corporation
North American Science Associates,
Inc.
Northrop Grumman Corporation
NYNEX Corporation Science &
Technology
Olivetti Spa.
Pennsylvania Electric Company
Pfizer Inc.
Pfizer Central Research Division
Philips Electronics Laboratories
Division
Philip Morris USA
Phillips Petroleum Company
PG&E Corporation

Polaroid Corporation
PQ Corporation
Procter & Gamble Company
Procter & Gamble Laundry Cleaning
Procter & Gamble Pharmaceuticals
Profound Quality Resources
Public Service Electric & Gas
Company
Quaker Chemical Corporation
Quaker Oats Company
Raytheon Company
Reckitt & Colman Incorporated
Rhone-Poulenc S.A.
Rhone-Poulenc Ltd. Rorer Project
Management
Rockwell International Corporation,
Science Center
Rockwell International Corporation
Rogers Corporation
Rohm and Haas Company
Samsung Hewlett-Packard
Sandoz Corporation
Sandoz Corporate Project
Management
Schering-Plough HealthCare
Products
Schuller International Incorporated
Shell Chemical Company
Shell Development Company
Shell International Petroleum
Research
Siecor Corporation
Smith & Nephew PLC
SmithKline Beecham
Sony Corporation Research Center
Southern California Edison Company
Southern California Gas Company
Southern Company
Southern Company Services
Incorporated
Sprint Corporation
Steelcase Incorporated
Stentor Research Centre
Sumitomo Chemical Tsukuba
Research Center

Sumitomo Electric Industries Ltd.
Sun Company
Svenska Cellulosa Aktiebolaget
Syncrude Canada, Ltd.
Syntex Corporation
Tektronix, Incorporated
Texaco, Incorporated
Texas Instruments, Inc.
Texas Instruments Central Research
  Laboratories
Texas Instruments Systems &
  Software R&D
Thomas J. Lipton Company
3M Company
3M Corporate Research Process
  Technology Lab
3M I, I, & E Sector
3M Speciality Films
U.S. Department of Energy
Unilever PLC

Unilever Research & Development
United States Borax Inc.
United Technologies
UOP
USG Corporation
Varian Associates, Inc.
Varian/Gould
Vickers, Inc.
Vulcan Chemicals Inc.
Washington Gas Company
Weyerhauser Company
Xerox Corporate Engineering
Xerox Corporate Research &
  Technology
Xerox Corporation
Xerox Corporation, Palo Alto
  Research Center
Xerox High Volume Reprographics
Zeneca Group PLC

APPENDIX B

Organizational IQ Test*

B - 1

SCORESHEET

Name: Address:

Organization:

                                             Phone:

Title: Fax:

Date: E-mail:

PRINCIPLE	A	B	C	D	E	TOTAL SUM	SUM POSITIVE	SUM NEGATIVE
Value Creation Culture Value creation is a compelling argument for change.								
Creating Alternatives Multiple alternatives are created and evaluated.								
Continual Learning Improvements are continually identified and acted on.								
Embracing Uncertainty Uncertainty is understood, communicated, and managed.								
Outside-In Strategic Perspective Meaningful information is available from the outside.								
Systems Thinking People understand complex cause-and-effect relationships.								
Disciplined Decision Making Systematic decision processes are used routinely.								
Alignment and Empowerment A common understanding of strategies for value creation coordinates the organization.								
Open Information Flow People have rapid, unrestricted access to information.								

*See instructions on page 162 of Chapter 8.

Total Score

Divided by 9

VALUE CREATION CULTURE

How do you know?	Scale $\vdash\!\!-\!\!+\!\!-\!\!+\!\!-\!\!+\!\!-\!\!+\!\!-\!\!+\!\!-\!\!+\!\!-\!\dashv$ $-3 \qquad 0 \qquad +3$	
	NOT SMART ORGANIZATION	**SMART ORGANIZATION**
A. Ask people how the organization creates value.	People focus on their own jobs and lack an understanding of how the organization ultimately creates and captures value.	People know who the customers of the organization are and how the organization captures value by serving them.
B. Look for formal measures of value creation.	There are no measures of value creation, or there are so many that people do not know which ones are important.	There are a few common measures of value creation that are used as the basis of decision making and compensation.
C. Determine how conflicts are resolved.	Conflicts are resolved through organizational power or turf. Often the conflicts get personal, and people lose track of the larger picture.	Conflicts are resolved through appealing to a shared understanding of value creation and through examining what actions create the most value for customers and the organization.
D. Examine how decisions are evaluated.	Evaluations do not measure ultimate value creation, or measures are used that are not translated into ultimate value (e.g., intuitive scoring systems).	Evaluations trace actions through to results measured by value creation, using either ultimate measures like NPV or translated measures (e.g., NPV loss per day of delay of launch).
E. Ask people if they feel empowered to question activities that they (or others) are doing that they think are not contributing to value.	People feel discouraged from questioning the value of a task. They fear (or have experienced) unresponsiveness or political backlash.	People provide examples of situations in which they have questioned activities. Inquiring into how the task creates value is a legitimate way to question activities. Tasks not creating value are modified or abandoned.

CREATING ALTERNATIVES

How do you know?

Scale

−3   0   +3

	NOT SMART ORGANIZATION	SMART ORGANIZATION
A. Examine the number and range of alternatives considered in recent decisions.	Only one option is developed (perhaps with some minor variations), or there is no perception of a choice other than go or no go.	There is ample evidence of a wide range of good options that were carefully considered and rejected in favor of even better ones.
B. Examine the doability of the alternatives considered in recent decisions.	Alternatives either specify high-level goals without giving people guidance about what to do, or they are detailed plans of the only alternative under consideration.	All alternatives are developed enough to be doable, yet they are not overspecified. People understand the effort and resources involved for implementation, but detailed plans are developed only for the selected alternative.
C. Examine how disagreement is resolved.	Disagreement escalates to conflict that is resolved by power or politics. All ideas but one are suppressed.	When people have different ideas about what to do, the ideas are incorporated into separate alternatives and objectively evaluated.
D. Examine how alternatives are evaluated.	People use raw judgment to pick their preferred alternative and are often dominated by internal political considerations. The general emphasis is on developing a social and political consensus.	People use systems thinking to connect alternatives to measures of value creation. Alternatives are ranked and refined by their ability to create value.
E. Look for the use of alternative-generating technology.	Creative tools are perceived as flaky and are not used to develop better alternatives.	There is ample evidence of formal tools and creative know-how. People readily use strategy tables, brainstorming, and other creative techniques.

CONTINUAL LEARNING

How do you know?

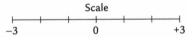

Scale

-3   0   +3

	NOT SMART ORGANIZATION	SMART ORGANIZATION
A. Ask people how change relates to the purpose of the organization.	People see that the purpose of the organization is to continue to do what it has always done. Change is viewed as necessary evolution forced on them by circumstances.	People see that the purpose of the organization is to continually learn how to create more value and make the required changes.
B. Listen to stories about the organization's history.	Stories are either about relatively modest changes or about failed attempts to change. Some stories may convey pride in being unchanged (e.g., tradition); others may convey fundamental barriers to change.	There is ample evidence of successful changes, including several changes that required paradigm shifts.
C. Ask people how they feel about recent changes.	People view the changes as forced on them. People are motivated by avoiding negative consequences.	Change is viewed as positive and productive, even if it was painful at the time. Changes are generally motivated by opportunity.
D. Observe how people react to new ideas or criticisms.	People are inflexible. They are unable to understand the new idea, regard it as dangerous or threatening, and reject it with prejudice. There is little experimentation with new approaches or organizational structures. People tend to shoot the messenger.	People are excited by the prospect of learning and growing. They explore ideas to find their value, possibly testing them out in small groups to discover their value and determine their applicability.
E. Look for formal or informal activities to search for new approaches, practices, and ideas.	The organization lacks such activities and inhibits people who try them.	People actively seek opportunities for improvement, such as benchmarking or performance measurement. Quality programs are an integral part of the company.

B - 5

EMBRACING UNCERTAINTY

How do you know?

Scale

−3   0   +3

	NOT SMART ORGANIZATION	SMART ORGANIZATION
A. Ask people to forecast an uncertain variable in which they have some degree of expertise.	People give a point estimate without acknowledgment of uncertainty. They have little awareness of factors that might upset their forecast. They may even view the forecast as a decision under their control.	People give you a range or a probability distribution. They might offer insights into the key influences or scenarios that would affect the result.
B. Review planning documents, how they are made, and how they are used.	Plans focus on a baseline set of assumptions. Forecasts are negotiated numbers or conservative estimates. Often, these numbers evolve to incorrect shared beliefs about the future.	Plans focus on major decisions and sources of uncertainty. Forecasts include ranges or probability assessments that reflect all sources of uncertainty.
C. Observe the process of setting budgets and estimating costs.	Budgets are rigid, and people are expected to promise accomplishments on fixed budgets. The "corporate lying game" is prevalent (people ask for too much, and their superiors cut them back). Often projects with the greatest overpromising win.	People recognize that the costs of making major accomplishments cannot be predicted. The budgeting process has the flexibility to adapt as new information is generated.
D. Observe how commitments are made and what people are held accountable for.	Information gathered for the purpose of communicating or understanding is used as the basis for commitments. This dual purpose biases communication of uncertainty.	Commitments are made based on achievable goals, and people are held accountable for things they can control. Assessments of uncertainty inform the organization of the risk it is undertaking.
E. Examine the assumptions in plans or decisions.	There are many assumptions, which may or may not be explicit. Often only one scenario is considered, usually implicitly.	The few assumptions are explicit and not crucial to the decisions at hand. Multiple scenarios representing the range of uncertainty are considered.

OUTSIDE-IN STRATEGIC PERSPECTIVE

How do you know?

Scale

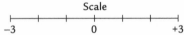

-3   0   +3

	NOT SMART ORGANIZATION	SMART ORGANIZATION
A. Ask people how the business environment is changing.	Answers are framed in terms of the organization's existing business and incremental trends—an inside-out perspective.	People have a broad view of the forces changing the industry and customers, the positions and strategies of the competition, and the implications for their organization.
B. Look for evidence of formal tools and processes to develop and communicate an outside-in perspective.	It is difficult to find staff, processes, or documents portraying an outside-in perspective. The focus is on pressing current issues, and outside information is in the form of undigested reports.	There are specialized staff, processes (e.g., global technology planning), and documents portraying an outside-in perspective.
C. Observe the assumptions people make when they plan or make decisions.	There are many assumptions based on extending current business success such as rates of growth of shares or markets will increase; we are technically ahead of the competition; with a better mousetrap, the world will beat a path to our door; and present markets and competition will change slowly.	The few assumptions are grounded in a solid understanding of industry change.
D. Examine peoples' experience and participation in perspective-expanding activities outside the organization.	People focus on their existing jobs to the exclusion of building a broader perspective based on outside information. The company discourages this outside perspective.	Most people participate in activities that broaden their perspective (e.g., job rotation, professional and industry meetings). The organization supports and values this perspective.
E. Ask people to interpret or comment on some recent event that impacts their industry.	People have trouble interpreting the event. They are overwhelmed by detail and have trouble relating it to their industry or organization.	Peoples' interpretations reflect a broad understanding of the industry. They are able to explain the event's significance to the industry and the organization.

SYSTEMS THINKING

How do you know?	Scale 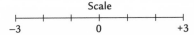 −3 0 +3	
	NOT SMART ORGANIZATION	**SMART ORGANIZATION**
A. Examine a recent decision, the factors considered, how people knew what was important, and the ultimate recommendation.	Few factors are considered, or so many are considered that people are overwhelmed. Recommendations are based on implications for only a few aspects of the business.	Many factors are considered, then narrowed down to a list of important factors based on the implications for value creation. The recommendation is based on its full implications.
B. Ask people what factors they look at in making a decision.	There is no checklist and different people have substantially different lists of factors to consider.	People know or immediately draw on a thorough checklist that covers all major aspects of the business system (e.g., technical, competitive, market, manufacturing, and regulatory issues).
C. Observe how peoples' different perspectives, such as marketing and technical, are integrated into a decision.	Few perspectives are represented in decisions. People with different perspectives develop into camps, each thinking it has the only right view.	Different perspectives are represented in each decision, and an integrated view is developed. Peoples' different perspectives are respected and used to broaden understanding.
D. Look for formal models of important systems such as business models showing the pathway to commercial profits for projects, industry dynamics, and the portfolio pipeline.	Systems models are rare, and if they exist are used infrequently or only by closed, specialized groups. The models often are too complex to be useful, perhaps taking days to run.	Many systems models exist and are routinely used to develop insight and conduct sensitivity analysis.
E. Ask people a complex question, and observe how they answer it. Ask them to articulate their thinking as they work.	People make snap judgments based on gut feelings or personal perspective, without acknowledging their limitations. Alternatively, they are overwhelmed and unable to make any progress without drawing on extensive resources.	The thought process represents a broad perspective on the question, and people can come up with a partial or rough answer. They are able to draw on the resources required to address the most important issues (e.g., other people, checklists, and model results) and extend their thinking.

OPEN INFORMATION FLOW

How do you know?

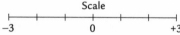

	NOT SMART ORGANIZATION	SMART ORGANIZATION
A. Ask people about their ability to get information they need.	People must work hard to extract the needed information. They may need authorization to use various sources.	People get the organization's best information quickly (e.g., find the right person to talk to in two phone calls).
B. Ask people how they feel about secret information.	People feel they are out of the loop on critical issues. The competition may have better information about their organization than they do.	There are few secrets. Those that exist are regarded as properly secret in the minds of people from whom the information is withheld (e.g., for competitive, legal, or personal reasons).
C. Ask people how much information they have received from others lately.	People have trouble getting information from others and must work hard to get the most basic information. Information is used as a source of personal power.	People have plenty of information—perhaps erring on the side of too much—and report that colleagues have been forthcoming and helpful.
D. Look for formal channels of communication and ask people how they use them.	The few channels that exist are viewed as not relevant to creating value. Informal channels are discouraged.	Channels are abundant and not restricted. People testify to their usefulness. Informal channels, such as networks, are fostered and encouraged.
E. Ask people about their contributions to communication channels or to helping others.	Contributions are limited, and opportunities to contribute are few.	People explain their recent contributions and feel they have been formally or informally rewarded for them.

ALIGNMENT AND EMPOWERMENT

How do you know?

Scale

| | −3 | 0 | +3 |

	NOT SMART ORGANIZATION	SMART ORGANIZATION
A. Examine the strategies at different levels (e.g., technology strategy to portfolio strategy to project strategy).	There may not be any strategies. If there are, they provide little guidance for decision making. They are viewed cynically, as corporate PR. The links among strategies are absent, unclear, or ambiguous.	There are clear strategies at all levels that provide useful guidance for decision making. Strategies at one level are clearly linked to strategies at the next. Lower-level strategies interpret and carry out the implementation of higher-level strategies.
B. Examine the value measures used to evaluate decisions at different levels (e.g., technology strategy to portfolio strategy to project strategy).	There may not be any value measures. If there are, each level sets its own values or decision criteria, with no special requirement that they be related to values and strategies at other levels.	There are clear measures of value at all levels. Value measures at one strategic level are clearly linked through the strategy to measures at the next level.
C. Examine the approvals required to make or carry out important decisions.	Decisions require many levels of approval. Review meetings are perceived as wasting time. Often meetings with upper management are feared because it may redirect efforts and change priorities without clear reason. Upper management often feels overloaded with the need to check on subordinates.	Decisions require few approvals because people understand the strategy and are trusted to carry it out. Meetings with upper management are viewed as adding value.
D. Examine the roles of people involved in a recent important decision.	Either few people participated in the decision or so many did that the process bogged down. Typically, lower level employees make proposals to upper levels for approval or rejection.	Many people participated in the decision process, at multiple levels in the organization. A dialogue was carried out in the process that continually aligned and refined the vertical links. Management at different levels collaborated to build a high-quality decision and achieved aligned commitment to action.
E. Examine a recent decision that was controversial.	The decision did not stick and was undone or remade over and over again.	People unified around the decisions and carried it out with little intervention. They understood the reasons for the decision and believe the organization is carrying out a sensible strategy for creating value.

DISCIPLINED DECISION MAKING

How do you know?

Scale

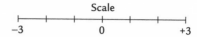

−3   0   +3

	NOT SMART ORGANIZATION	SMART ORGANIZATION
A. Ask people how a recent strategic decision was made.	Decisions are often made without much conscious choice. If there was a choice, the reasons for it are often unclear and undocumented. Perhaps someone in authority simply "made the call."	They explain that it was done by a conscious decision, and they show the documentation of its basis. They can also explain the process that led to the decision.
B. Ask people what the process is for making a decision.	People are either unable to identify the true decision maker(s) or they admit the real decision process is at variance with the nominal process.	They provide consistent explanations of a systematic decision process, which focuses on building a quality decision and incorporates many best practices.
C. Observe the types of decisions made.	These types of decisions are unclearly delineated, or whole categories are absent (e.g., the portfolio is simply the sum of individually considered project decisions, or the business strategy is redefined to pursue whatever new R&D results have been achieved).	People readily make distinctions among types of decisions such as project, portfolio, and technology strategy.
D. Ask people to critique the organization's decision processes.	People frequently believe that processes yield poor decisions, thereby wasting potential value creation and their personal time. Critiques are sometimes destructive or cynical and convey a sense of hopelessness.	People recognize the value added by the process and their criticisms will be couched as potential improvements.
E. Examine the formal tools used to support the process.	These tools will not be apparent, or if they can be found they will not often be used to support decisions. They may be used to justify decisions after they have been made.	You can find modern decision technology such as decision analysis, decision quality spider diagrams, portfolio grids, cumulative R&D productivity curves, and strategy tables.

Notes

Chapter 1

1. Most examples are taken from the public literature or from presentations made by executives of the named companies. Because the benchmarked companies were promised anonymity, we have disguised actual situations, made up composites, and changed some numerical and verbal conclusions. However, all of the examples are based on real situations.

2. For details of the NCR case, see Richard Foster, *Innovation: The Attacker's Advantage* (New York: Summit Books, 1986), 139–141.

3. Peters and Waterman correlated "excellence" with eight management principles such as leadership, being close to customers, entrepreneurship, and so forth. (See *In Search of Excellence*, New York: Harper & Row, 1981.) Other researchers associated corporate excellence with other factors: organizational design, strategy, and R&D investments. See Noel Capon, John U. Farley, James M. Hulber, and David Lei, "In Search of Excellence Ten Years Later: Strategy and Organization Do Matter," *Management Decision*, 29 (July 1991): 12.

4. Karen Bemowski, "Carrying on the P&G Tradition," *Quality Progress,* 23 (May 1992): 21–25.

5. "The Cracks in Quality," *The Economist*, 323, no. 7755 (18 April 1992): 67–68.

6. Betsy Weisendanger, "Deming's Luster Dims at Florida Power & Light," *Journal of Business Strategy*, 14, no. 15 (September–October 1993): 60–62.

7. "Cracks in Quality," 67.

8. Robert X. Cringley, *Accidental Empires* (Reading, MA: Addison-Wesley Publishing Company, 1992), 91.

9. See Tim Stevens, "Tool Kit for Innovators," *Industry Week* (5 June 1995): 28–33.

10. Robert T. Fraley and Charles S. Gasser, "Transgenic Crops," *Scientific American,* 266 (June 1992): 62 (6).

Chapter 2

1. From Buckler's speech to Strategic Decision Group Executive Forum in November, 1995.
2. Also called the Deming Wheel and the Plan-Do-Check-Act Cycle. For discussion see Thomas F. Wallace, Ed., *World Class Manufacturing* (Essex Junction, VT: Omneo, 1994), 217.
3. James M. Utterback, *Mastering the Dynamics of Innovation* (Boston: Harvard Business School Press, 1994), 112–116.
4. Peter Senge, *The Fifth Discipline* (New York: Doubleday/Currency, 1990).
5. "Putting the Idiot in Idiot Savant," *Fortune*, 133, no. 1 (15 January 1996), 46.
6. J. Edward Russo and Paul J. H. Shoemaker have an excellent description of the psychology of framing and its leverage in decision making in their book *Decision Traps* (New York: Doubleday, 1989).

Chapter 3

1. Michael Hammer and James Champy, *Reengineering the Corporation* (New York: HarperBusiness, 1993), 24.
2. Many R&D organizations separate their project work into a series of stages, such as discovery, development, scale up, and initial commercialization. Between each stage is a "gate" where a decision is made to advance the project to the next stage, terminate the project, or ask for further development in the present stage. Such a process provides natural breaks in which to make strategic decisions. For more information on stage gate processes, see Robert G. Cooper, *Winning at New Products*, 2nd Ed. (Menlo Park, CA: Addison-Wesley, 1993).
3. Russell L. Ackoff, "Systems and Organizations and Interdisciplinary Research," in F. E. Emery, Ed., *Systems Thinking* (Middlesex, England: Penguin, 1969).
4. For details on the inventive work of Xerox PARC, see Douglas K. Smith and Robert C. Alexander, *Fumbling the Future* (New York: William Morrow & Co., 1989).
5. For a full and exciting recounting of the solution to the problem of longitude, see Dava Sobel, *Longitude* (New York: Walker Publishing, 1996).
6. Details on assessment procedures can be found in C. S. Spetzler and C. S. Staël von Holstein, "Probability Encoding in Decisions Analysis" in *Readings on the Principles and Applications of Decision Analysis*, James Matheson and Ronald Howard, Eds. (Menlo Park, CA: Strategic Decisions Group, 1984).

7. Ronald A. Howard, Unpublished Course Notes, Stanford EES 231, 1988.

8. For an introduction to this vast literature, see Daniel Kahneman, Paul Slovic, and Amos Tversky, Eds., *Judgment Under Uncertainty: Heuristics and Biases* (Cambridge, England: Cambridge University Press, 1986).

9. There is a large literature on appropriate ways to measure shareholder value. The current consensus points to NPV of cash flows as the best. The terms of that literature are beyond the scope of this book .

10. James W. Tipping, Eugene Zeffren, and Alan R. Fusfield, "Assessing the Value of Your Technology," *Research Technology Management*, 38, no. 5, Industrial Research Institute (September–October 1995): 22–39.

11. Chapter 11, Project Strategy, gives a detailed case study with a well-established process for making this link.

12. According to *Parexel's Pharmaceutical R&D Statistical Sourcebook* (Waltham, MA: Paraxel, 1996), the average cost of a drug can be as high as $597 million and a large firm takes 128 months to develop it. This results in an average expenditure of $233,000 per working day.

13. Leigh Thompson, former CTO of Eli Lilly and Company, private communication, 1993.

14. The "naive NPV approach" is discussed in Avinash Dixit and Robert Pindyck, "The Options Approach to Capital Investment," *Harvard Business Review* (May-June 1995). The correct approach shown in the text is equivalent to an option approach to NPV calculations.

15. The term *expected value* is a bit misleading, but is the standard terminology. There is nothing expected about the expected value. Indeed, it might be a value that can never be achieved. It represents the probability-weighted average of all the possibilities. Also called *mean value*, it is a good first measure of the value of an investment when the range of possible outcomes is modest compared to the financial capacity of the organization. In general, the expected value should be replaced by a figure called the *certain equivalent*, which takes into account the organization's capacity to bear the associated risk. There is an extensive literature and well-established practice for doing this, which is beyond the scope of this book. The interested reader should see James Matheson and Ronald Howard, Eds., *The Principles and Applications of Decision Analysis* (Menlo Park, CA: Strategic Decisions Group, 1984), or Robert Clemens, *Making Hard Decisions* (Belmont, CA: Duxbury Press, 1991), for an introduction to this vast literature.

16. There is a vast literature on decision analysis. For an introduction, see Matheson and Howard, *The Principles and Applications of Decision Analysis;* Clemens, *Making Hard Decisions*; Steven Watson, *Decision Synthesis* (Cambridge: Cambridge University Press, 1987); or Ronald Howard, *Decision Analysis*, unpublished manuscript in progress.

Chapter 4

1. Product Development Management Association.

2. More detail on the study can be found in David Matheson, James E. Matheson, and Michael M. Menke, *R&D Decision Quality Benchmarking Study, Volume I* (Menlo Park, CA: Strategic Decisions Group, 1995).

3. Because the nominating process was done in 1990, experienced R&D managers reading this chapter today may quibble with the high ranking of one or more firms.

4. The astute reader will notice that since our criterion for a best practice company is based on a self-assessment, it is possible that our method has identified those companies that most exaggerate their capabilities. We have conducted audits to test this, and have found that when companies rate themselves highly, an outside panel also rates them highly. We worked with the Quality Directors Network of the Industrial Research Institute to study the implementation of four specific best practices in depth. Panels of interviewers went to ten companies that rated themselves highly on various practices. Nine of the ten were truly excellent, and only one had overstated its actualization.

5. We reported on this paper company in chapter 2. There we emphasized the qualitative aspect of the diagnosis based on the decision quality spider; here we emphasize the quantitative aspect of the diagnosis based on the survey instrument.

Chapter 5

1. See Richard Luecke, *Scuttle Your Ships before Advancing: And Other Lessons from History on Leadership and Change for Today's Managers* (New York: Oxford University Press, 1994), 146–153.

2. Ibid., 150.

3. Paul Lawrence, "How to Deal with Resistance to Change," *Harvard Business Review* (1 January 1967): 9.

4. See Lynn Lander, David Matheson, Michael Mence, and Derek Ransley, "Improving the R&D Decision Process," *Research Technology Management* (January–February 1995): 40–43.

5. For large multidivision companies like these, we conducted our analysis at the level of an appropriate R&D group, not for the entire company. Sometimes this group was a central lab, at other times it was a lab in a major division.

6. The astute reader will note that this is not exactly a measure of value creation, because it does not take costs into account. An overall measure of value creation, NPV of cash flows, had been translated into revenue terms to be more useful for R&D. In this particular business,

margins were quite stable so revenues were a reasonable surrogate for value creation.

Chapter 6

1. See in particular Chris Argyris, *On Organizational Learning* (Cambridge MA: Blackwell Publishers, 1992); Chris Argyris, *Knowledge for Action* (San Francisco: Jossey-Bass, 1993); and Peter M. Senge, *The Fifth Discipline* (New York: Doubleday, 1990).

2. Russell L. Ackoff, *Creating the Corporate Future* (New York: John Wiley & Sons, 1981); *Management in Small Doses* (New York: John Wiley & Sons, 1986); *The Democratic Corporation* (New York: Oxford University Press, 1994).

3. See James C. Collins and Jerry I. Porras, *Built to Last* (New York: Harper-Collins, 1994); and G. Bennett Stewart III, *The Quest for Value* (New York: HarperCollins, 1991).

4. Ronald A. Howard and James E. Matheson, *Readings on the Principles and Applications of Decision Analysis*, vols. I, II (Menlo Park, CA: Strategic Decisions Group, 1983); J. Edward Russo and Paul J. H. Schoemaker, *Decision Traps* (New York: Doubleday, 1989).

Chapter 7

1. Collins and Porras found that companies that survived and dominated their industries over time pursued customer value creation as a first objective. They were more successful than those that put shareholder values ahead of customer values. See James C. Collins and Jerry Porras, *Built to Last* (New York: HarperCollins, 1994).

2. *The Hawk Eye*, Burlington, Iowa (20 January 1940).

3. Some of the dangers of a naive application are discussed by Avinash Dixit and Robert Pindyck, "The Options Approach to Capital Investment," *Harvard Business Review* (May–June 1995).

4. See G. Bennett Stewart, III, *The Quest for Value: The EVA™ Management Guide* (New York: HarperBusiness, 1991).

5. Tim Stevens, "Tool Kit for Innovators," *Industry Week* (5 June 1995): 28–35.

6. From "Improving Research Using Total Quality Management (1993 Update)" presentation by Phillip Griswold, Director, Polymers Research Division, Eastman Chemical Company.

7. Marvin Weisbord, *Productive Workplaces* (San Francisco: Jossey-Bass, 1987), 175.

8. Based on a presentation by Ed Finein to the DQA forum in 1992 in Menlo Park, CA.

9. Ibid.

10. Chris Argyris, "Teaching Smart People How to Learn," *Harvard Business Review* (May–June 1991).

11. Ibid.

12. "Probability Encoding in Decision Analysis," paper presented at the ORSA-TIMS-AIEE 1972 Joint National Meeting, Atlantic city, New Jersey, 8–10 November, 1972. Reprinted in "Readings on the Principles and Applications of Decision Analysis," pp. 601–625, published by Strategic Decisions Group, Menlo Park, California. "Judgment Under Uncertainty: Heuristics and Biases," *Science* 185 (27 September 1974): 1124–1131.

13. "Adventures with Capital," *The Economist* (25 January 1997): 15.

14. Gary Hamel and C. K. Prahalad, *Competing for the Future* (Boston: Harvard Business School Press, 1994).

15. There is a vast literature on systems thinking and systems dynamics. See Daniel H. Kim, *Systems Thinking Tools, A User's Reference Guide* (Cambridge: Pegasus Communications, 1994) for a nonmathematical introduction; see David Luenberger, *Dynamic Systems* (Reading, MA: Addison-Wesley, 1979) for a textbook treatment. Peter Senge's *The Fifth Discipline* (New York: Doubleday, 1990) and *The Fifth Discipline Fieldbook* (New York: Doubleday, 1994) both provide many examples and applications of systems thinking to corporate settings and discuss the implications beyond the technical methodology.

16. Jesus Sanchez, "Firms Tell How Soft-Cookie Sales Crumbled after a Heated Battle," *Los Angeles Times* (6 July 1987) home edition, bus. sec., part 4, p. 1.

17. Ibid.

18. Ibid.

19. See Rebecca Henderson, "Managing Innovation in the Information Age," *Harvard Business Review* (January–February 1994): 100–105.

20. Ibid., 102.

21. William Freedman, *Chemical Week*, 157, no. 11 (27 September 1995): 35.

22. George Labovitz and Victory Rosansky, *The Power of Alignment* (New York: John Wiley & Sons, 1997): 1–2.

23. Ibid., 2.

24. For more detail see Marvin L. Patterson, *Accelerating Innovation* (New York: Van Nostrand Reinhold, 1993): 3f.

25. W. Leigh Thompson, *Fractal Portfolio Resourcing* (Charleston, SC: Profound Quality Resources, 1995): 3.

26. Ibid, 34.

27. Ibid, 3.

Chapter 8

1. Based on a January 1996 meeting with twenty-seven companies convened by the Quality Directors Network

Chapter 9

1. Vincent P. Barabba, *Meeting of the Minds* (Boston: Harvard Business School Press, 1994).
2. Chapter 2 explains our approach to value measures and more advanced measures of risk aversion such as the certain equivalent.
3. This assumes that the NPV increases or decreases consistently over the range of values, which is almost always the case for business models.
4. Technically the most important uncertainties are the ones whose resolution would cause a change in the best decision. Determining these involves simultaneously comparing sensitivity charts from several strategies. Also sometimes sensitivities need to be examined for more than one variable at a time. But for exposition, we assume the simpler analysis will suffice.
5. A common misconception is that incorporating greater expertise will narrow the range of uncertainty. The true expert realizes how unknowable an uncertainty is and gives it a wide range, while a naive expert may try to predict it too narrowly. This is the most common form of probability assessment bias, as mentioned in chapter 3. Embracing uncertainty means being able to understand and express your true range of uncertainty and make the best decision in the face of it.
6. Figure 9-10 is an abbreviated tree. In the full tree the second node should appear three times, once at the end of each strategy branch, making six partial end points, then the third node should appear at the end of each of these, resulting in twenty-four partial end points, and so on. The fully developed tree is very bushy, in this case with 1,296 ($3 \times 2 \times 4 \times 3 \times 3 \times 3 \times 2$) end points. We cannot discuss here the many nuances of trees or the merits of several other methods of analysis to reach identical results.

Chapter 10

1. This qualitative approach might be a reasonable starting point for a broader discussion and to develop an initial mutual understanding. However, this superficial consensus should not be used as the main input for decision making.
2. For the full story on the Swatch Watch, see Marc Meyer and Alvin Lehnerd, *The Power of Product Platforms* (New York: The Free Press, 1997)

and William Taylor, "Message and Muscle: An Interview with Swatch Titan Nicolas Hayek," *Harvard Business Review* (March–April 1993): 103.

3. Strict financial theory would suggest funding all projects with a positive incremental productivity ratio. As a practical matter, organizations do not usually go that far because they feel constrained by resources or because of unmodeled transaction costs. They need to be careful not to demand *only* high-ratio projects or they might shortchange the future.

Chapter 11

1. It is usually better if R&D fails earlier. Project leaders often work on the easy challenges to show that they are making progress. If the project is destined to fail, this only prolongs the inevitable and consumes resources. Thus, it is much better to tackle the challenging hurdles first.

2. The fact that 493 possible outcomes existed in the decision tree analysis of these three strategies underscores the benefits of modeling the entire business model on a computer spreadsheet. The same spreadsheet used for the base case and tornado diagrams can be used to evaluate all of these scenarios as well.

3. Curves of the general shape illustrated here occur in virtually every R&D project strategy.

4. See discussion in chapter 3.

Chapter 12

1. One of us (Jim) used to keep detailed personal financial accounts on his personal computer. He typed in each bank and credit card transaction and carefully categorized them and reconciled them against the statements. After several years of doing this, Jim asked, "How does this create value?" He realized that all of the discrepancies he had ever discovered were due to his own errors, never the bank's. He could figure his net worth fairly quickly by adding up numbers from his brokers and banks. He realized that these institutions did a better job of tracking his finances than he did. It short, Jim's attempt to keep his own financial accounting was not adding value to his life. So he stopped doing it, and is creating more personal value with the time he freed up.

2. This section draws heavily on "Syncrude: A Transformation Success Story," by Carl Spetzler of SDG and Phil Lachambre, CFO of Syncrude Canada (Menlo Park, CA: Strategic Decisions Group, 1996).

INDEX

Accountability, embracing uncertainty and, 127–30
Ackoff, Russell, 36, 99
Acting smart, defined, 1
Action, commitment to, for decision, 26, 57–59
Actualization, 75–79
Adobe, 5
Advocates and politics, 54–55
Aggressive analog strategy, 187, 193–95, 197
Agreement, superficial, 57–58
Alignment and Empowerment (AE), principle of, 98, 140, 146–53, 159, 164
Alternatives
    avoiding, 19
    choosing carefully among, 21
    creative, doable, for decision, 24, 40–44
    and decision quality, 29
    requirements for high quality, 43–44
    See also Creating Alternatives (CA), principle of
Ambivalent principles, 164–67
Analysis
    decision, 55, 56
    deterministic, 228–34
    quantitative project, 70–73
    robustness, 241–43
    sensitivity, 190–92, 232–34
Apple, 5
Argyris, Chris, 99, 121–22
Arthur D. Little, 5
Artzt, Edwin, 4
Assessment phase of dialogue decision process, 181–85
Assumptions hiding uncertainty, 48–49
AT&T, 63, 66, 88, 113
    Bell Laboratories, 23
Atari, 4
A. T. Kearney, 5
Attention, managing focus of, 56
Attila the Hun, 47–48
Avery Dennison, 88

Baldrige Award, *see* Malcolm Baldrige Quality Award

Barabba, Vince, 247, 251–55
    Meeting of the Minds, 176
Barriers
    to implementation of best practices in decision making, 84–88, 89
    lessons from companies about overcoming, 88–91
    removing, with continual learning, 120–21
    removing, with free-flowing information, 144–45
    removing, with systems thinking, 140
Base case scenario, 231
Being smart, defined, 1, 97
Benchmarking, 59
    application of, to R&D decision making, 63–67
    for best practices, 74–81
    at Xerox Corporation, 3, 120, 121
Bernoulli, Daniel, 99
Best practices for R&D decisions, 63
    barriers to implementation of, 84–88, 89
    benchmarking for, 74–81
    blueprint of, 68–70
    lessons from companies about overcoming barriers to, 88–91
    listing of, 63–64, 70–74
    methodology of study of, 64–67
Bias
    avoiding, 48
    overconfidence, 48
Bismarck, Otto von, 173
Bread-and-butter projects, 203
British Columbia, University of, 142
Brown, John Seely, 142
Buckler, Sheldon, 17
Business strategy, 10

Capital investment, 250
Carter, Jim, 258
Causes, treating, not symptoms, 138–40
Census Bureau, U.S., 251
Champy, James, 35
Change, resistance of people to technological, 83–84

Honeywell, 113
Horizons, considering long time, 21
Horizontal organization, concept of, 256

IBM, 63
Ideas, good, and resources, 117–18
Improvement, 18–21
Industrial Research Institute (IRI), Quality Director's Network of, 67, 88, 91, 160
Influence diagrams, 45, 183–85
Information
    and decision quality, 29
    meaningful, reliable, for decision, 24–25, 44–50
    requirements for high-quality, 49–50
    See also Open Information Flow (OIF), principle of
Information age strategy, 187, 193–95, 196
In Search of Excellence (Peters and Waterman), 4
Intel, 63
Interlude, strategic, 157–58
Internal customers, relationship with, as best practice for R&D decisions, 64
IQ test, organizational, 100, 109, 160, 161–62, 169, 170
    profile, 163–65
    score, 162–63
Issues, focusing on important, 21

John Deere, 82
Juran, Joseph, 99, 158

Kahnaman, Daniel, 125
Keynes, John Maynard, 54

Labovitz, George, 147–48
Lachambre, Phil, 257, 258–60
Laplace, Pierre-Simon, 99
Lawrence, Paul, 83
Learning
    double-loop, 106
    single-loop, 106
    See also Continual Learning (CL), principle of
Linvill, William K., 247
Lister, Joseph, 41
Logic, scientific, 55
    See also Reasoning

Long-range planning (LRP) case, 102–5, 169
Luecke, Richard, 82, 83

McGraw, Gary, 143
Machiavelli, Niccolò, 83
Malcolm Baldrige Quality Award, 4, 114, 170
Master process, decision making as, 5
Means versus ends, 51–52
Measurement, 18–21
    of decision quality, 27–30
    perceived difficulties in, 87
Merck, 63, 66
Methodology, engaging at level of, 108–9
Metrics
    for implementing best practices, 90–91
    of value, 90–91, 113–15
Mies van der Rohe, Ludwig, 199
Monsanto, 11, 113
Motorola, 3, 63

Nabisco, 137–38
Napoleon, 47
NBC, 183
NCR, 3–4
Net present value (NPV), 90, 113, 114, 190–91, 193–95
Newell, Eric, 257, 260
Newton, Sir Isaac, 41–42
Noyce, Robert, 221

Open Information Flow (OIF), principle of, 98, 140, 141–45, 159, 160
Organizational boundaries, 87
Organizational identity, 9
Organization and process, as best practice for R&D decisions, 64
Outcomes, embracing uncertainty and, 127–30
Outside-In Strategic Perspective (OISP), principle of, 97, 122, 132–35, 159, 160, 248
Overconfidence bias, 48
Oysters, 204
    understanding risk of, 208–11

PG&E, 66
Pasteur, Louis, 41
Patterson, Marvin, 155
Pearls, 203–4

ABOUT THE AUTHORS

David Matheson is a principal of Strategic Decisions Group, an international management consulting firm headquartered in Menlo Park, California. Based in SDG's London office, he has conducted extensive research into decision making in a variety of industries. Through this research, SDG has been able to improve organizations' abilities to create value from research and development. In addition to his strategy consulting, David conducts frequent seminars for executives.

Jim Matheson, a founding director of Strategic Decisions Group, is a recognized leader in the development and application of decision analysis. He has conducted strategy work with companies from a variety of industries, including chemical, electronics, pharmaceutical, and entertainment. Jim was recently recognized by the Institute for Operations Research and Management Sciences (INFORMS) for his work in the field of decision analysis. Before cofounding SDG in 1981, Jim directed SRI International's Decision Analysis Group.